Lawrence Buckley Thomas

Genealogical notes

Containing the pedigree of the Thomas family of Maryland

Lawrence Buckley Thomas

Genealogical notes
Containing the pedigree of the Thomas family of Maryland

ISBN/EAN: 9783337257293

Printed in Europe, USA, Canada, Australia, Japan

Cover: Foto ©Andreas Hilbeck / pixelio.de

More available books at **www.hansebooks.com**

CAREW CASTLE.

GENEALOGICAL NOTES:

CONTAINING THE PEDIGREE OF THE

THOMAS FAMILY,

OF MARYLAND,

AND OF THE FOLLOWING CONNECTED FAMILIES:

SNOWDEN — BUCKLEY — LAWRENCE — CHEW — ELLICOTT —
HOPKINS — JOHNSON — RUTHERFURD —
FAIRFAX — SCHIEFFELIN —
TYSON

AND OTHERS.

ILLUSTRATED BY VIEWS AND COATS OF ARMS.

BY

LAWRENCE BUCKLEY THOMAS.

———

BALTIMORE:
LAWRENCE B. THOMAS.
1877.

CHARLES HARVEY & CO.

FINE BOOK AND JOB PRINTERS,

BALTIMORE, MD.

PREFACE.

—

This book is mainly compiled from four distinct sources of information, and is complete or the reverse, in accordance with them.

These sources are the printed publications of the Record Commission of Great Britain, containing Calendars of State papers, and in some instances, full reprints of the same; the papers at the Office for the Registry of Wills in Annapolis, Md.; the Manuscript Records of the Society of Friends in Maryland; and Family Bibles. I have also, in a few cases, been aided by the personal knowledge of living members of some of the families noticed. Where so many are concerned, it may seem invidious to select any for acknowledgment; but I must be permitted to express my feelings of especial gratitude to Mrs. Edward Snowden, of Baltimore; Mrs. Edward P. Thomas and Dr. Francis Thomas, of Montgomery County, Md.; Mr. Richard L. Schieffelin, of New York; Mr. Samuel Chew, of Germantown; Mr. William G. Thomas, of Perth Amboy, N. J., and to the memory of his father, the late Philip E. Thomas, of Baltimore, whose family tree first suggested my present book.

In the course of my labors it has been necessary for me to visit members of the different families with whom I had no previous acquaintance; but, in every instance, I have been received in the most cordial manner, and every facility afforded me for making the desired researches. Indeed, I may say, with truth, that the pleasant acquaintances thus made would alone repay me for the labor incident to the compilation of my book.

In conclusion, I would ask the genealogist, as with "a critic's eye" he scans my pages, and dips his pen in gall, before exposing "its many inaccuracies," to remember that in most of the pedigrees I am the "Columbus of a new America," and working in absolutely virgin soil.

He should, also, bear in mind not only the great scarcity of printed books on pedigree in our libraries, but the incompleteness of the original MSS. sources of information, and the carelessness or culpable negligence that some families show in the preservation of their records. The latter cause will account for the fragmentary character of several of the pedigrees I print.

Any one who can supply corrections of, or additions to these pedigrees, will confer a favor by sending them to the compiler, duly authenticated by dates and authorities; as it is his intention to print a supplement containing such alterations.

LAWRENCE BUCKLEY THOMAS.

54 McCulloh Street, Baltimore, Md.

July 12th, 1877.

ABBREVIATIONS.

The abbreviations used in this book are the following: ap.—son of; b.—born; d.—dead, died, &c.; dau.—daughter; d. s. p.—died without issue; md.—married; and q. v.—a reference to the Index.

THOMAS.

THIS FAMILY is of great antiquity in Wales, claiming descent from the ancient kings of Britain. Its authentic history may be said to commence with Uryan or Urien Rheged who lived in the sixth century after Christ. The latest and best authorities on the History of Wales seem to confirm this date, which is also the traditional one, although some writers would put his birth as late as the eighth or ninth century. Urien is said to have been the son of Cynvarch Oer ap Meirchion Gul, a Prince of the North Britons, who was expelled from his principality by the Saxons and took refuge in Wales. This Prince's name appears on the Pillar of Eliseg near Llangollen. Urien his son is said to have driven out the Gwyddelians, or Irish Scots, from Rheged, a district of country lying between the Tawe and the Tavy rivers, and to have been granted the sovereignty of that principality in reward. It comprised Gowerland, Cydweli, Carynwllion, Iscenen, and Cantrev Bychan. He waged war for many years against Ida the Saxon King of Northumberland, and is said to have been treacherously slain by Llovan Llawdivo in the year 575 while besieging Ida's son Deoric in the Isle of Lindisfarne. He was a munificent patron of the bards, one of the greatest of whom, Llywarch Hen, has celebrated his prowess and death in his verse. By the Welsh Triads he is ranked as one of the three Bulls of Conflict; and several early romances speak of him under the name of Sir Urience. He married Margaret La Faye, dau. of Gorlois Duke of Cornwall, and had issue: a dau. Elwri, who married Morgan Morganwdd; and two sons Pasgen, and Owain who slew Ida King of Northumberland in battle. Pasgen was the lineal ancestor of Rhys ap Goronwy, ap Einion, ap Lloarch, ap Kymbathwye, ap Gurwared, ap Syssylt, ap Rhyne, ap Llarch, ap Mor, ap Pasgen, of all of whom nothing more than their names is recorded on the pages of history. Rhys married Margaret, dau. and heiress of Griffin ap Kiddy, Lord of Gwynvey, and had issue: Elider ap Rhys married Gladwys dau. of Philip ap Bah, ap Gwath Voed, Lord of Esginbrath, and had issue: Sir Elidur Ddu, Knight of the Holy Sepulchre. He married Cecily dau. of Sysillt ap Llewellyn, Lord of Cantrescliffe, and had issue: Katherine married David Morthye, Lord of Odyn Castle and Fountain Gate; and Philip married Gladys dau. of David Vras and was the father of Philip who had issue: Crisley married Richard Aubrey; Gwylliam; and Nicholas. Nicholas married Janet dau. and heiress of Gruffyd ap Llewellyn Voethes, descended from Elystan Gloddryd, Prince of Ferlys, and had issue: Gruffyd ap Nicholas who was a remarkable and most ingenious gentleman. The possessor of an ample fortune and allied by marriage with some of the principal families both in North and South Wales, his power and influence in Caermarthenshire was very great.

His hasty spirit and violence of temper often involved him in complications with his neighbours, to extricate himself from which required the exercise of all his ingenuity. He drew upon himself the enmity of no less a personage than Richard, Duke of York, by witholding from him a piece of land in Herefordshire, and he insolently and peremptorily refused to obey the summons of the Sheriff to answer for his conduct. At the head of a numerous and warlike clan, which was strongly attached to him, he gave shelter and encouragement to innumerable Welsh thieves, who were in the constant habit of plundering and ravaging the English border. The frequency and severity of these predatory incursions raised against him a host of enemies; the most powerful of whom, Humphrey, Duke of Buckingham, Richard of York, Jasper Tudor, Earl of Pembroke, and the Earl of Warwick made such representations to the King, Henry VI., accusing him of being an encourager and harbourer of thieves, that he was deprived of the Commission of the Peace and Captaincy of Kilgarran Castle, which that Sovereign had granted him. It is alleged that his hatred of the English was Gruffyd's reason for harbouring those who ravaged their territory. A commission was finally appointed by the King to arrest the accused and investigate the charges against him, at the head of which was placed the Lord Whitney. Gruffyd, who had heard of the Commission, but was not informed of its exact object, laid his plans with the craftiness and executed them with the boldness peculiar to his character. He met the Commissioners on their entry into Caermarthenshire, himself meanly dressed, and accompanied only by four or five attendants raggedly attired, and as miserably mounted. Right glad was Lord Whitney to find the truculent Welshman apparently in his power, and not a little astonished was he also to hear him offer his services to guide him to Caermarthen, the place of his destination. Their road followed the windings of the Bran to where that river unites with the Gwydderig in its confluence with the Towey. On the Western bank, on a rocky eminence, was Gruffyd's Castle of Abermarlais, hidden from the Commissioners by the thick woods, which lined the shores of the river. A graceful curve of the road, however, brought them to the foot of the gentle eminence on which the Castle stood, and Gruffyd, then turning to the surprised Commissioners and pointing to the open postern, invited them with a smile to enter and refresh themselves. They were received with demonstrations of extreme respect by Gruffyd's son Thomas at the head of one hundred horsemen handsomely dressed and gallantly mounted, and began to open their eyes to the real power and consequence of their companion. After having well refreshed themselves, the whole party, including Thomas, ap Gruffyd, and his armed retinue left the Castle. A little further on their way they came to the ancient fortress of Dinevawr, not far from the town of Llandelo Fawr, then the stronghold of Owen, Gruffyd's son. He received them at the head of a chosen body of two hundred armed horsemen, and played the part of host with such address that he contrived to draw from his guests the secret of their commission. The whole party then proceeded on their way, leaving the mountains for the plain where the Towey meets, the Gwili, at the little village of Abergwili. Here they were met by a splendid body of five hundred "tall men" on foot, well armed and accoutred, and led by Gruffyd's eldest son. Thus magnificently attended the Commissioners entered Caermarthen, then the Capital of South Wales. Gruffyd now excused himself from attendance on the Commissioners and committed to his sons the care of attending them to the banquet prepared in their honor at the Guild Hall. Lord Whitney privately sent for the Mayor and Sheriffs, and showing his commission, demanded their assistance to arrest Gruffyd, which it was determined should be done on the following morning.

The banquet was now prepared, and the Commissioners were escorted to it with much pomp by the sons of Gruffyd. The tables had been arranged along the centre of the floor, and according to the architecture of the time a row of pillars separated the upper end of the room, which was slightly elevated, from that part which was assigned to the less distinguished members of the Assembly. Lord Whitney was conducted to a seat on the dais, splendidly hung with cloth of gold, and Owen placed himself upon his right hand. On either side of this elevated dais, galleries had been raised, in which were placed the bards of that land of Minstrelsy. The guests betook themselves with right good-will to the noble cheer provided, and Owen in particular plied them with Ypocras, Garhiofilac, and other delicate and precious drinks, which soon produced the desired effect upon the Commissioners. Lord Whitney, after his conference with the authorities, and exhibiting to them his commission, carelessly placed it in his sleeve, which was made after the then fashion, very wide, and often used for such purposes. During the revel, Owen abstracted it from its hiding place, while Lord Whitney was in that state of mental obscuration from the strong potations that had been pressed upon him, that he not only did not notice its loss at the

2

time but retired to bed without doing so. Owen communicated to his father the success of their plans, but Gruffyd abated nothing of his formal courtesy to the Commissioners, and the next morning presented himself before them in the Guild Hall splendidly dressed and attended by his sons and armed retainers. He was immediately arrested by the officers of the Court, to which he made no resistance, but with an air of great humility requested that the proceedings against him might be conducted according to law, and asked to see their commission. Lord Whitney readily assented to his request, but upon putting his hand into his sleeve and finding the warrant gone, his consternation may be easily imagined. "Methinks Lord Whitney," said Gruffyd, "if he comes here as he says, by the King's grace, must have valued his commission too highly to have committed it to the safe keeping of that ruffle or carelessly to have lost it." Then dropping his assumed deference, clapping his hat upon his head, and turning to his friends and followers, he exclaimed: "What! have we cozeners and cheaters come hither to abuse the King's Majesty's power and to disquiet his true hearted subjects." Then looking on the commissioners with a bitter frown, he said, "By the mass, before the next day come to an end, I will hang up all your bodies for traitors and impostors." The commissioners were panic-struck, and entreated for their lives: which Gruffyd at last granted on condition that Lord Whitney should put on his livery coat of blue and wear his cognizance, and be bound by an oath to go to the King so arrayed, acknowledge his own offences and justify the Welshman's proceedings.

Gruffyd continuing his depredations upon the Lord's Marchers was at length found guilty of felony on an indictment preferred against him in the County of Salop. This decision at once illumined his mind as to the rival claims of the Houses of York and Lancaster. A Lancastrian King had adjudged him a felon, the Duke of York was therefore of necessity the champion of a good cause and him should he support. He joined Edward of March, the Duke's son, at Gloucester, with eight hundred men well armed and provisioned, and marched with him to Mortimer's Cross, in Herefordshire. Here on the 2nd of February, 1461, a battle was fought between the Yorkists and the Lancastrians under Jasper, Earl of Pembroke, in which Gruffyd was mortally wounded, surviving only long enough to know that his friends were victorious. He had married Mabel, daughter of Meredith ap Henry Donne of Kidwelly, and was succeeded by his son Thomas ap Gruffyd, who married Elizabeth, daughter and heiress of Sir John Gruffyd of Abermarlais. He is described as a man of a character very different from his turbulent father, and one of the most accomplished gentlemen of the age, with a mildness of disposition and elegance of manners rarely found in those cruel times of civil warfare. To avoid taking part in the contests of the rival Houses of York and Lancaster, he withdrew to the accomplished Court of the Duke of Burgundy, in whose service he enrolled himself. Here he became famous for his boldness and skill in the tilt and tourney, and in single combat. After the death of his wife, his gallantry and gracious disposition won the affections of a niece of the Duke, and Thomas was compelled to return to England. There he had constant encounters with his neighbors, particularly Henry ap Gwilym of Court Henry in the Vale of Towey, between whom and his house there seems to have existed an ancient feud His last duel took place in Merionethshire, with one David Gough, whom he killed. Having laid aside his armor and thrown himself on the ground to rest after the combat, Thomas was treacherously run through the body by one of Gough's retainers. He was buried in the Abbey of Bardsey in Caermarvonshire. He was married first to Elizabeth of Abermarlais, and it is said secondly to another Elizabeth, a relative of the Duke of Burgundy. His only dau. md. Griffith ap Owen. His two eldest sons, Morgan and David, espoused opposite sides in the Wars of the Roses, and both perished in that murderous struggle. Rhys or Rees, his third son succeeded to the estate after their deaths. He was born in 1451, and was educated at the Court of Burgundy, where he held a post of honor in the Duke's household. This he relinquished to accompany his father on his banishment to England. His bravery was so noted, that after his death one of the Welsh bards lamented that a "drum had not been covered with his skin; the sound of which alone," he assures us, "would have always ensured the victory to the British." He seems to have been as wise and politic as brave. After the death of his first wife, the daughter and heiress of Sir John Ellis descended from Sir Henry Elys of Yorkshire temp. Richard the First, he put an end to the long established feud between his own family and that of Court Henry by marrying Eva, the only daughter and heiress of Henry ap Gwilym, the head of that House. By this marriage he added to his possessions a property not much inferior to his original patrimony, and became one of the most opulent subjects of the realm. His establishment and hospitality were in every respect suitable to his immense wealth, and displayed the magnificence of a prince, rather than of a private gentleman. He acquired unbounded popularity, and by degrees very formidable power by re-establishing the games of his country on his estates, and by training the young men to the use of arms, under the guise of sham fights and spectacles. It is stated that he had nineteen hundred tenants bound by their leases to attend him at the shortest call, and that brief warning having been given he could bring into the field five

thousand disciplined men, mounted and armed. He was a great builder
or enlarger of Castles, built New Castle Emlyn, and enlarged Carew Castle,
which came into his possession by a mortgage from Sir Edmund Carew, and
which became his favorite residence. Besides these he also possessed Abermarlais, Dinevawr, Narberth, Whibley, and many others. Every effort was
made to interest him in the cause of Henry of Richmond, with whom he
was connected in blood; Rhys ap Thomas and Henry's father being descended from a common ancestor. Apprehensive of the success of these
efforts, Richard the Third sent Commissioners to him to demand his son as
a hostage and an oath of fidelity from the father. The former demand he
evaded in a wily letter still extant, but was compelled to take an oath
that Richmond should not enter England "except over his body." Offended
at the King's suspicions, and moved by a letter from Richmond, in which
he tells him that all his fortunes hang on Rhys ap Thomas' decision, the
chieftain called a council of his most trusty friends to consider the question.
At this were present the Abbot of Talley, the Bp. of St. Davids, several
of the more influential gentry and two of his father's veteran officers, in
whom he had great confidence. They advised his aiding Henry, and when
he spoke of his oath, the Churchmen silenced his scruples and one of them
proposed a method by which he might keep its letter while evading the
spirit. Still he hesitated, and it was not until he had consulted his sooth-
sayer or prophet, that he sent a messenger to Henry assuring him of his
assistance. The Earl immediately set sail for England, and was met on
landing at Milford Haven by Rhys ap Thomas at the head of two thousand
picked men. It is said that he carried out the suggestion of the Bishop
of St. Davids by crouching under one of the arches of a bridge over which
Henry rode, thus "passing over his body." Henry appointed Shrewsbury as
the place of rendezvous for his friends, and divided his army into two
bodies, one of which he led thither himself by way of Cardiganshire, and
the other he committed to Rhys ap Thomas. On the march the chieftain's
force was augmented by vast numbers of the Welsh, from whom he made
a selection of two thousand horse, the flower of his attendants, and five
hundred foot, dismissing the rest to their homes. The infantry he placed
under the command of his younger brothers, and left in the principality
to secure it for Henry. The horse he led himself to Shrewsbury, and
there joined the Earl.

King Richard, though taken by surprise, rose to the occasion, and
hastily gathering an army marched to meet them. The hostile forces came
in sight of each other on the field of Bosworth, near Leicester, August
22nd, 1485.

Richard, in the heat of the battle, made a desperate plunge at the Earl of Richmond; he killed with his own hands the Earl's standard-bearer, Sir William Brandon, dismounted Sir John Cheyney and many a high-born gentleman who attempted to stay him in his career. He had nearly reached the spot where Henry stood, when Rhys ap Thomas perceived the Earl's danger, and mounting his favorite charger, "Llwyd y Bacse," or Grey Fetter-locks, with Sir William Stanley, bore down between. The Welsh tradition asserts that it was Rhys who slew King Richard, fighting with him hand to hand. Whatever may be the foundation for this story, his conduct on this day was so distinguished that Richmond ascribed to it the issue of the battle and ever after in gratitude applied to him the title of "Father Rhys." He also knighted him on the field after the victory. Other honors were subsequently heaped upon him by the grateful monarch when established on the throne. He was appointed a member of the King's Council, and it is said that he declined the Earldom of Pembroke, alleging that knighthood was the greatest honor that could be conferred on a soldier. November 3rd, 1485, he received a grant for life of the offices of Constable, Lieutenant and Steward of Brecknock. November 6th, of the same year, he was appointed Chamberlain of Caermarthen and Cardigan and Steward of the Lordship of Builth. February 26th, 1485–6, he was appointed one of the commissioners of the King's mines. In the next year he was present at the Battle of Stoke, June 16th, and mainly instrumental in se-curing the victory. In 1492 he accompanied Henry to France, and the military appearance and handsome equipment of his soldiers is spoken of by Bacon in his history of the reign of Henry VII. June 22nd, 1497, with fifteen hundred horse, he was at the battles of Blackheath, fought between the King's forces and the revolted Cornishmen under Lord Audley; and after a fierce conflict took the latter prisoner. April 22nd, 1505, he was elected a Knight of the most noble order of the Garter, and occupied the twelfth stall of the Sovereign's side in St. George's Chapel, Windsor; where his arms were still visible when Anstis wrote his Memorials of the Garter. He was frequently employed by Henry in negotiations on the Continent; and the records of the Garter show that he was excused from attendance at several Chapters of the Order, as being absent on the King's business. In 1507 he gave a magnificent tournament at Carew Castle, in honor of his election to the Garter, the festivities at which lasted over a week. November 7th, 1509, he was appointed Justiciary for South Wales. May 12th, 1510, he was made Chamberlain of the same District. In a list of the Vanguard retinue of Henry in his French expedition, dated May 15th, 1513, appears Sir Ryce ap Thomas with captains and petty

captains, foot soldiers, demi-lances, in all 2,993. The MSS. diary of John
Taylor, Clerk of Parliament, under June 25th, of the same year, says:
"The French fled before Sir Rice ap Thomas;" June 29th Sir Rice recap-
tured one of the King's great guns which had been taken by the French.
At the battle of Guinegate or Spurs he took four French standards, and
was instrumental in the capture of the Duke of Longueville. August 22nd
he was present at the siege of Therouenne, and September 9th at that of
Tournay. June 4th, 1515, there is recorded a confirmation and quit-claim
from the King to Sir Rhesus ap Thomas son and heir of Thomas son and
heir of Griffin Nicholas, of the Castle and Lordship of Trayne March, and
third part of the Ville of St. Clair in Caermarthen. May 16th, 1517, he
was granted the offices of Steward and Chancellor, in survivorship with his
son, Sir Griffith, of Haverford West and Rowse in the Marches of Wales.
July 5th, of the same year, he was one of the witnesses to a treaty executed
between Henry, Maximilian, and Charles. In a list of the persons who
shall accompany the King to the Field of the Cloth of Gold, drawn up
March 12th, 1518-19, Sir Rhys is one of the four Knights of the Order,
i. e., the Garter, who are to go, each having 22 servants, 2 to be chaplains,
and 2 gentlemen, with 48 horses. In 1520, Henry writing to the Lord
Lieutenant of Ireland, says that he has "writen to our trusty and right
welbiloved Sir Rice ap Thomas to putt the nomber of fifte horsemen of
Walys in arredinesse for the Irish wars." May 27th, 1522, he was appointed
to attend the King at the visit of Charles the Fifth. The exact date of
his death I have not been able to ascertain, but it is on record that
February 2nd, 1526-7, he made his will, and died the following year, the
will being probated July 5th, 1527. He was buried in the Church of the
Grey Friars at Caermarthen: but his body was afterwards removed to the
eastern aisle of St. Peter's Church, in the same town, where his monu-
ment, a sculptured marble block, surmounted by recumbent figures of Sir
Rhys and his third wife, is the most remarkable which the Church contains.
He was married three times, first to the daughter of Sir John Ellis; second,
to Eva of Court Henry; and thirdly, to Elizabeth dau. of Sir William
Thomas of Ragland Castle, and sister to William Herbert, first Earl of
Pembroke, of that family; who was the widow of Sir Harry Stradling,
Knight of St. Donat's Castle Glamorgan, and died at Picton, in Pembroke,
February 5th, 1535. Sir Rhys left several natural children, for whom he
liberally provided. By his second wife, Eva, of Court Henry, he had one
son Griffith ap Rhys, born in 1478. He was once nominated as a candidate
for the Garter, but failed to secure an election. When Henry VII. revived
the order of the Bath, November 17th, 1501, on the marriage of his son,

Prince Arthur, to Katherine of Arragon, Griffith ap Rhys was created a Knight of that ancient order. In April of the next year at the funeral of Prince Arthur, he bore the Prince's banner before his bier. At his father's tournament, in 1507, he was one of the principal challengers.

TOMB OF SIR RHYS AP THOMAS, K. G., IN ST. PETER'S CHURCH, CARMARTHEN.

Sir Griffith ap Rhys md. about 1504, Katherine, dau. of Sir John St. John, and aunt to the first Lord St. John of Bletshoe: who after his death md. Sir Piers Edgecombe, ancestor of the present Earl of Mt. Edgecombe; but is buried with her first husband in Worcester Cathedral. By her Sir Griffith ap Rhys left issue at his death, in 1521:

1st. Agnes md. William VI., Lord Stourton, who d. in 1557, and his widow md. Sir Edward Baynton, Knt. of Rowden, in Hertfordshire, and d. in 1574.

2nd. Rice, who succeeded his grandfather Rice ap Griffith, b. in 1508, was a gallant youth, fond of splendor and display.

Brought up with a knowledge of his great wealth and position, and married to a daughter of the Duke of Norfolk, he seems to have shown an arrogant disposition, which made him dangerous enemies. With a numerous and devoted tenantry he felt secure and able to defy them; but in the end by obtaining the ear of the jealous King, they were able to effect his ruin. The history of his fall is a brief, though tragic, one. In the month of July, 1528, we find him in the height of his power, and in his loyalty writing from Caermarthen to Cardinal Wolsey to complain of the numbers of Irish rebels from Desmond's country who came into Pembroke-shire, and that the Mayor and Council of Tenby encourage them. March 3rd, 1528-9, he writes to Wolsey complaining that his tenants are disturbed by persons under Lord Ferrars, the King's Justiciary for South Wales; and reminding the Cardinal that he encouraged him to declare any grievance of himself or tenants, asks to be Lord Ferrars' Deputy. Would be content to give my Lord such sum as Wolsey thought convenient for it.

The eleventh of the same month he notifies Wolsey that he has taken a pirate vessel; and thanks the Cardinal for his continued goodness. July 8th he writes again, giving an account of the trial of the master of the pirate vessel, one William Hughes. Whether this is the same person afterwards concerned in Rice ap Griffith's treason I do not know. Between these two dates occurs an event which was probably the cause of Rice ap Griffith's conspiracy. June 16th of this year, Walter Devereux, Lord Ferrars, writes from "Kermarthen" to Wolsey "that during his sessions in that town, Rece Griffith, Esq., encouraged the malefactors by causing proclamation to be made in divers churches to induce the people to attend upon him, instead of the Justiciary, and by making quarrels in Kermarden. On Tuesday, June 15th, he came to the Castle with his armed servants; where I was with other gentlemen, and picked a quarrel with me about Thomas ap Howen, his kinsman, who was in ward for various misdemeanours, and hurting the people when they came to complain of him. Rece drew his dagger on me, and I took it from him and put him in ward. His friends stir up the people to rebellion, but he shall not be let out until he find security." The next day Lady Katherine Ryx writes Wolsey reminding him of his friendship for her family, and telling him that "his servant, master Ryx Griffith is in Caermarthen Castle on false surmise of desiring Thomas ap Owen, servant to the King, then in ward, to take out of the constable's hands one Jankyn, servant to Ryx, upon which Ferrers drew his dagger, and Ryx his also in self-defence. No harm was done except that Ryx was hurt in his arm and arrested, at which the county is greatly discontented. Great dissatisfaction has prevailed ever since Ferrers' coming to Caermarthen.

Ryx would have written, but is kept from pen and ink." In conclusion she begs that Wolsey will not allow them to have shame and rebuke.

The arrest seems to have caused a great disturbance among the people; and Lady Ryx and her friends seem to have attempted to release her husband by force without waiting for Wolsey's action, for we find Ferrers writing on June 18th, to Wolsey, about "the great insurrection in these parts at the instigation of Rece Griffith and Lady Haward. There has not been such in Wales in any one's memory. Everything is now quiet, and the captains and ringleaders have returned home."

From the fact of his presiding at the trial of William Hughes, master of the pirate vessel, Rice ap Griffith appears to have given the necessary security and been released by the Justiciary. The insult, however, no doubt rankled in his memory; and two years after, when he went up to London, predisposed him to listen to the proposals of some of the papal emissaries.

"The history of his conspiracy is a very mysterious one," says the historian Froude, and my investigation has enabled me to throw very little additional light on the subject. William Hughes called in the act of attainder, "gentleman of London," who was his partner in the plot, was actively engaged in behalf of Queen Katherine of Arragon at the time of the proceedings in regard to her divorce. From a conversation between two friars after the execution of Rice ap Griffith, reported in Froude's second volume, from the testimony of one who overheard them, it would appear that the unfortunate youth was in reality innocent of the crime charged against him. The conspiracy itself was one of the numerous out-croppings of the great papal movement of the Sixteenth Century. The intention seems to have been to assassinate the King, and in the uncertainty with regard to the succession, Rice ap Griffith was persuaded that his claim as a descendant of the British and Welsh Kings might be sufficient to give him the throne. An old prophecy that James of Scotland, with the bloody hand, and the Raven (Rice's crest) should conquer England, was also brought to mind to encourage him. Probably Rice was not guilty of doing more than listening to their treasonable propositions, but that was sufficient to ruin him. Some time in the autumn of 1531, probably October 2nd, he was arrested. His friends in Wales broke out in open insurrection, and we find that a warrant was addressed to Lord Ferrers, dated October 7th, 1531, directing the arrest of James ap Griffith, ap Howell sister's son to Sir Rhys ap Thomas, who had fortified himself in the Castle of Emlyn. He seems to have directed the revolt, and probably was the last of Rice's adherents to surrender. At its session of January 15th, 1531-2 Parliament passed an act forfeiting "Rychard ap Gruffyth late of London Esquire, otherwise Rice ap Griffith of Carewe and William Hughes late of London gentleman, as indicted and convicted in the Court of the King's Bench of having at Iseldon (or Islington) in Middlesex, on August 28th, 1531, and elsewhere compassed &c. the death of our Lord the King."

January 4th, 1531-2, Carlo Capello, their English Agent, writes as follows to the Signory of Venice: "The heretic friar was burnt alive; and, three days ago, they sentenced to death Master Ris, who had been put in the Tower before October 3rd, 1531, and this morning, on Tower Hill, he was beheaded in public, and one of his servants (presumably William Hughes) was hanged and quartered."

In the act of forfeiture the rights of Lady Katherine Rice were scrupulously reserved; but uselessly, for in the Parliamentary Session of 1541-2 we find her name, Katherine, Countess of Bridgewater, (she had md. 2nd Sir Henry Daubeney, Earl of Bridgewater) amongst others as attainted of misprision of treason, along with Queen Katherine, Howard.

Rice ap. Griffith md. Lady Katherine Howard, the sixth dau. of the second Duke of Norfolk of that Family by his second wife Agnes, dau. of Hugh Tilney and sister and heiress of Sir Philip Tilney of Boston, Knt., and had issue: Griffith, Agnes, and Thomas.

Griffith ap Rice (q. v.) was restored in blood, though not to the estates of his father, in the reign of Queen Mary, is said to have md. Eleanor, dau. of Sir Thomas Jones, Knt., and is claimed as the lineal ancestor of the present Lord Dynevor of Dynevor Castle, Caermarthenshire.

Thomas, youngest son of Rice ap Griffith, was a child at the time of his House's fall; I have reason to believe he was with his Cousin James Griffith at Emlyn at the time of his arrest, and in his suite when he escaped from the Tower and went to Scotland. When Griffith left the Scotch Court, Thomas was brought back to Wales, and growing up there as appears by the Proceedings in Chancery relating to a suit brought by one James Reade to recover a piece of property; occupied land in the Parish of Ebbernant, in Caermarthenshire. He married a dau. of Philip Scidamore, who brought him the demesne lands in Grosmont Manor, Monmouthshire, and a grist mill near by. Their son, John Philip Thomas, inherited this property before 1585, and in 1591 was Queen's Lessee of Mills at Kenchurch in the same shire. He seems to have married a wife from Swansea, as we find his son Evan b. in 1580 resided there. He may have been the Evan Thomas who was a member of the Awennydion or Bardic College of Glamorganshire in 1620.

He died in 1650, leaving issue: Philip, of whom presently, and possibly Capt. Evan Thomas who was one of the principal members of a Baptist

Thomas

congregation, near Swansea, in 1672, and Rice Thomas who was gunner of the tenth Lion's Whelp pinnace between 1632 and 1637, and served with John Mears whose namesake and grandson married Philip Thomas' daughter.

Philip, son of Evan Thomas, was in the East India Company's service in 1621, and possibly was the Messenger of the Commissioners for charitable uses in 1638; if so, he was in London that year. Afterwards he engaged in Mercantile life in Bristol, in partnership with one Devonshire.

Some time in 1651 Philip Thomas left Bristol, and with his wife Sarah Harrison and three children Philip, Sarah, and Elizabeth, came to Lord Baltimore's province of Maryland. Family tradition states that he first landed on Kent Island; but the earliest record of a land grant to him dated February 19th, 1651-2, conveys to him 500 acres of land called "Beckley" on the west side of Chesapeake Bay "in consideration that he hath in the year 1651 transported himself, Sarah his wife, Philip, Sarah, and Elizabeth his children into this our province." Between 1658 and 1661 he had granted him 100 acres called "Thomas Towne," in 1665 a grant of 120 acres called "Fuller's Poynt," in 1668 a grant of 300 acres called "The Planes," in 1672 a grant of 200 acres called "Phillip's Addición," and numerous other grants of unnamed tracts. This land lay mostly in Anne Arundel County and in the neighborhood of what is now known as West River. "Fuller's Poynt" between the Severn and South Rivers is now known as Thomas' Point, and is the site of a light-house. A man of character and position, he acquired considerable influence in the affairs of the Colony, and affiliating himself with the Puritan party, became one of its leaders. When under his friend, Capt. William Fuller, they gained possession of the Government, he appointed a member of the Provincial Council, and when in 1658 they were compelled to resign their control, he was one of the commissioners to make the surrender.

March 20th, 1658-9, says the old Council Record Book, Liber Hh. "Messrs. Wm. Fuller, Edward Lloyd, Richard Preston, Samuel Withers, Philip Thomas, and Thomas Mears came to St. Leonards in order to the performance of the Articles of Surrender of the Government as intended and arranged between Richard Bennet and others and the Lord Proprietary's Officers, November 30th, 1657.

After this he did not take an active part in the political affairs of the Colony, and seems to have joined the Society of Friends previous to his death. The celebrated George Fox visiting Maryland, Philip Thomas may have been converted to that persuasion by his preaching. His Will (a copy of which in the handwriting of one of his sons-in-law is in the possession of his descendants) was made September 9th, 1674, and probated July 10th,

1675. From this he appears to have disposed of by sale or otherwise of much of the land granted him, only mentioning "Beckley," "Fuller's Poynt," and the "Playns," and his two houses in Bristol, England. The clause in the Will making "the body of Quakers" a final Court of Appeal in the event of any dispute arising under its provisions, was a common one amongst the Society of Friends and in this case was had recourse to. After the death of his widow Sarah Thomas, his son Samuel claimed all her estates by virtue of a verbal will which he alleged she had made in his favor. This claim was resisted by his brother-in-law Edward Talbot, and the West River Meeting of Friends was appealed to, to decide the question. The Meeting decided that although she had expressed a wish that Samuel Thomas should be her sole heir, she had not given legal effect to it, and that the estate should be equally divided between her several heirs.

After her husband's death Sarah Thomas had been a prominent member of the Society of Friends, if not an accepted Minister. She died early in the year 1687 having had issue:

Born in Bristol before 1651:

i.   **PHILIP** d. without issue before 1688.

ii.   **SARAH** md. after 1674 **JOHN**, son of **Thomas** and **Elizabeth Mears**, who d. in May 1675, and his wife in the same year, leaving issue: an only dau. **SARAH**.

iii. **ELIZABETH** md. as his 3d wife **WILLIAM COALE**, (q. v.) he d. Oct. 30th, 1678, and his widow md. 2dly before 1683 **EDWARD**, 2d son of **Richard** and **Elizabeth Talbot**, (q. v.) who d. in Jan. 1692-3, his wife in 1726.

Born in Maryland after 1651:

iv.   **MARTHA** md. after 1672 **RICHARD ARNELL** or **ARNOLD** who d. in June 1684, his wife d. before 1688, having had issue; **SAMUEL** who d. in infancy; **SARAH**; and **ELIZABETH** md. Jany. 8th, 1701-2, **JACOB GILES** and had issue: Sarah md. September 2d, 1740, Samuel Hopkins. (q. v.)

v.   **SAMUEL** born about 1655, a prominent member of the Society of Friends, md. May 15th, 1688, by Friends' ceremony at his own house in Anne Arundel County, **MARY**, youngest dau. of **Francis** and **Elizabeth Hutchins** of Calvert County, who d. in July 1751, her husband d. before 1743, having had issue:

      i.   **SARAH** b. in 1689, md. October 25th, 1705, **JOSEPH**, son of **William** and **Eliza Richardson**. (q. v.)

      ii.   **ELIZABETH** md. December 19th, 1717, **RICHARD**, son of **Richard** and **Mary Snowden**. (q. v.)

iii.   **MARY** md. July 31st, 1718, **JOHN**, son of **Samuel** and Ann Galloway. (q. v.)

iv.   **PHILIP** b. in 1694, of whom presently.

v.   **JOHN** md. in 1727, **ELIZABETH**, dau. of Richard and Eliza Snowden. (q. v.)

vi.   **SAMUEL** b. in 1702. md. in 1730, **MARY**, dau. of Richard and Eliza Snowden. (q. v.)

vii.   **ANN** md. October 8th, 1730, **EDWARD FELL**, of Over Killet, Lancashire England, who d. in March 1743, his wife having predeceased him, leaving an only dau. **ANNE.**

viii.   **MARGARET** md. after 1735, **WILLIAM HARRIS.** (q. v.)

PHILIP, eldest son of **Samuel** and **Mary Thomas**, b. in 1694, md. 1st in March 1721, **FRANCES HOLLAND**, and had issue by her: **WILLIAM**, (q. v.) He married 2dly August 11th, 1724, **ANN**, dau. of **Samuel** and **Mary Chew**, and died in January 1763, his wife in July 1777, having had issue :

i.   **SAMUEL** b. June 4th, 1725. (q. v.)

ii.   **PHILIP** b. July 3d. 172—. (q. v.)

iii.   **MARY** b. Jany. 1st, 1730-1, md. 1st, May 12th, 1748, **HENRY HILL**, and had issue: **HENRIETTA MARGARET** md. **BENJAMIN OGLE**, of Annapolis, who d. in July 1809, his wife in Aug. 1815, having had issue: Ann md. John Tayloe, Mary and Benjamin. **MRS. HILL** md. 2dly February 7th, 1760, **ROBERT**, son of **John Pleasants** of Virginia, by whom she had issue: **Ann Thomas.**

iv.   **ELIZABETH** b. March 8th, 1732-3 md. **SAMUEL SNOWDEN.** (q. v.)

v.   **RICHARD** b. July 7, 1736 md. **DEBORAH HUGHES**, and had issue: **PHILIP** md. —— **MYERS**: and **ELIZABETH** md. **STEPHEN STEWART.**

vi.   **JOHN** b. Aug. 26th, 1743, resided at West River, in Anne Arundel County, Md. He wrote some very respectable poetry, mostly in the shape of occasional verses, twenty-two of which may be found in a Collection of Extracts and Original Verses printed at Annapolis in 1808. He was President of the Senate of Maryland ; md. Aug. 23d, 1777, **SARAH**, third child of **Dr. William Murray**, and d. Feby. 3d, 1805, having had issue :

   i.   **ANNE** b. July 6th, 1778, d. in April 1848, unmarried.

   ii.   **PHILIP JOHN** b. July 29th, 1782, of whom presently.

   iii.   **SARAH** b. Oct. 28th, 1784, d. Oct. 12th, 1860, unmarried.

iv.　JOHN b. April 27th. 1788, md. Dec. 31st., 1817. ELIZABETH, fourth dau. of Commodore Alexander Murray, of Philadelphia, and d. Dec. 27th, 1858. His wife is also d., having had issue: SALLY; JULIA MURRAY; ALEXANDER MURRAY; all unmarried and residing at "Lebanon" the family seat at West River; DANIEL MURRAY, an Attorney at Law of Baltimore City, and a prominent member of the Protestant Episcopal Church; MARY md. A. HAMILTON HALL, of West River, by whom she had two children; CORNELIA unmarried and resident at "Lebanon."

PHILIP JOHN, eldest son of John and Sarah (Murray) Thomas, b. July 29th, 1782, md. November 8th, 1804. CORNELIA, dau. of Thomas Lancaster Lansdale, and d. June 15th, 1859. having had issue: two daughters. MARY and CORNELIA; who both md. Dr. JAMES CHESTON; and a son, JOHN MOYLAN, b. September 26th, 1805, who practiced medicine in Washington, D. C., md. July 25th, 1829. SARAH BROOKE LEE, dau. of Tench Ringgold, and d. October 15th, 1853, having had issue:

i.　MARY b. May 11th, 1830.

ii.　ELIZA LEE b. August 8th, 1831, d. in October, 1865, unmarried.

iii.　JOHN MOYLAN b. Mch. 2d, 1833, an Attorney-at-Law, of Philadelphia, Pa., md. Oct. 24th, 1860. ADELE, dau. of Charles Ingersoll, of that city, and has issue: HELEN RINGGOLD b. Jany. 12th, 1862; CHARLES INGERSOLL b. Nov. 27th, 1865; and MARY GEORGINA LEE b. Sept. 9th, 1870.

iv.　CORNELIA LANSDALE b. Sept. 5th, 1834.

v.　LAWRENCE RINGGOLD b. in Sept. 1836.

vi.　SAMUEL SPRIGG b. Mch. 31st, 1838.

vii.　SARAH BROOKE LEE b. April 6th, 1840.

viii.　ANNA MARIA b. Jany. 19th, 1842.

ix.　WILLIAM LANSDALE b. June 26th, 1844, d. in infancy.

x.　CATHARINE LOUISA b. June 29th, 1845, d. in infancy.

SAMUEL, eldest son of Philip and Ann (Chew) Thomas, b. June 4th, 1725, resided at Perry Point, on the Susquehannah River, opposite Havre-de-Grace, and was proprietor of the Ferry rights on both sides of the River. He md. Oct. 23rd, 1750. his cousin MARY, dau. of Samuel and Mary (Snowden) Thomas; who d. Mch. 4th, 1770, and her husband d. July 17th, 1784. having had issue:

i.   **ANN** b. October 2d, 1751, md. **THOMAS RUSSELL.** (q. v.)

ii.   **PHILIP** b. August 12th, 1753, d. s. p.

iii.   **SAMUEL** b. June 20th, 1757, d. May 20th, 1759.

iv.   **RICHARD SNOWDEN** b. Feby. 25th, 1762, of whom presently.

v.   **JOHN CHEW** b. October 15th, 1764. (q. v.)

vi.   **SAMUEL** b. February 2d, 1776, was a Minister of the Society of Friends, md. September 17th, 1789, **ANNA**, dau. of Dr. **Charles Alexander Warfield**, also a Minister of the Society of Friends, who d. May 19th, 1820, her husband d. October 1st, 1820, having had issue: **ELIZABETH WARFIELD** b. November 14th, 1790, md. October 7th, 1806, **NICHOLAS SNOWDEN**, (q. v.); **HARRIET ANN** b. December 16th, 1793, d. January 16th, 1794; and **JULIANNA MARIA** b. January 16th, 1795, md. September 24th, 1811, **ISAAC KNIGHT.** (q. v.)

vii.   **EVAN WILLIAM** b. February 6th, 1769, resided first at "Richmond Hill," in Cecil County, Maryland, afterwards at "Mt. Friendship," near Havre-de-Grace, and then at "Whitby Hall," near Philadelphia, to which place he removed in 1802. He md. January 5th, 1792, **MARTHA**, dau. of George and Martha Gray of Whitby Hall, who d. February 9th, 1868, her husband d. August 27th, 1840, having had issue:

    i.   **MARY** b. March 15th, 1793, md. Oct. 27th, 1810, Dr. **GUSTAVUS WARFIELD.** (q. v.)

    ii.   **GEORGE GRAY** b. December 28th, 1794, d. July 17th, 1795.

    iii.   **EVAN WILLIAM** b. May 22d, 1796, md. May 13th, 1826, **ELIZA**, dau. of Gen. Josiah Harmar, of Philadelphia, and d. s. p. at "Greenwood," near "Whitby," September 17th, 1838.

    iv.   **GEORGE GRAY** b. October 5th, 1798, md. 1st September 29th, 1834, **JANE H. GRAFF**; 2d, **ANN GRAY**, dau. of Thomas and Elizabeth Leiper, of Philadelphia, and d. s. p. March 9th, 1854.

    v.   Dr. **SAMUEL** b. July 20th, 1802, md. April 11th, 1832, **HENRIETTA GRAFF**, who d. in 1876, he died February 17th, 1864, having had issue:

        i.   **HENRIETTA** md. June 7th, 1866, **CHARLES EASTWICK.**

        ii.   **WILLIAM HARMAR** b. March 22d, 1845, resides at "Whitby Hall," md. June 2d, 1870, **NANNIE**, dau. of Rev. John Chew and Annie Thomas, and has issue: **ANNIE HEATH**, and **JULIA VALENTINE.**

        iii.   **MARTHA** md. June 2d, 1866, **EVAN W. THOMAS.** (q. v.)

        iv.   **EMMA** md. June 2d, 1870, **WILLIAM EASTWICK**, and has issue: **LILLY, WILLIAM,** Jr.

RICHARD SNOWDEN THOMAS, eldest surviving son of **Samuel** and **Mary** (**Thomas**) **Thomas,** b. Feby. 25th, 1762, resided at Perry Point, near Havre-de-Grace. He md. December 13th, 1784, **MARY,** only dau. of **Sutherland Mifflin,** and d. July 29th, 1814, having had issue:

i. **SAMUEL** b. September 1st, 1785, d. s. p.

ii. **RICHARD SNOWDEN** b. January 11th, 1787, d. s. p. April 23d, 1871.

iii. **MARY** b. June 25th, 1788, md. **DAVID JONES.** (q. v.)

iv. **ANN** b. November 4th, 1789, d. February 7th, 1793.

v. **JOHANNAH** b. November 16th, 1790, d. October 13th, 1792.

vi. **DEBORAH** b. March 17th, 1792, md. **GUSTAVUS WRIGHT,** and had issue: **GUSTAVUS.**

vii. **WILLIAM** b. August 8th, 1793, d. s. p.

viii. **ELIZABETH** b. January 25th, 1795, d. s. p.

ix. **MIFFLIN** b. April 11th, 1796, d. s. p. October 9th, 1821.

x. **HENRY** b. September 15th, 1797, d. August 28th, 1798.

xi. **JOHN** of whom presently.

xii. **HENRY EDWARD** b. January 1st, 1802, d. September 11th, 1803.

JOHN, eleventh child of **Richard Snowden** and **Mary Thomas,** b. March 7th, 1799, md. in May or June, 1826, **HARRIET MARIA STRONG;** he died August 18th, 1837, and his wife January 7th, 1866, having had issue:

i. **MARY SUSANNA** b. in May 1829, d. in September 1829.

ii. **HENRY MIFFLIN** b. April 1st, 1831, md. November 27th, 1860, **SARAH LOUISA CHAMBERLAIN,** and has issue: **MIFFLIN WILBER** b. September 12th, 1861; **ELLA CHAMBERLAIN** b. May 7th, 1864; **RICHARD SNOWDEN** b. January 23d, 1866; **LAURA REBECCA** b. September 16th, 1867; and **JOHN ALEXANDER** b. June 8th, 1874.

iii. **JOHN EVAN** b. January 28th, 1834, md. February 22d, 1865, **LAURA CORNELIA TILDEN,** and had issue: **GEORGE HINES** b. February 23d, 1866; **JOHN EVAN** and **HARRIET MAUD,** twins, b. November 7th, 1867, the former d. August 23d, 1868; and **MARY MIFFLIN** b. December 12th, 1870.

iv. **LAWRENCE ALEXANDER** b. March 6th, 1837.

JOHN CHEW, fourth son of **Samuel** and **Mary Thomas,** b. Oct. 15th, 1764, resided after his marriage at "Fairland" in Anne Arundel County, which place he afterwards sold for $50,000. He was a man of high character, and an active member of the Society of Friends. In early life he took an interest in politics and was elected by the Federal party in Maryland one of their representatives in the Congress of 1799–1801. As a member of that House he took part in the celebrated election of President in the last named year, which after three days of intense excitement, and thirty-five ballots, resulted in the election of Thomas Jefferson. On marrying an heiress and becoming a slaveholder, he lost his membership in the Society of Friends, but Feby. 12th, 1812, he manumitted his slaves to the number of over one hundred and was received again into membership with the Society. He md. Sept. 18th, 1788, **MARY,** only daughter and heiress of **Richard** and **Eliza (Rutland) Snowden** of "Fairland," Anne Arundel County, Maryland, and died at his residence in Leiperville, Pennsylvania, May 10th, 1836. By his wife who died Nov. 13th, 1844, at the residence of her son **Dr. Richard H. Thomas,** he had issue:

i.   **MARY ANN** b. Jany. 23d, 1789, d. April 4th, 1790.

ii.   **ANN SNOWDEN** b. March 13th, 1791, d. Oct. 2d, 1791.

iii.   **ELIZA SNOWDEN** b. August 5th, 1792, md. May 3d, 1810, **GEORGE GRAY LEIPER,** of "Lapidea." (¶ v.

iv.   **SAMUEL** b. March 28th, 1794, d. Sept. 14th, 1804.

v.   **THOMAS SNOWDEN** b. February 19th, 1796, of whom presently.

vi.   **JOHN CHEW** b. August 21st, 1797, d. March 15th, 1799.

vii.   **HENRIETTA MARIA** b. July 30th, 1799, d. unmarried, Jany. 17th, 1874, at the residence of the family of her brother **Dr. Richard H. Thomas,** over which she had exercised a mother's care from the time of their own mother's death.

viii.   **MARY SNOWDEN** b. Sept. 22d, 1801, d. Aug. 13th, 1802.

ix.   **Dr. JOHN CHEW** b. September 22d, 1803, at "Fairland," was graduated an M. D. at the University of Pennsylvania, April 8th, 1824, and led a roving life in early manhood. He was for some time in the Government employ at the building of the Newcastle Breakwater on the Coast of Delaware and finally settled in Baltimore, practicing his profession there with success. In 1854 he injured one knee by a fall from his carriage, and further injury to the same limb resulted in Paralysis which confined him to his residence for several years previous to his death. He was md. March 2d, 1848, by the Mayor of New York to **JANE LAWRENCE,** dau. of **Thomas** and **Anna Buckley** of that city, and d. August 29th, 1862, leaving issue: **LAWRENCE BUCKLEY** b. December 6th, 1848; **JULIA;** and **WALTER WOOD** b. June 11th, 1852.

x.   Dr. **RICHARD HENRY** b. June 20th, 1805. (q. v.)

xi.   **SAMUEL EVAN** b. March 12th, 1807, d. in 1851, leaving issue : **ANNIE, JOHN CHEW,** and **MARY SNOWDEN.**

xii.   **JULIA** b. August 16th, 1808, a Minister of the Society of Friends, md. April 20th, 1845, **BOND VALENTINE** of Bellefonte, Centre County, Pa., a Minister of the Society of Friends, who has since d. s. p.

xiii.   **HARRIET** b. March 20, and d. March 27th, 1811.

xiv.   **MARIA RUSSELL** b. Aug. 29th, 1812, d. in Novr. 1816.

xv.   **CHARLES** b. August 18th, 1816, d. in 1817.

THOMAS SNOWDEN, eldest son of **John Chew** and **Mary** (Snowden) **Thomas,** b. Feby. 19th, 1796, was at one time a member of the Legislature of Maryland, md. Decr. 31st, 1819, by Rev. Wm. Duke, P. E. Minister of Elkton, Md., to **ANN,** dau. of **William** and **Frances** (**Russell**) **Sewall.** He resided at North East, Cecil County, Md., where he died May 21st, 1857, leaving issue :

i.   Rev. **JOHN CHEW** b. Nov. 9th, 1820, a minister of the Methodist Episcopal Church, to which denomination his parents belonged. He md. March 16th, 1847, **ANNIE HEATH WILLIAMS,** of Newtown, Bucks Co., Pa., and died at Stroudsburg in the same State, leaving issue : NANNIE and **WM. HARMAR THOMAS.** (q. v.) GRIFFITH WILLIAMS b. Feby. 10th, 1853, md. Feby. 10th, 1874, LIZZIE, dau. of Peter B. Melick, of Philadelphia, and has one child Mary ; and FANNY BOSWELL md. in 1876, HUBERT SMITH, of New Jersey.

ii.   **RUSSELL** b. Aug. 7th, 1822, md. **ELIZABETH A. MITCHELL,** of Elkton, Md., and and died April 22d, 1876, leaving issue : MARY ALICIA.

iii.   **NANCY** b. Sept. 30th, 1824, died unmarried in August 1873.

iv.   **FRANCES LOUISA** b. Aug. 26th, 1826, md. April 8th, 1851, Rev. **WILLIAM LAWS BOSWELL,** a minister of the Methodist Episcopal Church, and at one time a Professor in Dickinson College. She died after a short illness, April 17th, 1876, leaving issue : **Rev. JAMES IVERSON,** a minister of the Methodist Episcopal Church, b. Jany. 9th, 1852 ; THOMAS SNOWDEN b. Nov. 6th, 1856 ; WILLIAM LAWS b. July 18th, 1859 ; and RUSSELL THOMAS b. in November 1863.

v.   Rev. **THOMAS SNOWDEN** b. July 28th, 1828, a minister of the Methodist Episcopal Church, Chief Clerk of the Maryland House of Delegates 1860-61, Hospital Chaplain U. S. A. 1862-65, and now Pastor of a large Church in Philadelphia. He md. April 20th, 1854, **ANNA M. MILLER,** and has issue : JOSEPH MILLER b. Feby. 4th, 1855 ; MARY RUSSELL : ANN ELIZABETH : EMMA VIRGINIA ; FANNY BOSWELL ; HENRIETTA MARIA ; and MARTHA.

vi.   EVAN W. b. Sept. 13th, 1829, was a Lieutenant in the Maryland Volunteers U. S. A during the Civil War, md. June 2d. 1866, MARTHA GRAY, dau. of Dr. Samuel Thomas, of Whitby Hall, and has issue: EVAN, ANNIE and MARTHA.

vii. Rev. JAMES SEWALL b. Dec. 21st, 1831, a minister of the Methodist Episcopal Church, md. June 6th, 1863, EUNICE D. DRAKE, and has issue: EVAN WALDEN b. Feby. 26th, 1864; ANNIE HEATH b. May 3d, 1865; HELEN LOUISA b. Feby. 4th, 1867; THOMAS SNOWDEN b. March 17th, 1869; CARRIE RUSSELL b. Sept. 20th, 1871; GRACE WILBUR b. Jany. 24th, 1874.

viii. MARY RUSSELL b. May 24th, 1835, died Jany. 11th, 1849.

ix.   ELIZA SNOWDEN.

Dr. RICHARD HENRY, tenth child of John Chew and Mary Thomas, b. June 20th, 1805, was educated at the University of Pennsylvania, sharing the first honors, and was graduated in its Medical School in 1828. Afterwards he settled in Baltimore where he had one of the largest practices; was a Professor in the Medical School of the University of Maryland, and an eminent Minister of the Society of Friends, in which capacity he travelled extensively in Europe and America. He md. first May 13th, 1830, MARTHA, dau. of Jas. Carey, a Bank President and distinguished Merchant of Baltimore, and had issue: Dr. JAMES CAREY, a Minister of the Society of Friends and practicing Physician, who md. Oct. 31st, 1855, MARY, dau. of John M. Whitall, of Philadelphia, and has issue: MARTHA CAREY, JOHN M. WHITALL, HENRY M., BOND VALENTINE, MARY GRACE, MARGARET CHESTON, HELEN W., FRANK S., and DORA C.

Dr. R. H. THOMAS md. secondly Feby. 9th, 1842, PHEBE, dau. of John and Phebe (Hicks) Clapp, of New York, and had issue by her: JOHN CLAPP b. Dec. 11th, 1842, md. June 11th, 1873, EUGENIA, dau. of Richard Cromwell, of Baltimore; HENRY died in youth; ALLEN CLAPP b. Dec. 26th, 1846, md. August 20th, 1872, REBECCA H., dau. of Russel and Phebe A. Marble, of Woonsocket, R. I.; and has issue: EDWARD b. June 21st, 1877; MARY SNOWDEN; CHARLES YARNALL b. Oct. 16th, 1851, md. Aug. 16th, 1877, REBECCA S., dau. of Joseph and Mary Edge, of Deer Creek, Md.; and Dr. RICHARD HENRY b. Jany. 26th, 1854.

Dr. R. H. THOMAS md. thirdly Feby. 9th, 1859, DEBORAH C. HINSDALE, of New York City, a Minister of the Society of Friends, and died without further issue Jany. 15th, 1860.

PHILIP, second son of **Philip** and **Anne** (**Chew**) **Thomas**, b. July 3d, 172-, inherited from his father one-half of his estate at the Susquehannah Ferry called "Mount Ararat"; md. April 30th, 1754. **ANNE**, dau. of **John Harris** of Harrisburg, and widow of **Joseph Galloway**, and had issue an only son, **PHILIP**.

PHILIP md. in 1783, **SARAH MARGARET**, dau. of **William** and **Catherine** (**Crumpton**) **Weems**, of Crumpton Hall, Elkridge, Md., and d. in 1808 at Rockland, in Cecil Co., Md., having had issue:

i.   MARY F. C. md. Capt. JEREMIAH S. BOIES, and had issue: JEREMIAH S.; JAMES THOMAS; SARAH H. md. Professor R. A. F. PENROSE of Philadelphia, and WILLIAM HUBBARD.

ii.   PHILIP md. about 1805 FANNY LUDLOW, and had issue: PHILIP d. in childhood; ELIZABETH; SARAH md. ——— JONES; MARTHA md. as his second wife ——— JONES; CATHERINE md. ——— BONN and LUDLOW.

iii. JOHN WEEMS resided near Port Deposit, Cecil Co., Md., was manager of the Canal there, and at one time a member of the State Legislature. He md. ——— WEBSTER, and d. leaving issue: PHILIP; and ELIZABETH WEEMS md. Rev. OWEN PATTEN THACKARA of Florida, and has issue: Juan Serrano, John Weems; Elizabeth James md. June 11th, 1874, Arthur W. Palmer, of Baltimore, and has one child Emma Louise; Samuel, and Philip Thomas.

iv.   JAMES d. unmarried.

v.   CATHERINE md. ——————— DAVIDSON, and d. leaving issue: Dr. JAMES; PHILIP d. s. p.; SARAH, ELIZABETH, GEORGE, FANNY, and WILLIAM.

vi.   ANN WEEMS md. as his second wife ——— DAVIDSON, and had issue: CHARLES and MERRYMAN.

vii. GEORGE A. md. HENRIETTA MARIA, dau. of Samuel Chamberlain, of Talbot County, Md., and d. leaving issue: NANNIE.

JOHN, second son of **Samuel** and **Mary** (**Hutchins**) **Thomas**, md. in April 1727, **ELIZABETH**, dau. of **Richard** and **Mary Snowden**, and d. in Feby. 1749-50, having had issue by his wife who predeceased him:

i.   RICHARD of whom presently.

ii.   SAMUEL, d. s. p.

iii. ELIZABETH md. RICHARD RICHARDSON. (q. v.)

iv.   JOHN b. in 1734, md. MARGARET HOPKINS, who d. Mch. 16th, 1806, aged 75 years, and her husband Feby. 15th, 1826, without issue surviving.

RICHARD, eldest son of **John** and **Elizabeth** (Snowden) **Thomas**, b about 1728, md. **SARAH COALE**, and had issue:

i.   **SAMUEL** 3d b. Dec. 2d, 1753, of whom presently.

ii.   **ELIZABETH** b. Oct. 28th, 1755, md. **ROGER JOHNSON**. (q. v.)

iii.   **RICHARD** b. Feby. 21st, 1758. (q. v.)

iv.   **JOHN** b. Sept. 27th, 1760, d. s. p.

v.   **MARY** b. Mch. 12th, 1762, md. **WILLIAM ROBERTSON**, and had issue: **SARAH** md. **JOSEPH HOWARD** (q. v.); and **THOMAS** md. **JANE RITTENHOUSE**.

vi.   **SARAH** b. Nov. 26th, 1764, md. **BERNARD GILPIN**. (q. v.)

vii.   **HENRIETTA** b. Feby. 17th, 1767, d. in infancy.

viii.   **MARGARET** b. June 11th, 1769, md. **GERARD BROOKE**. (q. v.)

ix.   **WILLIAM** b. Dec. 11th, 1771. (q. v.)

x.   **ANN** b. May 25th, 1774, d. s. p.

xi.   **HENRIETTA** 2d, b. Mch. 7th, 1777, d. s. p.

SAMUEL, eldest son of **Richard** and **Sarah** (Coale) **Thomas**, b. Dec. 2d, 1753, settled in Montgomery County and md. Oct. 31st, 1775, **MARY**, dau. of **John Cowman**, at her father's residence, and had issue:

i.   **SAMUEL** b. Nov. 13th, 1776, of whom presently.

ii.   **JOHN** 3d, b, Jany. 30th, 1778. (q. v.)

iii.   **SARAH** b. Jany. 25th, 1781, md. **WILLIS CANBY**, and had issue: **SAMUEL** md. **JULIET COCUS**, and had issue: William T.

iv.   **HENRIETTA** b. Dec. 9th, 1782, md. **CALEB BENTLEY**. (q. v.)

v.   **ELIZABETH** b. April 28th, 1784, md. Oct. 13th, 1825, **JAZER GARRETTSON**, and d. s. p.

vi.   **MARY** b. Nov. 16th, 1785, md. **JOSEPH HOWARD**. (q. v.)

SAMUEL, eldest son of **Samuel** and **Mary (Cowman) Thomas**, b. Nov. 13th, 1776, md. **MARY**, dau. of **Joshua** and **Rebecca (Owings) Howard**, and had issue:

i.   **REBECCA OWINGS** b. Dec. 15th, 1797, d. s. p.

ii.   **MATILDA BEAL** b. Feby. 10th, 1800, d. s. p.

iii.   **MARY ANN** b. Dec. 27th, 1801, md. 1st **CHARLES WORTHINGTON**, and had issue: **JOSEPH WILSON**; and after his death md. 2d. **JACOB SCHLEICH**.

iv.   **JOSHUA HOWARD** b. Mch. 2d, 1804, md. 1st **LUCY COLSTON**, and had issue: **MARY ELIZABETH** md. Dr. **SAMUEL WATKINS**; **SUSAN MATILDA** 2d wife of Dr. **SAMUEL WATKINS**; **LUCY HOWARD** md. **WILLIAM EDSON**; **ANN REBECCA** md. her cousin **SAMUEL WALLACE THOMAS**, (q. v.;) **VIRGINIA YOUNG** md. —— **NALL**; **ALICE HENRIETTA** md. **JOHN G. CLOYD**, of Decatur, Ill.   **JOSHUA H. THOMAS** md. 2d **FANNY OWINGS**, and had further issue: **FANNY ZORAYDA** md. **SAMUEL ROBERTSON** of Elizabethtown, Ky.; and **SAMUEL HOWARD**.

v.   **JAMES BAYARD** b. Feby. 4th, 1806, md. **ELIZABETH J. A. GOODWIN** of Boston, Mass.

vi.   **HENRIETTA ELIZA** b. July 3d, 1809, md. **WILLIAM HENRY BRIGGS** of Brookeville, Md. (q. v.)

vii.   **SAMUEL BEAL** b. Aug. 4th, 1811, of whom presently.

viii.   **SARAH CATHERINE** b. Feby. 5th, 1814, md. **THOMAS B. MUNFORD**, and had issue: **THOMAS SAMUEL** b. in May, 1840, md. **ETTA GUNTER**; **SARAH ELIZA** b. in 1841 md. **W. H. BRENTZ**; **ZORAYDA OWINGS** md. **J. W. MATTHIS**; **ANN AMELIA** md. **GEORGE J BROWNFIELD**, **ELLEN BAYARD** md. **QWYMAN**; and **WILLIAM HENRY**.

ix.   **JOSEPH HENRY** b. Feby. 18th, 1818, md. **AMANDA LA RUE**, and had issue: **WARREN LA RUE** b. Jany. 25th, 1845, md. **MARY H. WARDROPER**; **MARY HELEN** b. Aug. 16th, 1847, md. **A. C. HODGES**; **ELIZA HOWARD** b. Nov. 14th, 1849, md. **CHARLES W. SWANSON**; **VIRGINIA BEAL** b. Sept. 15th, 1851, md. **SAMUEL V. LEIDOM**; **ANNA BROOKS** b. June 27th, 1853; **ELLA OWINGS** b. Sept. 26th, 1856; and **WILLIAM BAYARD** b. Feby. 14th, 1861.

x.   **SUSAN AMELIA** b. June 23d, 1821, md. **JAMES COX**, and had issue: **DAVID YOUNG**; **MARY THOMAS** md. —— **AYRE**; **ROLAND HUGHS**; **MEHETABLE**; **JAMES HENRY**; **BOYD**; **SAMUEL HENRY**; **ELI**; and **NANNIE**.

SAMUEL BEAL, third son of **Samuel** and **Mary** (Howard) **Thomas,** at the age of twenty removed to Kentucky, and went into the employ of Col. Edward P. Johnson, of Scott County, then the largest Stage Contractor in that State. Assisted by that gentleman, after a few years he went into the same business on his own account and soon became very successful, controlling a number of lines. He was among the first who suggested the Louisville and Nashville Railroad and afterwards was one of its most efficient directors. Some time since he originated the project of building a road at right angles with the Nashville one, and after years of labor and using liberally his money and influence in its favor, the Elizabethtown and Paducah railroad was built. Naturally he was made its first president, and after the election of Mr. Dulaney, he remained a director, which position he held up to the time of his death.

Col. Thomas amassed a large fortune during these busy years of his life. Much of his property was in the City of Louisville, and the splendid "Thomas Building" on Fourth Street near Walnut, will long remind the citizens of him. After the disastrous fire of 1869 which laid waste one half of the City, he procured money for the sufferers with which to rebuild, he himself going security without asking a guarantee in his favor, and to him is owing in a great measure the beautiful row of buildings which Main-Cross Street boasts to-day. He md. **ZORAYDA YOUNG,** who d. in Jany. 1873, and her husband d. Dec. 3d, 1874, having had issue:

i.   **JAMES HOWARD** b. in 1836, d. in 1856.

ii.   **SAMUEL WALLACE** b. in 1838, md. **ANNA REBECCA,** dau. of Joshua H. and Lucy Thomas, and d. s. p.

iii.   **MARY LIZZIE** b. in 1840, md. Col. **JAMES B. PAYNE,** of Elizabethtown, Ky., and had issue: **SAMUEL THOMAS, LIZZIE ROBINSON, ELLA THOMAS, ZORAYDA YOUNG, EDWARD CHURCHILL** d. ; **SUSAN CHURCHILL; MARY** and **JAMES B.** d. ; **ELIZA C.,** and **JULIA BLACKBURNE.**

iv.   **ANN ZORAYDA** b. in 1844.

v.   **ELLEN MATILDA** b. in 1846, md. **GEORGE W. WELCH,** Jr., Cashier First National Bank, Danville, Ky., and has had issue: **ZORADYA YOUNG, MARY BREATH;** and **SAMUEL THOMAS,** d.

JOHN, second son of **Samuel** and **Mary** (Cowman) **Thomas,** b. Jany. 30th, 1778, md. ———— **BERRY,** and had issue:

i.   **CHARLOTTE** md. **WALTER GODEY.** (q. v.)

ii.   **NICHOLAS** removed to Ohio, md. ——— **HIGGINS**, and had issue: **JOHN, MARY, NICHOLAS** and **WILLIAM**.

iii.   **MARY.**

iv.   **CAROLINE**, d. s. p.

RICHARD, Jr., second son of **Richard** and **Sarah (Coale) Thomas**, b Feby. 21st, 1758, resided at Brookeville, in Montgomery County, Maryland. He md. **DEBORAH**, dau. of **James** and **Deborah (Snowden) Brooke**, who d. Nov. 12th, 1814, and her husband Nov. 6th, 1821, having had issue:

i.   **ELIZA P.** b. Aug. 1st, 1784, md. **THOMAS P. STABLER.** (q. v.)

ii.   **FREDERICK AUGUSTUS** b. Sept. 27th, 1788, d. Aug. 16th, 1794.

iii.   **MARY** b. Oct. 18th, 1791, d. Aug. 21st, 1794.

iv.   **SARAH BROOKE** b. April 26th, 1794, d. Sept. 25th, 1826.

v.   **DEBORAH** b. Mch. 2d, 1796, d. May 27th, 1797.

vi.   **MARGARET E.** b. Mch. 3d, 1798, md. May 22d, 1816, **ROBERT H.**, son of **William** and **Hannah Garrigues**, of Philadelphia. (q. v.)

vii.   **ROGER BROOKE** b. April 9th, 1803.

WILLIAM, fourth son of **Richard** and **Sarah (Coale) Thomas**, b. Dec. 11th, 1771, md. **MARTHA PATRICK**, and had issue:

i.   **ANNE POULTNEY** b. April 14th, 1801, d. unmarried Mch. 5th, 1830.

ii.   **ELIZA** b. April 10th, 1803, md. **WILLIAM HENRY STABLER.** (q. v)

iii.   **MARIA R.** b. November 23d, 1804.

iv.   **HENRIETTA** b. Feby. 21st, 1807, d. Oct. 14th, 1821.

v.   **RICHARD** b. April 19th, 1809, d. Oct. 15th, 1820.

vi.   **EDWARD** b. June 22d, 1811, of whom presently.

vii.   **WILLIAM JOHN** b. Sept. 15th, 1813. (q. v.)

viii. **SAMUEL PATRICK** b. Jany. 23d, 1816, md. **ELIZA G. PORTER.**

ix.   **JANE** b. May 20th, 1818, md. **CHARLES G. PORTER.**

x.   **MARTHA** b. Feby. 3d, 1822, md. **THOMAS P. HARVEY**, and had issue: **GRACE, WILLIAM, CLARENCE, EUGENE**, and **SWANN.**

EDWARD, eldest surviving son of **William** and **Martha** (**Patrick**) **Thomas**, b. June 22d, 1811, resides at "Belmont," in Montgomery County, Maryland. He md. Apl. 25th, 1833, **LYDIA S.**, dau. of **Joseph** and **Sarah Gilpin**, and has had issue:

i.   **MARCELLA** b. Feby. 13th, 1834, md. in May 1853, **ROBERT SULLIVAN**.

ii.   **RICHARD PIERCE** b. Jany. 6th, 1836, removed to Baltimore and engaged in Mercantile life; md. Sept. 29th, 1857, **HARRIET**, dau. of **John** and **Mary E. Cowman**, of Alexandria, Virginia, who was born Dec. 17th, 1836, and has had issue: **HERBERT** b. Nov. 6th, 1859; **MARGARET** b. Oct. 25th, 1860, d. Oct. 7th, 1861; **MABEL** b. June 24th, 1862, d. Feby. 27th, 1865; **HARVEY** b. Aug. 5th, 1864; **LOUISA** b. Feby. 1st, 1867; and **RICHARD HENRY** b. Mch. 12th, 1876.

iii.   **JOSEPH GILPIN** b. Dec. 28th, 1837, d. July 7th, 1854.

iv.   **SAMUEL** b. Jany. 21st, 1840, d. Nov. 22d, 1875.

v.   **ALBAN GILPIN** b. April 29th, 1843, md. Sept. 12th, 1871, **SUSANNAH HAYDOCK**, dau. of **Thomas** and **Patience Leggett**, of New York, and has issue: **ANNA LEGGETT** b. Dec. 3d, 1872; and **HELEN LEGGETT** b. June 2d, 1874.

vi.   **LOUISA** b. Aug. 17th, 1845, md. Sept. 14th, 1871, **ROGER BROOKE**. (q. v.)

vii.   **MARY PHILLIPS** b. Dec. 8th, 1847.

viii.   **EMILIE** b. Sept. 6th, 1852, md. Sept. 5th, 1872, **J. LLEWELLYN**, son of **John E.** and **Margaret A. Massey**, of Virginia, and has issue: **MARY GERTRUDE** b. Dec. 7th, 1873; and **MARGARET** b. Aug. 10th, 1875.

WILLIAM JOHN, third son of **William** and **Martha** (**Patrick**) **Thomas**, b. Sept. 15th, 1813, resides at "Clifton," in Montgomery County, md. **REBECCA M. PORTER**, and has issue:

i.   **MARY ELIZABETH** b. Oct. 24th, 1838, md. **WILLIAM W. MOORE**, of Sandy Spring, and has issue: **CLARA PAINTER** b. June 16th, 1860, d. Aug. 8th, 1863; **ROBERT ROWLAND** b. April 15th, 1863; **SARAH THOMAS** b. Oct. 17th, 1865; **REBECCA THOMAS** b. July 9th, 1872.

ii.   Dr. **FRANCIS** b. Jany. 30th, 1840, md. **BEULAH L. HAINES**, and has issue: **WILLIAM FRANCIS** b. June 21st, 1871; and **ELLEN HAINES** b. Mch. 5th, 1875.

iii.   **SARAH T.** b April 12th, 1841, md. Sept. 15th, 1862, **BENJAMIN H. MILLER**, and has issue: **REBECCA T.** b. Feby. 1st, 1864; **ELIZABETH T.** b. Aug. 13th, 1867; and **MARTHA T.** b. July 2d, 1870.

5

iv.   **EDWARD PORTER** b. Jany. 16th, 1844, md. November 30th, 1865, **MARY THOMAS**, dau. of Richard T. and Elizabeth (Needles) Bentley, and has issue: **EDITH BENTLEY** b. Oct. 30th, 1866; **MARY E.** b. Feby. 28th, 1870; **RICHARD BENTLEY** b. Oct. 19th, 1873; **EDWARD CLIFTON** b. June 17th, 1875, and **AUGUSTA NEEDLES** b. June 12th, 1877.

v.   **JOHN** b. April 20th, 1846, md. in Nov 1876, **CATHERINE D. VICKERS**, of Baltimore.

vi.   **WILLIAM** b. Aug. 20th, 1848, d. May 30th, 1871.

vii.   **CHARLES** b. Aug. 3d, 1850.

viii.   **MARTHA** b. July 18th, 1852.

SAMUEL, third son of **Samuel** and (**Mary Hutchins**) **Thomas**, b. in 1702, md. in August, 1730, **MARY**, dau. of **Richard** and **Mary Snowden**, who d. August 15th, 1755, in her 43d year; her husband d. Feby. 3d, 1780, having had issue:

i.   **MARY** b. Nov. 3d, 1731, md. her cousin **SAMUEL THOMAS**. (q. v.)

ii.   **SAMUEL** b. Sept. 23d, 1733, d. s. p.

iii.   **PHILIP** b. April 18th, 1735, d. s. p. in November 1754.

iv.   **ELIZABETH** b. March 10th, 1736–7, md. **JOHNS HOPKINS**. (q. v.)

v.   **EVAN** b. Jany. 21st, 1738–9, md. Dec. 26th, 1766, at Indian Spring Meeting House, **RACHEL**, dau. of Gerard Hopkins. Both of them were Ministers of the Society of Friends, and persons of a great deal of character. Before his death, **EVAN THOMAS** freed his slaves, over 200 in number, and gave them small allotments of land to cultivate. He d. Nov. 10th, 1826, and his wife Dec. 3d, 1825, having had issue:

   i.   **MARY** b. Aug. 14th, 1768, md. **ELIAS ELLICOTT**. (q. v.)

   ii.   **ANN** b. Aug. 6th, 1771, md. **THOMAS POULTNEY**. (q. v.)

   iii. iv. **PHILIP** and **SAMUEL**, twins, b. Jany. 12th, 1774, both died in 1775.

   v.   **PHILIP EVAN**, of whom presently.

   vi   **ELIZABETH** b. Mch. 26th, 1779, md. **ISAAC TYSON**. (q. v.)

   vii.   **EVAN, Jr.,** b. Mch. 8th, 1781, d. s. p.

   viii.   **MARGARET** b. Sept. 26th, 1783, d. Oct. 5th, 1783.

PHILIP EVAN, third son of **Evan** and **Rachel** (Hopkins) **Thomas**, b. at Mt. Radnor, in Montgomery County, Md., November 11th, 1776, was educated at the District School under a Mr. Knox, at Bladensburg. Arriving at manhood he went to Baltimore, then a town of only 15,000 inhabitants, and was received into the store of his brother-in-law, Thomas Poultney. In 1800 he commenced business on his own account as a hardware merchant on Baltimore Street, afterwards taking into partnership his wife's brother, Wm. E. George, and finally his brother Evan. He early took an interest in municipal affairs and public charities, and was the first President of the Maryland Bible Society, and the Mechanical Fire Company, one of the founders of the Baltimore Library Company, for many years President of the Mechanic's Bank, and advanced the first $25,000 to enable the State to begin building the Washington Monument.

During the Fall of 1826 Philip E. Thomas held frequent conferences with George Brown, then a Director of the Mechanics' Bank, of Baltimore, in reference to the loss which Baltimore had sustained by the diversion of a large part of its Western trade to Philadelphia and New York through the Erie Canal, and similar facilities for internal navigation and traffic in the States of New York and Pennsylvania. Gen. Barnard's report, showing the cost of completing the Chesapeake and Ohio Canal, and the difficulties that lay in its way, convinced them it would not accomplish the desired end in directing the Trade. to Baltimore.

At this time Evan Thomas was in Europe, and wrote from England to his brother, giving him an account of the railroad just built from Stockton to Darlington, in Durhamshire, by the enterprise of Joseph Pease of the latter place. William Brown, of Liverpool, also forwarded to his brother various documents, giving valuable information in reference to the railways of England.

Philip E. Thomas at once saw the utility of railroads as a means of communication and carriers of passengers and freight, and resigning his position as a State Director of the Canal Company turned his whole attention to the projection of a railroad connecting Baltimore with the West.

February 12th, 1827, twenty-five of the most influential Merchants of Baltimore met at the residence of Mr. Brown, pursuant to a call issued by Messrs. Thomas and Brown. At this meeting Philip E. Thomas ably presented the various advantages the railroad system had over the Canal, and the old-fashioned turnpike in efficiency, rapidity of carriage and ultimate economy, and a committee was appointed to further examine the subject, and report to a public meeting. This committee consisted of Philip E. Thomas, Chairman, Benjamin C. Howard, George Brown, Talbot Jones,

Joseph W. Patterson, Evan Thomas and John V. L. McMahon. The following Monday, February 19th, the committee presented their report, written by their chairman, which was unanimously adopted, and ordered to be printed and widely distributed.

A charter for a Road having been obtained, largely through the instrumentality of John V. L. McMahon, and the proposed amount of stock speedily taken, a Company was duly organized April 24th, 1827, being the first one in America.

The first Board of Directors were: Philip E. Thomas, President; George Brown, Treasurer; Charles Carroll, of Carrollton; William Patterson, Robert Oliver, Alexander Brown, Isaac McKim, William Lorman, George Hoffman, Thomas Ellicott, John B. Morris, Talbot Jones, and William Steuart.

A committee of Engineers was appointed to make the necessary surveys for the route of the Road, consisting of Col. Stephen H. Long and Jonathan Knight, on the part of the Company, assisted by a number from the U. S. Topographical Corps; Philip E. Thomas being its chairman. April 5th, 1828, Messrs. Long and Knight reported the completion of their surveys, and choice of a route along the Valley of the Patapsco, and thence in the direction of Linganore Creek to the Point of Rocks. July 4th of the same year, the "first stone" was laid by Charles Carroll of Carrollton, with great ceremony and a magnificent procession of Associations, Trades and Professions. Before the road passed four miles from the city, it encountered a high dividing ridge, which had to be cut down fifty-four feet through a hard clay, involving an expense far beyond the estimates, and the funds prepared to meet them. The President and nine of the directors immediately advanced $20,000 each, which met the difficulty and the road was completed to the Point of Rocks. Here it was delayed by the action of the Chesapeake and Ohio Canal Company, and it was not until after long and vexatious litigation that a compromise was effected.

In June 1830, the road was opened for passenger travel as far as Ellicott's Mills, horse and mule power being used. Among other experiments in motive powers tried during this first year, Evan Thomas constructed a car with sails called the Æolus, which attracted much attention, and a model of it was sent to Russia.

April 1st, 1832, the whole line was opened to the Point of Rocks. In 1831 it was decided to adopt steam as a motive power, and Locomotives replaced the horses and mules previously employed.

In 1833 the dispute with the Canal Company was adjusted, and the Rail Road was soon open to Harper's Ferry. June 30th, 1836, Philip E. Thomas, against the earnest remonstrances of the Board, resigned the

Presidency of the Company, being compelled to do so by the state of his health.

In one of the resolutions passed by the Board on this occasion they say "On the commencement of this work of which he has been in fact the father and projector, everything connected with its construction was new, crude and doubtful, with little to guide the way, and that derived from distant and uncertain sources; now, such has been the increase of information and experience acquired under his auspices and direction as to ensure the completion and success of the undertaking if prosecuted with the same zeal, assiduity and integrity which have ever marked his course."

Philip E. Thomas was a prominent member of the Society of Friends, of which his father had been an eminent Minister; was much interested in the cause of the Indians, several of their young men were educated at the same school with his sons, and to his exertions it was owing that the remnant of the Six Nations residing in Western New York were not driven from their Reservation by the intrigues of the Ogden Land Company with their chiefs. The chiefs were deposed, and a republican form of government established. He was afterwards made a chief of the Swan tribe of Seneca Indians, by the name of "Sagouan" or bountiful giver, and represented them in their intercourse with the government at Washington. In the summer of 1861, he went, as was his usual custom, to his daughter's in Westchester County, New York. There he was taken with his last illness, and after much suffering patiently endured, d. there Sept. 1st, 1861. He md. in 1801, **ELIZABETH**, dau. of **Robert** and **Elizabeth (Edmonson) George**, of Kent County, Md., and left issue by her:

i. **ANN** b. Feby. 17th, 1803, md. **THOMAS E. WALKER**. (q. v.)

ii. **RACHEL** b. Feby. 1st, 1805, md. **J. J. WALKER**. (q. v.)

iii. **EVAN PHILIP** b. Nov. 19th, 1806, md. Nov. 17th, 1835, **ELIZABETH**, dau. of Joseph and Eliza (Onion) Todhunter, and d. leaving issue: **PHILIP WILLIAM** b. Mch. 21st, 1842, d. July 14th, 1861; **KATE TODHUNTER** md. Dec. 24th, 1866, **EDWARD GOODWIN DYKE** of Boston; and **JOSEPHINE**.

iv. **WILLIAM GEORGE** b. Feby. 9th, 1809, of whom presently.

v. **MARY** b. Oct. 11th, 1813, md. **JOHN WETHERED**. (q. v.)

vi. **ELIZABETH** b. Jany. 22d, 1817.

vii. **HARRIET** b. Oct. 25th, 1820, md. **JAMES C. BELL**, and has issue: **PHILIP THOMAS**, **JOHN WETHERED**, **JAMES CHRISTIE**, **JACOB HARVEY**, and **ELIZABETH**.

WILLIAM GEORGE, second son of **Philip E.** and **Elizabeth** (**George**) **Thomas,** b. Feby. 9th, 1809, was a prominent merchant of Baltimore, succeeding his father in the Hardware business on Baltimore street. To him the City of Baltimore is indebted for her first improved public square, Franklin Square in the Northwestern section of the City; her first charitable institution erected by private subscription, the Widow's Home, and her first line of Omnibuses. He md. **MARY LEWIN,** dau. of **Lewin** and **Elizabeth** (**Ellicott**) **Wethered,** and has issue: **ELIZABETH; PHILIP EVAN** of whom presently; **ANN** md. **WILLIAM BELL** of New York, and has issue: **MARY, LEWIN** and **REBECCA; LEWIN WETH-ERED; MARY LEWIN** md. in 1866, **ALEXANDER SMITH; EVAN; MATILDA** and **HARRIET GEORGE** twins; and **WETHERED BROTHERS.**

PHILIP EVAN, eldest son of **William G.** and **Mary** (**Wethered**) **Thomas,** b. April 28th, 1834, is a merchant of New York City. He md. April 30th, 1859, **MARIE SUZETTE,** dau. of **Mandeville de Marigny,** whose father Bernard de Marigny, of New Orleans, was a veteran of the war of 1812, and by birth a Duke and Marquis of France; Miss de Marigny was also a grand-daughter of William C. C. Claiborne, the first American Governor of Louisiana, and a great grand-daughter of Don Juan Ventura Morales, the last Spanish Governor of the Colony. The children of this marriage are **WILLIAMINE, PHILIP EVAN, MARIE SUZETTE, MARY LEWIN, MANDEVILLE DE MARIGNY, CLAIBORNE,** and **SOPHRONIE COLE.**

WILLIAM, only son of **Philip** and **Frances** (**Holland**) **Thomas,** md. **MARY WYAN,** and had issue:

i. **MARY ANN** md. Captain **JOSEPH LEONARD.**

ii. **PHILIP WILLIAM** md. **MARY WILLIAMS,** and had issue a dau., **HENRIETTA;** soon after her birth he removed to England, leaving her with her cousins Isaac and Elizabeth Tyson, who brought her up, and at whose house she md. **JAMES ELLICOTT.** (q. v.) After his removal to England P. W. THOMAS engaged in the Banking business in London, and d. at an advanced age, leaving issue: three sons, **HENRY** b. about 1786, md. and has several daughters, one of whom md. ―――― l'Ansen; **JOHN,** d. s. p.; and **WILLIAM ALEXANDER,** who resides near London, and has two sons, Percy and Alexander. **PHILIP W. THOMAS** had also several daughters, all now deceased, of whom one md. ―――― **FERN,** and another md. ―――― **BLAKEWAY** and had issue: Philip d. about 1871; John d. about 1860; and **William Evan** still living and the active partner in the Banking House.

ANDREWS.

Col. TIMOTHY PATRICK ANDREWS, of the U. S. Army, b. in 1794 in Ireland, served as aide to Commodore Barney in the War of 1812, was distinguished for bravery at the battle of El Molino, in Mexico, in 1847, and brevetted Brigadier-General for gallantry at Chapultepec. Appointed Paymaster-General of the Army September 6th, 1862. He md. EMILY ROSEVILLE, fourth dau. of Richard and Eliza (Warfield) Snowden, and d. March 11th, 1868, having had issue:

i.   Col. RICHARD SNOWDEN, a Civil Engineer by profession, md. MARY LEE, and has issue: LOUISA, CHARLES, EMILY, CAROLINE, and GEORGE.

ii. LOUISA md. SAMUEL S. EARLY, and has issue: EMILY, JACOB, SAMUEL and CHARLES.

iii. EMILY ROSALIE md. CHARLES MARSHALL, and d. leaving one dau., EMILY ROSALIE; her husband md. 2d SARAH REBECCA, dau. of Thomas and Ann Rebecca Snowden.

iv. CAROLINE.

v.   ALBERT.

BENTLEY.

CALEB, son of Joseph and Mary Bentley, md. 1st April 20th, 1791, SARAH, dau. of Roger Brooke, who d. Sept. 9th, 1805, and her husband md. 2d Aug. 26th, 1807. HENRIETTA, second dau. of Samuel and Mary (Cowman) Thomas, and had issue by her:

i.   MARY THOMAS b. Aug. 29th, 1808, of whom presently.

ii. SARAH BROOKE b. Nov. 16th, 1814, md. Dr. GEORGE WARFIELD, and had issue: LOUIS M. b. Oct. 27th, 1837, resides at Savannah, Georgia, md. Jany. 6th, 1875, PHEMIE D. WAYNE, and has issue: Louis M. Jr., b. May 15th, 1876.

iii. RICHARD THOMAS b. July 20th, 1819, resides at Sandy Spring, Montgomery County, Maryland; md. June 20th, 1842, EDITH D. NEEDLES, and has had issue:

  i. ELIZA NEEDLES b. Aug. 25th, 1843.

  ii. MARY H. b. Dec. 14th, 1845, md. EDWARD P. THOMAS. (q. v.)

iii. SARAH BROOKE b. Feby. 26th, 1848, md. June 21st, 1867, Lieut. WILLIAM
LEA, and has issue: JENNIE L. b. June 3d, 1868; EDITH BENTLEY b. in
April 1872; and EDWARD THOMAS b. Nov. 13th, 1873.

iv. ANNA M. b. Feby. 26th, 1850, md. Nov. 12th, 1872, WILLIAM J. PARKER, and
has issue: MARY b. Nov. 17th, 1873; RICHARD BENTLEY b. Nov. 13th,
1875; and HENRY MELVILLE b. Dec. 28th, 1876.

v. JOHN CALEB b. April 30th, 1852.

vi. EDWARD NEEDLES b. Sept. 16th, 1854.

vii. EDITH HELEN b. Aug. 26th, 1856.

viii. RICHARD LOUIS b. Oct. 28th, 1859,

MARY THOMAS, eldest dau. of Caleb and Henrietta (Thomas) Bentley,
b. Aug. 29th, 1808, md. 1st LAWRENCE MOORE, and had issue:

i. FREDERICK LAWRENCE b. June 4th, 1835, md. Sept. 18th, 1855, C. VIRGINIA
CAMPBELL, and has had issue: MARY ELLA b. June 27th, 1856; JULIA BENTLEY
b. Nov. 2d, 1857; ELOISE C. d. in infancy; LAWRENCE C. b. Oct. 23d, 1860;
WILLIAM P. b. Nov. 22d, 1862; and EDITH BENTLEY; VIRGINIA; and LEON
who all d. in infancy.

Mrs. MARY BENTLEY MOORE md. 2d EBEN G. BROWN, and had
issue:

ii. SARAH BENTLEY md. JOHN PARKES, and has issue: LAWRENCE E; MABEL;
HOWARD; HENRIETTA; ANNA V.; FRANK THOMAS; and EDITH E.

iii. HENRIETTA E. md. DARIUS CLAGGETT, and has issue: MARY ETHELYND.

BORDLEY.

Rev. STEPHEN BORDLEY, Prebendary of St. Paul's Cathedral, London,
England, had with other issue: STEPHEN, who settled in Kent County,
Md.; and THOMAS b. in 1682 removed with his brother to Maryland
in 1694, practised Law at Annapolis, and became very celebrated in his
profession. Was Attorney General of Maryland from 1715 until his
death. He md. 1st RACHEL BEARD, of Annapolis, and had issue by

her: STEPHEN b. in 1709, practised Law at Annapolis, and d. s. p. Dec. 6th, 1764; WILLIAM b. in 1716 md. —— PEARCE, and had a son and daughter, who both d. in infancy: ELIZABETH b. in 1717 d. Nov. 28th, 1789, at her brother Beale's residence unmarried: and JOHN b. in 1721 md. and settled near Chestertown, Md.; d. s. p. in 1761.

THOMAS BORDLEY md. 2d, Sept. 1st, 1723, Mrs. ARIANA FRISBY, and d. Oct. 11th, 1726, having had further issue: THOMAS b. in 1724, practised Law, and d. s. p. in England in 1747: MATTHIAS b. in 1725 at Annapolis, md. PEGGY BIGGER, who d. in childbirth in 1756, and her husband followed her in a few months leaving no issue; and JOHN BEALE b. Feby. 1st, 1726-7, in 1753 appointed Clerk of Baltimore County, which then included Harford, and removed to a farm near Joppa, where he resided some twelve years. In 1765 removed to Baltimore City, and practised Law there; in 1766 appointed one of the Judges of the Provincial Court; in 1767 Judge of Admiralty. In 1770 removed to Wye Island to an estate bequeathed his wife by her brother, Philemon Lloyd Chew, who d. s. p. that year. In 1774 he was a member of the Committe of Public Safety, and in 1777 appointed one of the Judges of the General Court. In 1791 he removed to Philadelphia, and resided there during the rest of his life.

He md. 1st in 1751 MARGARET, dau. of Samuel and Henrietta Maria (Dulany) Chew, and had issue by her: Thomas b. in 1755, d. in 1771: Matthias b. in 1757 md. Susan Heath; and John.

J. BEALE BORDLEY was md. 2d Oct. 8th, 1776, at Philadelphia, by Rev. William White, afterwards Bishop of Pennsylvania, to Mrs. SARAH MIFFLIN, dau. of William and Jane (Roberts) Fishbourne, and had further issue: Elizabeth b. Oct. 21st, 1777, md. James Gibson, and d. Jany. 26th, 1804.

BOWIE.

WALTER WILLIAM WEEMS BOWIE, md. Sept. 1st, 1836, at Laurel, ADELINE, dau. of Nicholas and Elizabeth Snowden, who d. at Eglington, Jany. 8th, 1865, having had issue: WALTER WILLIAM WEEMS b. June 25th, 1837, a Captain in Mosby's Guerrillas during the Civil War, and killed Oct. 6th, 1864, while on a raid in Maryland: NICHOLAS

DE WILTON b. Jany 27th, 1839, d. May 15th, 1845; **THOMAS RICHARD** b. Nov. 23d, 1840, drowned June 20th, 1853, trying in vain to rescue two of his companions; **ELIZABETH** b. Oct. 25th, 1842, d. April 30th, 1845; **HENRY BRUNE** b. Jany. 26th, 1845, fought on the side of the Confederacy during the Civil War, md. Nov. 4th, 1872, **FLORENCE REESE**; **ROBERT** b. Dec. 22d, 1852, md. in June 1873, **ALICE EARLY**; **AMELIA**; **MARY** md. in Oct. 1870, **THOMAS FRANKLIN, C. E.**; **ADA** md. Nov. 24th, 1874, Prof. **B. MAURICE**; **REGINALD**; and **EMILY** who d. in infancy.

BOWNE.

THOMAS BOWNE, baptized May 25th, 1595, at Matlack, in Derbyshire, England, had issue: **JOHN** b. March 9th, 1626–7, and **DOROTHY** b. Aug. 14th, 1631, who left England for Boston in 1649, and another dau. **TRUTH** who remained at Matlack.

JOHN, his only son md. Aug. 7th, 1656, **HANNAH FIELD**, and had issue :

i.   **JOHN** b. in 1657, d. in 1673.

ii.   **ELIZABETH** b. in 1658, md. **SAMUEL TITUS**, and d. in 1691.

iii. **MARY** b. in 1660.

iv.   **ABIGAIL** b. in 1662, md. **RICHARD WILLETTS**.

v.   **HANNAH** b. in 1665, md. **BENJ. FIELD**.

vi.   **SAMUEL**, of whom presently.

vii. **DOROTHY** b. in 1669, md. **HENRY FRANKLIN**.

viii. **MARTHA** b. in 1673, md. **JOSEPH THORNE**.

JOHN BOWNE afterwards md. **HANNAH BICKERSTAFFE**, who d. in 1690, and her husband md. **MARY COCK**, and d. Oct. 20th, 1695.

SAMUEL, second son of **John** and **Hannah** (Field) **Bowne**, b. in 1667, md. Aug. 4th, 1691, **MARY BECKETT**, and had issue:

i.   **SAMUEL** b. in 1692, md. **SARAH FRANKLIN**, and d. in 1769.

ii. **THOMAS** b. in 1694, md. **HANNAH UNDERHILL**.

iii. **ELEANOR** b. in 1695, md. **ISAAC HORNER**.

iv. **HANNAH** b. in 1696, md. **RICHARD LAWRENCE**, (q. v.) and d. in 1748.

v.   **JOHN** b. in 1697, md. in 1736, **DINAH UNDERHILL**, and d. in 1757.

vi. **MARY** b. in 1698, md. **JOHN KEESE**.

vii. **ROBERT** b. in 1700, md. **MARGARET LATHAM**, and d. in 1743.

viii. **WILLIAM**.

ix. **BENJAMIN** d. in childhood.

x.   **ELIZABETH** b. in 1704.

SAMUEL BOWNE afterwards md. **HANNAH SMITH**, and 3d **GRACE COWPERTHWAITE**, and d. in 1745.

BROOKE.

ROBERT BROOKE, b. June 3d, 1602, at London, md. 1st Feby. 27th, 1627, **MARY BAKER**, who was b. at Battel, and 2d May 11th, 1635, **MARY**, dau. of **Roger Mainwaring, D. D.,** Dean of Worcester, and grand-daughter of the Bishop of St. David's. June 29th, 1650, **ROBERT BROOKE** arrived out of England in Maryland, bringing his family with him, and his family record says "was the first that did seat Patuxent about 20 miles up the river at Della Brooke. In the year 1652, he removed to Brooke Place being right against Della Brooke. July 20th, 1655, he departed this world, and lyeth buried at Brooke Place Manor, and his wife **MARY** departed this life Nov. 29th, 1663." By his first wife he had issue: **BAKER** b. Nov. 16th, 1628, at Battel; **MARY** b. Feby. 19th, 1630; **THOMAS** b. June 23d, 1632; and **BARBARY** b. at Wickham.

By his second wife he had further issue: **CHARLES** b. April 3d. 1636, at St. Giles in the fields Middlesex: **ROGER** b. Sept. 20th, 1637, of whom presently: **ROBERT** b. April 21st, 1639, at London, in St. Bride's Parish; **JOHN** b. Sept. 20th, 1640, at Battel: **MARY** b. April 14th, 1642, at Battel: **ANN** b. Jany. 22d, 1645, at Bretnoe: **FRANCES** b. May 30th, 1648, at Worwell, in Hamtshire: **ELIZABETH** and **HENRY** b. Nov. 28th, 1652, at Patuxent: and **BASIL** b. in 1654 at Della Brooke, and d. same day.

Of **ROGER**, second son of **Robert** and **Mary** (**Mainwaring**) **Brooke**, b. Sept. 20th. 1637. at Bretonew College, the family record says "Roger Brooke, Sr., son of Robert Brooke, died April 8th, 1700, and lyes buried in the graveyard at his own Plantation on Battel Creek, between his two wives, Dorathy Neal and 2d Mary Wolsley. Where also lyes buried his two daughters by his 2d wife, Cassandra and Mary, and his grandson Roger, son of Roger, Jr."

    ROGER BROOKE, Jr., eldest son of **Roger** and **Dorothy** (**Neal**) **Brooke**, b. April 12th, 1673, md Feby. 23d, 1702. **ELIZA**, third dau. of **Francis** and **Eliza Hutchins**, and had issue: **ROGER** b. Dec. 3d, 1703, d. May 28th, 1705; **JAMES** b. Feby. 21st, 1705, of whom presently: **ELIZA** b. Nov. 23d, 1707: **DOROTHY** b. July 3d, 1709; **MARY** b. Dec. 29th, 1710: **ANN** b. Mch. 29th, 1712: **ROGER** b. June 10th, 1714: **CASSANDRA** b. April 3d, 1716: **PRISCILLA** and **BASIL**, twins, b. Nov. 16th, 1717.

JAMES, eldest surviving son of **Roger** and **Eliza** **Hutchins**) **Brooke**, b. Feby. 21st, 1705, "came to housekeeping 25th day of November, 1723," and md. June 21st, 1725. **DEBORAH**, eldest dau. of **Richard** and **Eliza** (**Coale**) **Snowden**, and had issue:

i.   **JAMES** b. in 1731 md. and had issue at his d., Aug. 21st, 1767: **AMOS** d. the same year; **ELIZA** md. **GEORGE ELLICOTT**, (q. v.); and **DEBORAH** md. **GEORGE CHANDLEE**, and d. Dec. 31st, 1790, leaving issue: **Brooke** b. in 1785, d. March 24th, 1798.

ii.   **ROGER** b. Aug. 9th, 1734, of whom presently.

iii.   **RICHARD** b. July 8th, 1736, md. and had issue: **ELIZA**: and **ANN**.

iv.   **BASIL** b. Dec. 13th, 1738, (q. v.)

v.   **ELIZABETH** b. Mch. 22d, 1740-1, md. June 2d, 1761, **THOMAS PLEASANTS**, and had issue: **JAMES BROOKE**; **DEBORAH** md. **WILLIAM STABLER**, (q. v.); **THOMAS SNOWDEN, WILLIAM HENRY, MARY,** and **ELIZABETH.**

vi.   **THOMAS** b. Mch. 8th, 1743-4.

ROGER, second son of **James** and **Deborah (Snowden) Brooke,** b. Aug. 9th. 1734, md. **MARY** ———, who d. Apl. 25th. 1808, having had issue:

i.   **SAMUEL** b. Dec. 9th, 1755, md. **SARAH GARRIGUES**, and had issue: **WILLIAM** md. Aug. 22d, 1832, **LYDIA S.**, dau. of Bernard and Sarah Gilpin; and **ABRAHAM** md. Nov. 11th, 1829, **ELIZABETH**, dau. of Samuel and Hannah Y. Lukens, and had issue: Harriet b. Oct. 18th, 1831.

ii.   **MARY** b. July 27th, 1760.

iii.   **JAMES** b. Mch. 13th, 1762, d. Mch. 9th, 1764.

iv.   **DEBORAH** b. Feby. 6th. 1764.

v.   **MARGARET** b. Nov. 23d, 1765.

vi.   **SARAH** b. Dec. 29th, 1767. md. **CALEB BENTLEY**. (q. v.)

vii.   **HANNAH** b. June 5th, 1770, md. Aug. 27th, 1794, **ISAAC BRIGGS**, printer, and had issue: **ANNA** b. May 18th, 1796; **MARY BROOKE** b. Feby. 17th, 1798, md. **RICHARD BROOKE**, (q. v.); **DEBORAH** b. Aug. 19th, 1799; **SARAH BENTLEY** b. Aug. 9th, 1801; **ISAAC** b. Oct. 15th, 1803; **ELIZABETH** b. Oct. 5th, 1807; **MARGARET** b. Sept. 24th, 1812; and **WILLIAM HENRY** b. May 6th, 1815, md. **HENRIETTA E.**, fourth dau. of Samuel and Mary (Howard) Thomas, and had issue: Mary Z., Edward Thomas md. Fanny Beckwith, and has issue: Charles Edward, Samuel Thomas, William, Arthur, and Clara; Hannah B., Susan, and Sarah Ellen.

viii.   **ELIZABETH** b. Aug. 25th, 1772, d. Jany. 21st, 1774.

ix.   **ROGER** b. Nov. 24th, 1774, of whom presently.

x.   **DOROTHY** b. Dec. 24th, 1776, md. **GERARD T. HOPKINS**. (q. v.)

ROGER, third son of **Roger** and **Mary Brooke,** b. Nov. 24th, 1774, md. Aug. 22d, 1804, **MARY PLEASANTS,** dau. of Isaac Younghusband, and had issue:

i.   **SARAH** b. Sept. 14th, 1805, md. **CHARLES FARQUHAR**. (q. v.)

ii.   **MARTHA** b. Nov. 17th, 1807.

iii.   **MARY MATTHEWS** b. Jany. 5th, 1809.

iv.   **ROGER** b. Oct. 5th, 1810, md. May 13th, 1840, **SARAH THOMAS**, dau. of **Bernard** and **Sarah Gilpin**, and had a son **ROGER** md. Sept. 14th, 1871, **LOUISA**, second dau. of **Edward** and **Lydia Thomas**, and has issue: Emilie b. May 30th, 1873; Sarah b. Feby. 9th, 1875; and Jane Porter.

v.   **GEORGE** b. Nov. 27th, 1812.

BASIL, fourth son of **James** and **Deborah** (Snowden) **Brooke**, b. Dec. 13th, 1738, md. May 1st, 1764, **ELIZABETH**, dau. of **Gerard** and **Mary Hopkins**, who d. Aug. 17th, 1794, and her husband the 22d of the same month, having had issue:

i.   **JAMES** b. May 5th, 1766, md. **HESTHER**, dau. of **Isaiah** and **Hannah Boone**, and had issue **BASIL** b. Oct. 19th, 1798, d. in infancy; **ISAIAH BOONE** b. Dec. 30th, 1800; and **BASIL** 2d b. Feby. 5th, 1803.

ii.   **GERARD** b. Aug. 12th, 1768, of whom presently.

iii.   **DEBORAH** b. Sept. 4th, 1770, md. ———— **PLEASANTS**, and d. Feby. 21st, 1835.

iv.   **BASIL** b. April 25th, 1772, md. **MARY** ———— and had issue **ELIZA CUMMINS** b. Sept. 26th, 1798; **JAMES HARVEY** b. May 15th, 1801; **THOMAS** b. Aug. 18th, 1805, d. May 19th, 1831, **DEBORAH** b. July 24th, 1807, and **JANE** b. June 12th, 1812.

GERARD, second son of **Basil** and **Elizabeth** (Hopkins) **Brooke**, b. Aug. 12th, 1768, md. April 22d, 1789, **MARGARET**, fifth dau. of **Richard** and **Sarah** (Coale) **Thomas**, who d. Mch. 5th, 1797, her husband d. in 1821, having had issue:

i.   **RICHARD** b. Jany. 6th, 1790, of whom presently.

ii.   **JOHN THOMAS** b. Nov. 12th, 1791.

iii.   **ELIZABETH P.** b. Aug. 12th, 1794, md. **THOMAS P. STABLER**. (q. v.)

RICHARD, eldest son of Gerard and Margaret (Thomas) Brooke, b. Jany. 6th, 1790, md. April 21st, 1824, MARY BROOKE, second dau. of Isaac and Hannah Briggs, and had issue:

i. HENRY BRIGGS b. April 30th, 1828.

ii. HANNAH BRIGGS b. Sept. 18th, 1829.

iii. CHARLES H. b. July 26th, 1831, md. ANNA FARQUHAR, and has issue: HENRY b. Sept. 16th, 1866; EDITH b. May 30th, 1869; SARAH B. b. July 7th, 1872; and MARY B. b. May 10th, 1875.

BROWN.

WILLIAM BROWN b. about 1656, came from England to America about 1682, and settled at West Nottingham, in Pennsylvania. He md. 1st DOROTHY ———, who d. at sea on the voyage from England to America; 2d, in 1684 ANN MERCER; 3d in 1699 CATHERINE WILLIAMS of Philadelphia, and 4th in 1711 MARY MATTHEWS; and d. Aug. 23d, 1746. By his second wife he had with other issue: an eldest son, MERCER, b. Feby. 27th, 1685–6, md. 1st in 1710 JANE RICHARDS, and 2d Apl. 11th, 1728, DINAH, dau. of John and Hannah Churchman, and d. about 1733. His widow md. 2d MORDECAI JAMES of Goshen, and d. Jany. 1st, 1766, leaving issue by her 1st husband:

i. JOHN b. in 1729 md. Nov. 21st, 1751, JANE, dau. of John and Jane Pugh.

ii. DAVID b. about 1731 md. 1st Nov. 3d, 1757, SARAH, dau. of Joshua and Hannah Brown, of West Nottingham, and 2d ELIZABETH ———, who d. Mch. 3d, 1802, and her husband about 1781, leaving issue:

    i   David b. Dec. 18th, 1758.

    ii.   Uriah b. Apl. 18th, 1769, md. Jany. 10th, 1793, Mary, dau. of Jacob and Mary Brown, and d. having had issue: Elizabeth b. Aug. 1st, 1794; Sarah b. Jany. 23d, 1796; David Uriah b. Jany. 25th, 1798, md. Rachel, dau. of Thomas and Ann Poultney, and d. s. p.; Mary b. June 14th, 1800; and Diana b. Apl. 30th, 1805.

ARMS FROM A VISITATION.

BUCKLEY,

OF LANCASHIRE.

The hamlet of Buckley in Hundersfeld, Lancashire, gave residence and name to a family descended from John De Buckley, whose brother Geoffrey was Dean of Whalley in the reign of Stephen. This John had a son Geoffrey whose son Geoffrey was slain at the battle of Evesham in the year 1265. Adam de Buckley attests deeds in 1323 and 1325. John de Buckley does the same in 1339 and 1359; and another John in in 1370 and 1390, this latter was probably son of a Robert Buckeley and married Alice Wolfenden. Elias Buckeley in 1424, might be a son of John and Alice Buckeley, and was father of Rafe who married Katherine ———— Thomas Bucley witness to a deed May 18th, 1507, was probably a descendant. James Bucley, of Bucley, of this family, it appears Nov. 12th, 1512, married Alice Howarth of Howarth, and had issue: Thomas, and Catherine who married Thomas Chadwike. This Thomas Bucley attests deeds January 1st, 1534-5, and again May 16th, 1561, Aug. 16th, 1580, and Oct. 22d, 1581. He married Grace, daughter of Arthur Ashton, of Great Clegg. James Buckley who was another witness of the deed in 1581, was probably his son. Of the same family was Lawrence Buckley, who with one Edmund Ashton in 1567, was sued by Sir John Byron (ancestor of the poet) and others, the inhabitants of Rochdale, in Lancashire, about a right of way over property at Butterworth and other common rights. Two years later Barnarde Buckley, apparently his brother, had to establish his right to his inheritance by suit at law against Roger Gartside and John Holte, and lost part of it consisting of land at Castelton. This Barnarde was probably a cousin of Catherine Buckely of Chedale, aunt of Sir Richard Buckely, Knt., who made her will November 16th, 1559, in which she mentions by name her brothers Thomas, Robert and William, (the latter deceased,) her nieces Ellen Arderon, Elizabeth, and Kate Buckley, and her nephews John Buckley and Thomas, the son of William Buckley, "who is now with Dr. Pole." William Buckley died in the early part of Elizabeth's reign possessed of lands at Quicke and Saddleworth in Yorkshire, and Abell his great grandson became the heir general of the family in King Charles 1st reign.

Robert Buckley appears to have been the eldest of Catherine Buckely's brothers, and died apparently without issue in 1577, possessed of Messuag, Terr. Bosc. &c., at Buckley Maner and Hundersfelde in Lancashire. Twelve years later his brother Thomas leaves the same estates with the addition of land at Sportlande to his son Thomas; whose brother Robert at his decease in 1601, was possessed of the same estates. Abell great grandson of William Buckley, and their cousin inherited the property. He seems to have married a daughter and co-heiress of Edward Lord, who brought him lands at Butterworth and Todmerden in Lancashire. Sir Richard Buckley, Knt., living in 1619, who married Anne, sister of Sir Thomas Wilsford, was probably his father. Abell Buckley died in 1640, possessed of lands at Buckley Maner, Hundersfelde, Todmerden, and Butterworth in Lancashire, and Quicke and Saddleworth, Yorkshire. Edward Buckley who was buried in Trinity Church, Rochdale, in 1687, was I believe a lineal descendant of Abell Buckley, probably his grandson. Thomas Buckley who died at Rochdale in 1697, was his son, (i. e. Edward's.) He left a daughter who carried the estates to a Forster of Preston, whose son Thomas Forster Buckley had a son Edward who sold the property and died in 1816.

BUCKLEY,

OF NEW YORK.

This family so far as at present known had its origin with Phineas Buckley, supposed to be a cadet of the Lancashire family of the same name; who was a native of London, and a trader to the West India

Islands and the North American Provinces, and came in that capacity to Philadelphia in the year 1713.

There he md. Sarah, dau. of Elias Hugg, of Gloucester County, New Jersey, then in the nineteenth year of her age.

Not long after this he went on a trading voyage to Charleston, South Carolina, and is said to have died of the yellow fever in that city.

WILLIAM, his only child was b. Nov. 13th, 1715, in the City of Philadelphia. Left an orphan during his infancy parental care seems to have been well supplied by his mother's sister Elizabeth and her husband Ennion Williams of Bristol, Pennsylvania. He was educated in Philadelphia, and served his apprenticeship with Joshua Maddock, a noted merchant of that city. Inheriting perhaps from his father some predilection for a seafaring life, he made a few voyages to the West Indies, but it appears he soon became weary of this vocation, and we find it recorded that he married, May 21st, 1741, **RUTH**, daughter of **Thomas** and **Sarah Leach**, of Newport, Rhode Island. In those early days of our country, a journey from Newport to Philadelphia was a momentous event, and family tradition informs us that an elderly gentleman who had accompanied William Buckley to Newport brought the bride home in his tandem, while the groom rode alongside on horseback. After their marriage, William and Ruth Buckley settled at Bristol, and he engaged in the milling business of the place. In the year 1759 he entered into a partnership with Reese Meredith, of Philadelphia, and while assisting in taking an account of their stock, which was very large, he was seized with pleurisy, the effect of over exertion and exposure, and died in Philadelphia March 3d of the same year. He left a large family, many of whom died in infancy or childhood. Those who arrived at mature years were:

i.   **PHINEAS**, of whom presently.

ii.   **WILLIAM** b. July 19th, 1745, md. **SARAH**, dau. of **Anthony** and **Sarah Morris**, of of Philadelphia, and d. Oct. 17th, 1815, having issue:

    i.   **ELIZABETH** md. **LUKE MORRIS**. (q. v.)

    ii.   **SARAH PEROT** md. 1st, **JOSEPH COOPER**, and 2d. **THOMAS HOWARD**, of Philadelphia, and d. Nov. 18th, 1847, having had issue by her second husband: **Anthony Morris** d. unmarried Apl. 6th, 1845; **Emma** md. **William L. Edwards**; and **Elizabeth** md. **Samuel H. Edwards**.

iii.   **ELIZABETH** d. unmarried Nov. 7th, 1826.

iv.   **REBECCA** md. **JAMES FERGUSON**, and had issue **WILLIAM, JAMES,** and **SAMUEL B.**

PHINEAS, eldest son of **William and Ruth Buckley**, was born at Bristol, April 17th, 1742. Having no children of their own, his father's Uncle and Aunt, Ennion and Elizabeth Williams, adopted him. An interesting memorial of this connection is now in the possession of his great grandson, the compiler of this history. It is a copy of Cranmer's Bible, given Phineas Buckley by his adopted father, and containing the autographs of its various possessors beginning with Ennion Williams' father of the same name in 1702, and also having pasted inside of one cover the original certificate of marriage between Ennion Williams and his first wife, Mary Hugg, dated 21st of second month, 1726.

Phineas Buckley was carefully educated by his adopted parents in the principles of the Society of Friends, and led a quiet regular life in accordance therewith. In December 1765, he married **MARY ANNA**, daughter of **William** and **Mary Redman**, of Bristol. She only lived six months after her marriage, dying of consumption.

He married secondly May 12th, 1768, at Friends' Meeting House in Wilmington, Delaware, **MARY**, daughter of **Thomas** and **Mary Shipley**, of Brandywine, (q. v.) She died very suddenly in New York, (whither her husband had removed) October 29th, 1795. He survived her thirty-one years, dying in Philadelphia at the house of his son-in-law, Peter Thomson, November 21st, 1826.

By his second wife he had issue:

i.   **ENNION** born October 22d, 1769, named for his father's Great Uncle **ENNION WILLIAMS**, Jr., who died February 25th, 1780, in the eighty-fifth year of his age. Ennion Buckley died April 2d, 1775.

ii.   **THOMAS**, of whom presently.

iii.   **ELIZABETH WILLIAMS** md. 1st, in June 1796, **SAMUEL UNDERHILL**, and had issue: **ANDREW** d. s. p.; and **MARY BUCKLEY** md. June 5th, 1831, **WILLIAM HUTCHIN**. He d. August 15th, 1833, and she md. March 25th, 1857, **EDWARD H. BONSALL**, and d. s. p. surviving, September 13th, 1870. **ELIZABETH UNDERHILL** md. 2d, December 16th, 1807, **PETER THOMSON**, and d. August 5th, 1856, leaving issue by him: **PETER** md. November 7th, 1843, **CAROLINE BROWNE**.

iv.   **MARY** d. unmarried July 6th, 1788.

v. **SARAH** md. in 1825, **ISRAEL COPE**, of Philadelphia, and d. p. November 19th, 1852.

vi. **DEBORAH** d. unmarried February 3d, 1796.

vii. **REBECCA** d. in infancy.

viii. **ANN** d. unmarried Oct. 24th, 1837.

ix. **WILLIAM** d. in infancy.

x. **PHINEAS WILLIAM** b. Oct. 20th, 1791, d. at New Orleans April 29th, 1827.

THOMAS, second son of **Phineas** and **Mary Buckley**, was born at Bristol, Jany. 29th, 1771. He removed to New York and engaged in mercantile life there, becoming a prominent merchant; being for many years President of the Bank of North America, and connected with many charitable institutions of that city. He md. Sept. 11th, 1793, by Friends' ceremony at their Meeting-house in Pearl Street, New York, **ANNA**, dau. of **John L.** and **Ann (Burling) Lawrence**, who d. July 11th, 1846. Her husband d. at Manhattanville, April 28th of the same year, having had issue:

i. **WILLIAM LAWRENCE** b. Oct. 6th, 1794, d. Sept. 9th, 1812.

ii. **JOHN LAWRENCE** b. July 31st, 1797, of whom presently.

iii. **PHINEAS HENRY** b. March 3d, 1800. (q. v.)

iv. **MARY ANNA** b. July 22d, 1802, md. May 9th, 1821, **WALTER R.** son of **Jacob** and **Mary Wood**. He d. May 19th, 1830, and his wife July 24th, 1873, having had issue: **ANNA BUCKLEY** d. in infancy; **THOMAS BUCKLEY** d. at the age of 8; **MARIANA** md. May 9th, 1855, **EDWARD THORNTON BROWN**, and has had issue: Thornton Edward b. July 24th, 1857, d. Oct. 17th, 1876, and Anna b. Feby. 27th, 1863; and **WALTER RALEGH** b. May 28th, 1830, md. Jany. 17th, 1857, **EMILY**, dau. of **Charles West Hornor**, and has issue: Nellie, Josephine and Daisy.

v. **ELIZABETH WILLIAMS** b. July 31st, 1805, d. unmarried in 1841.

vi. **EFFINGHAM LAWRENCE** b. May 10th, 1808, md. June 11th, 1835, **HANNAH ANN**, dau. of **Luke** and **Ann Morris**, of Philadelphia, and d. at Troy, New York, leaving issue: **EDWARD MORRIS** md. **GERTRUDE ONDERDONK**, and d. s. p. on the coast of Africa; and **ANNIE MORRIS** md. Dec. 3d, 1855, her cousin **ISRAEL W. MORRIS**. (q. v.)

vii. **JANE LAWRENCE** b. Jany. 14th, 1812, md. **Dr. JOHN CHEW THOMAS**. (q. v.)

JOHN LAWRENCE, second son of **Thomas** and **Anna** (Lawrence) **Buckley,** b. July 31st, 1797. md. Jany. 21st, 1821, **SARAH ANN TAYLOR,** and d. March 13th, 1857. leaving issue:

i.   **THOMAS CROWELL TAYLOR** b. Aug. 19th, 1826, a distinguished lawyer of New York; md. 1st in Oct. 1859, **JULIETTE ANN GERARD,** of that city who d. July 27th, 1866, leaving issue; **MARY DICKINSON KEMBLE;** and **JULIAN GERARD** b. July 3d, 1866. **T. C. T. BUCKLEY,** md. 2d Sept. 17th, 1873, **KATHERINE LEE YOUNG,** of Geneseo, N. Y., and d. July 12th, 1874, without further issue.

ii.   **SARAH TAYLOR** md. Jany. 14th, 1857, **DAVID LORD TURNER,** of New York, and has issue: **ELINOR BUCKLEY, JULIET LORD** and **JEANIE.**

iii.   **JOHN LAWRENCE** b. Oct. 1st, 1831, md. February 22d, 1854, **SOPHIE PRICE,** and has had issue: **SARAH ANN, FLORENCE,** and **AGNES** who all d. in infancy or childhood; **MARIE ADELE** and **FREDERICK.**

PHINEAS HENRY, third son of **Thomas** and **Anna** (Lawrence) **Buckley,** b. March 3d, 1800, md. 1st. May 12th, 1834, **PHEBE,** daughter of **Townsend** and **Sarah McCoun,** of Troy, N. Y., and by her who d. March 15th, 1838, he had issue born at Troy:

i.   **SARAH McCOUN** b. Feby. 14th, 1825.

ii.   **ANNA LAWRENCE** b. April 19th, 1827, md. October 17th, 1848, at St. Mark's Church, New York City, **ROBERT WALTER RUTHERFURD,** of Edgerston, near Belleville, New Jersey. (q. v.)

iii.   **TOWNSEND McCOUN** b. May 25th, 1829, d. August 29th, 1831.

iv.   **TOWNSEND McCOUN** b. September 19th, 1831, d. at Mobile, Alabama, September 26th, 1862.

v.   **THOMAS** b. July 16th, 1833.

vi.   **PHEBE McCOUN** b. May 11th, 1836, md. June, 2d, 1855, **THOMAS M. WIGHAM,** of New York City, and has had issue: **MAY; EDITH;** and **EDGAR CARTERET** b. in December 1871, d. in December 1875.

vii.   **ELIZABETH WILLIAMS** b. March 4th, 1838, md. June 29th, 1869, **EASTMAN JOHNSON,** of New York City, the distinguished painter of "Genre" pictures, and has issue: **ETHEL EASTMAN** b. May 2d, 1870. **EASTMAN JOHNSON** was b. July 29th, 1824, in the little town of Lovell, near Fryeburg, in Maine. His father was an officer in the employ of the United States Treasury Department. The son was first know to fame as a crayon limner, being so successful in that art, that in a few years he was enabled to visit Europe. There he commenced an earnest system of study and began to practice in Oil; at Dusseldorf he remained two years and then started for

Italy, stopping to examine the galleries in Holland. At the Hague he fell in with Mignot, and tarried there ostensibly to copy a remarkable picture in the Royal Collection. His stay lasted four years. He met with flattering success in portraiture, painting many of the wealthy citizens and nearly all of the maids of honor. At the Hague he also painted his first pictures in oil. On his return to the United States he turned his attention with great success to native subjects, "and no one of our painters," says Henry Tuckerman in his Book of the Artists, "has more truly caught and perfectly delineated the American rustic and negro, or with such pathetic and natural emphasis put upon canvas, bits of household and childish life, or given such bright and real glimpses of primitive human nature."

PHINEAS HENRY BUCKLEY md. 2d, in August 1843, **JULIA,** dau. of **Nathaniel** and **Catherine Lawrence,** of New York City. and d. at Newark, New Jersey, having had issue by his second wife, who d. December 31st, 1854.

i.   **KATHERINE LAWRENCE** b. in June 1844, md. **LAWRENCE HOPKINS,** of New York City, and has issue: **KATE** and **JENNY.**

ii.   **JANE LAWRENCE** md. December 6th, 1865, **JAMES SHEAFE SATTERTHWAITE,** of New York City and East Hampton, and has issue: **KITTY; JULIA;** and **JAMES SHEAFE** b. Jany. 8th, 1873.

CAREY.

JAMES CAREY, of Baltimore County, b. Feby. 22d, 1751-2, md. **MARTHA,** second dau. of **John** and **Cassandra Ellicott,** and had issue:

i.   **JOHN C.** d. in infancy.

ii.   **JOHN ELLICOTT** b. Feby. 2d, 1789, of whom presently.

iii.   **SAMUEL** b. Mch. 6th, 1791, d. s. p.

iv.   **MARGARET** b. Nov. 22d, 1791, md. **GALLOWAY CHESTON.** (q. v.)

v.   **JAMES** b. Mch. 10th, 1793.

vi.   **HANNAH** b. Aug. 7th, 1795, md. **WILLIAM E. COALE.**

vii. GEORGE b. Sept. 9th, 1800. (q. v.)

viii. MARTHA b. May 12th, 1805, md. Dr. RICHARD H. THOMAS. (q. v.)

JOHN ELLICOTT, second son of James and Martha (Ellicott) Carey, b. Feby. 2d, 1789, md. NANCY IRWIN, and had issue:

i. JAMES md. SUSAN KIMBER, and has issue: THOMAS KIMBER, JOHN ELLICOTT, JAMES, Jr., MARY IRWIN, FRANK, and MAURICE.

ii. THOMAS IRWIN md. MARTHA GRAY, dau. of George G. and Eliza S. Leiper, and has had issue: ELIZA d. in infancy; NANCY IRWIN; GEORGE LEIPER b. Feby. 5th, 1858; MARY THOMAS; THOMAS IRWIN b. Oct. 12th, 1862; JAMES b. Aug. 16th, 1864; MARTHA; CHARLES HAMILTON b. Oct. 3d, 1868; HELEN and JOHN, twins, of whom the latter d. in infancy.

GEORGE, fifth son of James and Martha (Ellicott) Carey, b. Sept. 9th, 1800, md. MARY GIBSON, and d. leaving issue a dau. SUSAN and four sons:

i. GEORGE GIBSON md. JOSEPHINE POE, and has issue: JOSEPHINE GIBSON, GEORGE, MARIA GIBSON, NEILSON POE, and MARGARET CHESTON.

ii. JAMES md. MATTIE WARD, and has since deceased.

iii. HENRY GIBSON md. GRACE GIBSON.

iv. ALEXANDER GIBSON md. ELEANORA COALE, and has one child.

CHESTON.

Dr. DANIEL CHESTON md. FRANCINA AUGUSTINA, dau. of James and Ariana Frisby, and widow of William Stephenson. She d. in July 1766, having had issue by her second husband:

JAMES, of whom presently; DANIEL d. unmarried; and FRANCINA AUGUSTINA b. in 1752 md. WILLIAM BENSLEY, of England, and d. s. p.

JAMES, eldest son of **Dr. Daniel** and **Francina A.** (Frisby) Cheston,
b. in 1747 md. **ANNE,** dau. of **James** and **Anne Galloway,** and had
issue: **DANIEL** b. in 1776, d. in 1811 unmarried; **FRANCINA AUGUSTINA**
b. in 1777, d. s. p.; and **JAMES** b. in 1779, a merchant of Baltimore,
md. **MARY ANN,** dau. of Samuel Hollingsworth, of that city, and d. in
1843, having had issue:

Dr. JAMES of whom presently, GALLOWAY md. MARGARET, dau. of James
Carey, who d. s. p.; SAMUEL d. in March 1875, unmarried; ANN md. Dr.
CASPAR MORRIS. (q. v.;) MARY md. Dr. JAMES MURRAY, and d. leaving a son
Daniel; FANNY HENRIETTA md. Dr. JAMES MURRAY, as his second wife; JOHN;
SAMUEL and ELIZA, who all d. s. p.

Dr. **JAMES,** eldest son of **James** and **Mary Ann** (Hollingsworth) Cheston,
b. in 1804, md. 1st **MARY,** dau. of **Philip John** and **Cornelia Thomas,**
and had issue by her:

i.   CORNELIA, d. s. p.

ii.   MARY md AUGUSTUS HALL, and has issue: HENRY, CHESTON, EDWARD, MARY,
      and ANNIE.

iii. JAMES, Jr. md. CHARLOTTE RATCLIFFE, dau. of Dr. Charles H. and
      Charlotte Steele, and has issue: JAMES, RATCLIFFE, MARY STEELE, CHARLOTTE
      RATCLIFFE, and MARGARET CAREY.

Mrs. **MARY** (Thomas) **CHESTON,** d. in 1834, and **Dr. JAMES
CHESTON** md. 2d **CORNELIA,** another dau. of **Philip John** and
Cornelia Thomas, who d. in 1839, having had issue: a dau. **NANCY**
md. **FENWICK HALL,** and had issue: NANNIE, CORNELIA, and SALLY.

Dr. **CHESTON** md. 3d **SARAH SCOTT,** dau. of **Daniel** and
Mary Murray, and has had further issue: DANIEL MURRAY, GALLOWAY,
SALLY MURRAY, ROBERT MURRAY, and CASPAR MORRIS.

ARMS FROM A SEAL.

CHEW.

JOHN CHEW, said to be a cadet of the family of **CHEW** of Chewton, in Somersetshire, England, who was a member of the Virginia House of Assembly in 1623 as a Burgess from Jamestown, appears to have been the first of this name in America. In a land grant of the same year he is described as "John Chew, Merchant."

He is said to have come over in the "Charitie" and his wife **SARAH**, to have followed him in the "Sea Flower" which returned to England in 1622. He was afterwards a Burgess from Hogg's Island, and was in the Assembly until 1643. **JOHN** and **SARAH CHEW** it is said had five sons, **SAMUEL**, **JOSEPH**, and three of whose descendants nothing is known.

JOSEPH, the second son md. Nov. 17th, 1685, in Maryland, **MARY SMITH**, and d. in the same Province, Feby. 12th, 1715-16. He is also said to have married a **MISS LARKIN**, of Annapolis, and to have had by her a son, **LARKIN CHEW**. (q. v.)

SAMUEL, eldest son of John and Sarah Chew, removed to Maryland before 1655, received large grants of land there, and settled at Herring Bay in Calvert County. He md. **ANNE AYRES**, who was a prominent member of the Society of Friends, whose business meetings were long held at her house. **SAMUEL CHEW** d. Mch. 15th, 1676-7, and his wife April 13th, 1695, having had issue:

i. **SAMUEL** b. in 1660. (q. v.)

ii. **JOSEPH** md. **ELIZA** ——— and d. Feby. 11th, 1704-5. his wife d. in May 1716, having had issue: **JOSEPH** who md. and had issue: Joseph, Henry, and Eliza; **HENRY**; and a daughter md. **SAMUEL BATTEE**.

iii.   **NATHANIEL**, who deceased before 1694.

iv.   **WILLIAM** md. December 20th, 1690, **SIDNEY**, dau. of **Thomas** and **Martha Wynn**, of Pennsylvania, and d. February 25th, 1709-10, leaving issue: a son **BENJAMIN** who d. in Jany. 1763, leaving issue by his wife **SARAH** ———; Benjamin; Sarah who md. a **Johns**; Phinehas; Mary; Ann who md. **Capt. Isaac Van Biber**; Henrietta md. **Benjamin Galloway**; and a dau. who md. a **Crockett**.

v.   **BENJAMIN** b. Feby. 12th, 1670-1, of whom presently.

vi.   **JOHN** who d. Feby. 19th, 1696-7.

vii.   **CALEB** who d. May 8th, 1698.

viii.   **SARAH** md. a **BURGES**.

ix.   **ANNE**.

BENJAMIN, fifth child of **Samuel** and **Anne Chew**, b. Feby. 12th, 1670-1, md. Dec. 8th, 1692, **ELIZABETH BENSON**, and d. March 3d, 1699-1700, having had issue:

i.   **ELIZABETH** md. Sept. 24th, 1702, **RICHARD BOND**.

ii.   **MARY**.

iii.   **SAMUEL** b. Oct. 30th, 1693, was a physician by profession, and Chief Justice of the three lower counties of Pennsylvania, Newcastle, Kent and Sussex, now included in the State of Delaware. **Dr. CHEW** md. 1st Oct. 22d, 1715, **MARY**, dau. of **Samuel** and **Anne Galloway**, and by her (who d. May 26th, 1734) had issue:

   i.   **SARAH** b. July 23d, 1716, d. in Feby. 1717-18.

   ii.   **ANN** b. Jany. 4th, 1718-19, d. Oct. 2d, 1723.

   iii.   **ELIZABETH** b. Nov. 25th, 1720, md. in 1749, **Col. EDWARD TILGHMAN**, of Wye. (q. v.)

   iv.   **BENJAMIN** b. Nov. 29th, 1722, of whom presently.

   v.   **ANN** b. May 13th, 1725, md. **SAMUEL GALLOWAY**. (q. v.)

   vi.   **MARY** b. June 27th, 1727, d. May 28th, 1728.

   vii.   **SAMUEL** b. April 29th, 1728, d. June 29th, 1729.

   viii.   **SAMUEL** b. August 3d, 1730, d. Nov. 3d, 1730.

   ix.   **HENRIETTA** b. March 17th, 1731-2, d. in June 1732.

Dr. **SAMUEL CHEW** md. 2d Sept. 28th, 1735, Mrs. **MARY GALLOWAY**, dau. of **Aquila Paca**, and widow of **Richard Galloway**, and d. June 16th, 1744, having had further issue by her:

x.   SAMUEL b. Aug. 24th, 1737. for many years Attorney General of the Colony, and Judge of the Supreme Court of the State of Delaware. md. ANNA MARIA. dau. of Peregrine Frisby, and d. s. p. May 25th, 1809, at Chestertown, Md.

xi.   MARY b. September 6th, 1739. d. May 1st, 1740.

xii.   JOHN b. March 21st, 1739-40. d. Dec. 15th, 1807, unmarried.

BENJAMIN, fourth son of **Dr. Samuel Chew**, b. November 29th, 1722, studied law under Andrew Hamilton of Philadelphia, and in London; was Speaker of the Lower House of the Three Lower Counties (now Delaware,) Attorney General of Pennsylvania, Jany. 14th, 1755, a member of the Provincial Council the same year. Recorder of the City of Philadelphia in 1756, which position he held for twenty years; Register General of Wills about 1770, and April 29th, 1774, appointed Chief Justice of the Province of Pennsylvania. When the Revolution took place Chief Justice Chew sympathized with the mother country, although he took no active part in the contest. In 1777 when Congress arrested a number of prominent Philadelphia Friends and banished them to Fredericksburg, Virginia, Chief Justice Chew and his friend John Penn the Proprietary of Pennsylvania, were also put under arrest, but were allowed to retire to Mr. Chew's property, Union Forge, near Burlington, New Jersey, and released from arrest the next year. In 1791 Mr. Chew was appointed President of the High Court of Errors and Appeal of the State of Pennsylvania and retained the position until the Court was abolished in 1806. He md. 1st June 13th, 1747, **MARY**, dau. of **John** and **Mary Galloway**, who d. November 9th, 1755. leaving issue :

i.   MARY b. Mch. 10th, 1748, md. ALEXANDER WILCOCKS, and had issue : BENJAMIN md. SARAH WALN; SAMUEL; ELIZABETH; ANN md. an INGERSOLL; and MARY md. CHARLES J. INGERSOLL.

ii.   ANNA MARIA b. November 27th, 1749. d. in 1812.

iii.   ELIZABETH b. Nov. 10th, 1751, md. EDWARD TILGHMAN. (q. v.)

iv.   SARAH b. Nov. 5th, 1753. md. JOHN GALLOWAY. (q. v.)

v.   HENRIETTA b. in Sept. 1755. d. in 1756.

Chief Justice CHEW md. 2d, September 12th, 1757, **ELIZABETH OSWALD**, who d. in 1819. The Chief Justice d. Jany. 20th. 1810. having had further issue :

vi.   BENJAMIN b. September 30th, 1758, of whom presently.

vii.   **MARGARET OSWALD** b. Dec. 17th, 1760, md. in 1787. **Col. JOHN EAGER HOWARD**, of Maryland, and had issue: **JOHN EAGER** b. June 25th, 1788, md. Dec. 20th, 1820, **CORNELIA ANNABELLA READ**, and d. Oct. 18th, 1822; **GEORGE** b. Nov. 21st, 1789, Governor of Maryland, md. Dec. 26th, 1811, **PRUDENCE GOUGH RIDGELY**, and d. Aug. 2d, 1846; **BENJAMIN CHEW** b. Nov. 5th, 1791, md. Feby. 24th, 1818; **JANE GRANT GILMOR**; **WILLIAM** b. Dec. 16th, 1793, md. April 14th, 1828, **REBECCA ANN KEY**, and d. Aug. 25th, 1834; **JULIANA ELIZABETH** b. May 3d, 1796, md. Dec. 7th, 1818, **JOHN McHENRY**, and d. May 22d, 1821; **JAMES** b. Dec. 17th, 1797, md. 1st **SOPHIA GOUGH RIDGELY**, and 2d, **CATHERINE M. ROSS**; **SOPHIA CATHERINE** b. March 6th, 1800, md. April 7th, 1825, **WILLIAM GEORGE READ**; **CHARLES** b. April 26th, 1802, md. Nov. 9th, 1825, **ELIZABETH PHŒBE**, dau. of **Francis Scott Key**, the celebrated author of the "Star Spangled Banner," and d. June 15th, 1869; and **MARY ANNE** b. Feby. 16th, 1806, and d. the same year.

viii.   **JOSEPH** b. March 9th, 1763, d. in Sept. 1764.

ix.   **JULIANNA** b. April 8th, 1765, md. **PHILIP NICKLIN**.

x.   **HENRIETTA** b. Sept. 15th, 1767, d. in 1845.

xi.   **SOPHIA** b. Nov. 13th, 1769, md. **HENRY PHILLIPS**.

xii.   **MARIA** b. Dec. 22d, 1771.

xiii.   **HARRIET** b. Oct. 22d, 1775, md. in 1799, **CHARLES**, the only son of **Charles Carroll**, of Carrollton, and had issue: **CHARLES** b. in July 1801, md. in Oct. 1825, **MARY DIGGS LEE**; **MARY** md. **RICHARD H. BAYARD**; **LOUISA** md. a **JACKSON**; **HARRIET** md. **Hon. JOHN LEE**; and **ELIZABETH** md. **Dr. RICHARD TUCKER**.

xiv.   **CATHERINE** b. May 3d, 1779.

BENJAMIN, sixth child of **Chief Justice Chew**, b. Sept. 30th. 1758. md. Dec. 11th. 1788, **KATHERINE BANNING**, and had issue:

i.   **SAMUEL** b. December 8th, 1789, d. in infancy.

ii.   **ELIZA** b. May 4th, 1791, d. in infancy.

iii.   **BENJAMIN** b. Dec. 5th, 1793, md. **ELIZABETH**, dau. of Chief Justice Tilghman, and had one child, which d. in infancy.

iv.   **SAMUEL** b. June 19th, 1795, d. unmarried in 1842.

v.   **JOHN** b. Jany. 23d, 1797. Midshipman U. S. N. Lost at sea in the "Epervia."

vi.   **ELIZA** b. Nov. 19th, 1798, md. **Hon. JAMES MURRAY MASON**, of Virginia, for many years U. S. Senator from that State, and Commissioner with John Slidell from the "Confederate States" to England, whose capture by Capt. Wilkes of the U. S. Navy, while on their voyage to that country in an English vessel, came so near causing a war between the United States and England. Mr. Mason d. April 29th, 1871, having had issue: ANNA md. JOHN AMBLER; BENJAMIN; CATHERINE md. JOHN THOMAS B. DORSEY; GEORGE; VIRGINIA; IDA; JAMES MURRAY md. Miss HILL; and JOHN.

vii.   HENRY BANNING b. Dec. 11th, 1800, of whom presently.

viii.   WILLIAM WHITE b. April 12th, 1803, Secretary of Legation to Hon George M. Dallas, American Minister to Russia, and chargé d'affaires after Mr. Dallas' return, d. in November 1851.

ix.   ANNA SOPHIA PENN b. March 18th, 1805, now residing at "Cliveden" with her nephew Mr. Samuel Chew.

x.   JOSEPH b. December 12th, 1806, d. in 1837.

xi.   ANTHONY BANNING b. Jany. 24th, 1809, d. in 1854.

xii.   CATHERINE MARIA b. May 12th, 1811, d. in infancy.

xiii.   OSWALD b. May 23d, 1813, drowned while bathing in the Schuylkill River, June 8th, 1824.

HENRY BANNING, seventh child of Benjamin and Katherine Chew, b. December 11th, 1800, md. HARRIET, youngest dau. of Gen. Charles Ridgely, of Hampton, who was Governor of Maryland in 1815; and had issue:

i.   CATHERINE b. April 19th, 1823, d. in infancy.

ii.   PRISCILLA RIDGELY b. Dec. 3d, 1824, d. Feby. 11th, 1837.

iii.   CHARLES RIDGELY b. Jany. 20th, 1827, md. HARRIET GREEN, and d. November 28th, 1875, leaving issue now living at "Epsom" near Towsontown, Maryland.

iv.   BENJAMIN b. May 27th, 1828, d. in infancy.

v.   BENJAMIN b. June 21st, 1830.

vi.   SAMUEL b. Jany. 28th, 1832, living at "Cliveden" Germantown, Pennsylvania, the "Chew House" celebrated in the History of the American Revolution as the scene of the successful defence made by a small body of British troops Oct. 4th, 1777, which decided the battle of Germantown. The Americans were in full pursuit of the defeated British when they reached the "Chew House" into which a small party had thrown themselves to protect the retreat. Gen. Knox it is said refused to leave a fortified place behind him, and attempting to take it, found it so well defended that time was given the British to rally and turn their defeat into a victory. Mr. CHEW md. June 20th, 1861, MARY, dau. of David S. Brown, of Philadelphia, and has issue: ANNA SOPHIA PENN the 3d, b. June 17th, 1862; ELIZABETH BROWN b. November 19th, 1863; DAVID SANDS BROWN b. March 3d, 1866; and SAMUEL, Jr. b. April 28th, 1871.

vii.   **ACHSAH CARROLL** b. Jany. 22d, 1834, d. in infancy.

viii.   **HENRY BANNING** b. Oct. 19th, 1835, studied medicine and was graduated at Jefferson College, Philadelphia, in 1855 appointed resident physician to the Baltimore Almshouse, where he was taken ill with Typhus fever and d. April 29th, 1855.

SAMUEL, eldest son of **Samuel and Anne (Ayres) Chew,** b. in 1660, md. 1st, April 14th, 1682, **ANNE** — — and had issue by her who d. April 8th, 1702.

i.   **SAMUEL** b. May 28th, 1683, of whom presently.

ii.   **ANN** b. July 2d, 1685, d. Jany. 28th, 1694-5.

iii.   **JOHN** b. April 8th, 1687. (q. v.)

iv. v. **JOSEPH** and **BENJAMIN,** twins, b. April 1st, 1689, the latter d. April 18th, 1698.

vi.   **NATHANIEL** b. August 5th, 1692, md. **MARY** ——, who d. in Sept. 1728; he d. in Feby. 1727-8, leaving issue: **NATHANIEL, JOSEPH** and **ANN.**

vii.   **JOSEPH** b. Apl. 25th, 1696, md. **SARAH** ——, and d. in Feby. 1754, leaving issue: **THOMAS, ELIZABETH,** and **SUSANNAH.**

SAMUEL CHEW md. 2d, June 29th, 1704, **Mrs. ELIZABETH COALE,** widow, who d. Feby. 27th, 1709-10, and d. without further issue Oct. 10th, 1718.

SAMUEL CHEW, his eldest son, b. May 28th, 1683, md. **MARY** and d. Oct. 1736, leaving issue:

i.   **SAMUEL,** of whom presently.

ii.   **ANN** md. August 11th, 1724, **PHILIP THOMAS.** (q. v.)

iii.   **JOHN** d. Mch. 2d, 1726, aged 15.

iv.   **MARY** b. in 1714 md. **JOHN HEPBURN,** and d. Aug. 10th, 1770.

v.   **RICHARD** b. in May 1716, md. **Mrs. SARAH (Lock) CHEW,** widow of his cousin Samuel Chew, of John; and d. June 24th, 1769. His wife d. Feby. 1st, 1791, having had issue: **PHILEMON LLOYD;** Capt. **SAMUEL** b. in Jany. 1755, d. Feby. 1st, 1785; **LOCK** d. in 1794; **MARY** md. 1st —— **SMITH,** and had issue: Upton and Sarah; md. 2d —— **LYLES; SARAH LOCK** md. —— **LANE;** and **RICHARD** b. in 1753, d. in 1801, leaving issue: Richard; Mary md. —— Mackall; Thomas H.; William H. Philemon b. in 1789, d. leaving a son Richard B. B., Sarah and Frances.

vi. **FRANCIS** b. in 1721. md. Feby. 26th, 1749-50, **MARY LINGAN**, who d. Feby. 12th, 1764. He d. Nov. 11th, 1775. leaving issue: **SAMUEL** b. Jany. 29th. 1755; **ANN** b. May 15th, 1759, and **RICHARD** b. Oct 19th, 1761.

JOHN, second son of **Samuel** and **Anne Chew**, b. April 8th, 1687. md. **ELIZA** ——— and dying before 1718. his widow md. **ELIHU HALL** in 1722. By her first husband she had issue:

i. **SAMUEL** md. **SARAH LOCK**, and d. in London in 1749. leaving issue:

    i. **SAMUEL** b. in 1737. md. **PRISCILLA**, dau. of **Rev. Samuel Claggett**, and descended from Col. Edward Claggett, of Canterbury, England, who md. Margaret, dau. of Sir Thomas Adams, founder of a professorship of Arabic at the University of Cambridge. **SAMUEL CHEW** d. Feby. 20th, 1790, leaving issue a son: John Hamilton b. Sept. 14th, 1771. md. his cousin Priscilla E., dau. of Rt. Rev. Thomas John Claggett, D. D., first Bishop of Maryland, and the first Bishop of the Protestant Episcopal Church, consecrated in the United States. **John H. Chew** d. March 22d, 1830, leaving issue: Dr. Samuel b. April 29th, 1807, Professor of the Principles and Practice of Medicine in the University of Maryland, d. Dec. 26th, 1863; Thomas; William P.; and Rev. John H. a clergyman of the Protestant Episcopal Church.

    ii. **JOHN** d. May 26th, 1785. leaving issue: John Lane, Samuel, Nathaniel Lane, and William Lock.

    iii. **WILLIAM**.

    iv. **ELIZABETH** md. 1st, ——— **SMITH**, and 2d, ——— **SPRIGG**.

ii. **ANN** md. Aug. 17th, 1727. **JOSEPH**, son of Gerrard and Margaret Hopkins. (q. v.)

iii. **MARY**.

SAMUEL, eldest son of **Samuel** and **Mary Chew**, md. **HENRIETTA MARIA**, dau. of **Philemon Lloyd**, and d. Jany. 15th, 1736-7, having had issue:

i. **SAMUEL**, called of "Herring Bay."

ii. **HENRIETTA MARIA** md. **EDWARD DORSEY**.

iii, iv. **PHILEMON LLOYD** and **BENNET**, twins, the former d. s. p. in March 1770, the latter md. **ANNA MARIA**, dau. of Edward Tilghman, and had issue: **EDWARD**, d. s. p.

v. **MARGARET** md. **JOHN BEALE BORDLEY**. (q. v.)

vi. **MARY** md. 1st, **WILLIAM PACA**, signer of the Declaration of Independence, and had issue: **JOHN**. Mrs. **PACA** md. 2d, **DANIEL DULANY**, and had issue: **LLOYD** and **WALTER**.

LARKIN CHEW, said to be the son of **Joseph Chew** and a **Miss Larkin,** of Annapolis, was in Virginia before 1700; his connection with the Chews of Maryland, is I think sufficiently authenticated by a correspondence between the Madisons and Taylors of Virginia, and the Chews of Maryland, which I have seen.   He md. **HANNAH,** dau. of **John Roy,** of Port Royal, Virginia, and had issue:

i.   **JOSEPH** d. in infancy.

ii.   **THOMAS,** of whom presently.

iii.   **ANN** md. **WILLIAM JOHNSTON.**

iv.   **JOHN.** (q. v.)

v.   **LARKIN** md. **MARY BEVERLY,** and had two daughters.

THOMAS, eldest surviving son of **Larkin** and **Hannah (Roy) Chew,** md. **MARTHA,** dau. of **Col. James Taylor,** of York River, and sister of Mrs. Ambrose Madison, President Madison's grandmother, and had issue:

i.   **JOSEPH** md. **GRACE DESHON,** of New London, Conn., and had issue

    i.   **JOSEPH** d. in Jamaica unmarried.

    ii.   **WILLIAM JOHNSTON,** an officer in the British army, and killed at Niagara.

    iii.   **JOHN** d. at Montreal unmarried.

    iv.   **FRANCES** md. **GABRIEL SISTAI,** of New London, Conn., and d. in 1820.

    v.   **GRACE** d. at Montreal unmarried.

ii.   **LARKIN** d. in 1796 unmarried.

iii.   **FRANCES** md. **HENRY DOWNS.**

iv.   **HANNAH** d. unmarried.

v.   **THOMAS** d. in youth.

vi.   **COLEBY,** killed at Fort Du Quesne in 1755.

vii.   **ELIZABETH** d. unmarried.

viii. **ALICE** md. her cousin, **ZACHARY TAYLOR,** of Virginia, grandfather of **President Taylor,** and d. in 1796.

ix.   **MILDRED** md. —— **COLEMAN.**

x.   **SAMUEL,** of whom presently.

xi.   **JAMES** md. in 1765 **MARY CALDWELL,** of Virginia.

SAMUEL, tenth child of **Thomas** and **Martha (Taylor) Chew**, was an officer in the American Navy, and d. while on active service in 1779. He md. **LUCY MILLER**, of New Haven, Conn., and had issue:

i.   **COLEBY** md. **FRANCIS LARNED**, of New London, and d. in 1803, his wife d. in 1846, having had issue:

    i.   **FRANCES** b. in 1800 md. **LEONARD COIT**, of New London, and d. in 1866.

    ii.   **COLEBY** b. in 1802 md. **MARY CECELIA LAW**, and d. in 1850.

ii.   **SAMUEL** md. **MARY SABIN**, and d. in 1834, his wife d. in 1855, having had issue: **LUCY** md. **JAMES MORGAN SMITH**, of Georgia, and d. s. p.; **SAMUEL COLEBY** d. in 1832; **THOMAS JOHN**; **ANTHONY SANDFORD**; and **JAMES SMITH**.

iii.   **THOMAS JOHN** b. in 1771, entered the U. S. Navy in 1799, and resigned in 1832. He was on the "Chesapeake" when attacked by the "Shannon," and Capt. James Lawrence, when mortally wounded and supported in his arms, gave him his dying command: "Don't give up the ship." He md. **ABBY HORTENSE HALLAM**, and d. in 1846, having had issue:

    i.   **JAMES LAWRENCE** d. in 1829.

    ii.   **BETSEY P.** d. in infancy.

    iii.   **ELIZABETH HALLAM.**

    iv.   **LUCY** d. in youth.

    v.   **ABBY HORTENSE** md. **McCREA SWIFT**, of New Brunswick.

    vi.   **MARY HALLAM** md. **GEORGE R. LEWIS**, of New London.

    vii.   **LUCY** md. **M. LUDLOW WHITLOCK**, of Great Barrington, Mass.

JOHN, second surviving son of **Larkin** and **Hannah (Roy) Chew**, md. **MARGARET**, dau. of **Col. Robert Beverly**, Clerk of the Council of Virginia in 1697, and author of the History of Virginia, by R. B., Gent., published in 1705: and had issue:

i.   **ROBERT** md. **MOLLY PARROT**, of Middlesex, and had issue: **ROBERT BEVERLY** d. unmarried; **JOHN** md. **ELIZABETH SMITH**; **HENRY** d. unmarried; **ELIZABETH** md. **LARKIN STANARD**; and **JOSEPH** md. **MARY WINSLOW**.

ii.   **MARY BEVERLY** md. **JOSEPH BROCK**, of Spotsylvania.

iii.   **MARGARET** d. in youth.

iv.   **JOHN**, of whom presently.

v.   **HANNAH** md. **JOHN CARTER.**

JOHN, second son of John and **Margaret** (Beverly) Chew, was a Colonel in the Revolutionary Army, md. in 1772, **ANN**, dau. of **Thomas Fox**, and d. in 1799, his wife d. in 1820, having had issue:

i.   **BEVERLY** b. in 1773, of whom presently.

ii.   **JOHN** d. in 1835, unmarried.

iii.   **PHILADELPHIA CLAIBORNE** md. **BROOKER WALLER**.

iv.   **ANN** md. her cousin Capt. **JOSEPH BROCK**, U. S. A.

v.   **THOMAS** d. unmarried.

vi.   **ELIZABETH** md. **ROBERT CAMMACK**

vii.   **ROBERT** md. **LOUISE DE MARCELLON**, and d. s. p.

viii.   **CLAIBORNE** d. unmarried.

ix.   **MARY** d. in 1871, unmarried.

x.   **LUCY** d. unmarried.

xi.   **CAROLINE MATILDA** md. Col. **JOHN STANARD**.

xii.   **MARGARET** d. in infancy.

BEVERLY, eldest son of John and Ann (Fox) Chew, b. in 1773, removed to New Orleans in 1797, was Collector of the Port from 1817 to 1829, President of the Branch Bank of the United States, and Vice Consul of Russia. He md. Jany. 14th. 1810. **MARIA THEODORA DUER**, dau. of **Col. Wm. Duer**, of New York City, and grand daughter of Lord Stirling, of the Revolutionary Army, and d. in 1851, having had issue:

i.   **BEVERLY** d. in 1825, unmarried.

ii.   **CAROLINE** d. in 1823, unmarried.

iii.   **LUCY** md. **WILLIAM DUER**, son of Judge John Duer, of New York City.

iv.   **WILLIAM**.

v.   **KATHERINE** md. Judge **THOMAS KENNEDY**, and d. in 1863.

vi.   **ROBERT** d. in infancy.

vii.   **ALEXANDER LAFAYETTE**, of whom presently.

viii.   **MARY VIRGINIA** md. **MARTIN G. KENNEDY**, and d. in 1863.

ix.   **MORRIS ROBINSON** md. April 10th, 1860, **MARY MEDORA KENNEDY**, of New Orleans, La., and has had issue: **MARY MEDORA** b. in 1861; **JOSEPH WITHERS** b. in 1862; **JOSEPH BEVERLY** b. in 1865; **MARY ROSE** b. in 1868; **MARY VIRGINIA** b. in 1869; **MORRIS ROBINSON** b. in 1874, d. the same year.

ALEXANDER LAFAYETTE, seventh child of **Beverly** and **Maria Theodora** (**Duer**) **Chew**, md. in 1849, **SARAH AUGUSTA**, dau. of **Phinehas Prouty**, of Geneva, N. Y., and has issue:

i.   **BEVERLY** b. in 1850, md. in 1872, **CLARISSA**, dau. of Rev. **Job Pierson**, of Ionia, Mich.

ii. **HARRIET HILLHOUSE** b. in 1852, md. in 1874, **ERNEST CLEVELAND COXE**, son of Rt. Rev. **A. Cleveland Coxe**, Bishop of Western New York.

iii. **PHINEAS PROUTY** b. in 1854.

iv. **THOMAS HILLHOUSE** b. in 1856.

v.   **ALEXANDER DUER** b. in 1858.

vi. **KATE ADELAIDE** b. in 1860.

vii. **THEODORA AUGUSTA** b. in 1862, d. in 1874.

viii. **LILLIAN** b. in 1864.

[For the descendants of the three younger sons of John and Sarah Chew of Virginia, and those of John Lane eldest son of John Chew, who d. May 26th, 1785, and other additions to this Pedigree, see Addenda and Corrigenda, the information being received too late for insertion in its proper place.]

COALE.

WILLIAM COALE, of Anne Arundel County, Md., who d. Oct. 30th, 1678, in his will made Oct. 26th of the same year, mentions his son **WILLIAM** begotten of **HESTHER**, his wife, his son **WILLIAM** begotten of **HANNAH**, his second wife, and the children of his third wife **ELIZABETH**, dau. of Philip Thomas: **SAMUEL**; **PHILIP** of whom presently; and **ELIZABETH**.

The elder **WILLIAM** md. an **ELIZABETH**, surname unknown, and d. in October 1700, his wife afterwards md. **SAMUEL CHEW**. (q. v.) The younger md. **ELIZA** —— and d. in June 1715, leaving three sons, **WILLIAM**, **SAMUEL** and **THOMAS**, and seven daughters, **ELIZA** md. **RICHARD SNOWDEN**, (q. v.;) **MARY**, **HANNAH**, **PRISCILLA**, **SARAH**, **ANN**, and **MARGARET** who md. **GERARD HOPKINS**.

ELIZABETH, the only dau. md **NATHAN SMITH**, who d. in January 1710-11, leaving issue: five sons, JOSEPH, NATHAN, WILLIAM, THOMAS and PHILIP, and five daughters ELIZABETH, SUSANNAH, SARAH, CASSANDRA, and MARY. After her first husband's death, Mrs. **ELIZABETH** (Thomas) **COALE** md. **EDWARD TALBOT**. (q. v.)

PHILIP, second son of **William** and **Elizabeth** (**Thomas**) **Coale**, was an officer in the British Army, md. April 6th, 1697, **CASSANDRA**, dau. of **Sir George** and **Lady Bridget Skipwith**, and had issue a son SKIPWITH who md. **MARGARET HOLLAND**, and removed to Baltimore County in 1732. They had issue: PHILIP, WILLIAM of whom presently; SAMUEL, CASSANDRA, SARAH and SUSAN.

WILLIAM, second son of **Skipwith** and **Margaret** (Holland) **Coale**, md. **SARAH WEBSTER**, settled in Harford County, and had issue: JOHN. and ISAAC who was a farmer and miller at Deer Creek, in Harford Co., md. RACHEL, dau. of William and Mary (Goldhawk) Cox, of that County, but originally of Egham, in England, and had issue: SKIPWITH, WILLIAM ELLIS of whom presently: SARAH, ELIZABETH, JOHN WEBSTER, MARY, SUSAN HOLLAND and ISAAC.

WILLIAM ELLIS, second son of **William** and **Rachel** (**Cox**) **Coale**, md. **HANNAH ELLICOTT**, dau. of **James** and **Martha Carey**, who d. in 1837, having had issue:

i. JAMES CAREY b. May 25th, 1825, md. Aug. 2d, 1847, KATHARINE, dau. of George Baily, of Chester Co., Pa., and has issue: ELIZABETH BAILY md. Oct. 19th, 1876, EDWARD BLAKE BRUCE, of Boston, Mass., and has issue Edward Skipwith b. Aug. 1st, 1877.

ii. ISAAC, Jr. b. in 1827, md. 1st MARY GABLE, and had issue ALFORD G.; and JAMES CAREY d. in infancy; md. 2d HELEN McDOWELL, and d. in 1875, having had further issue: HELEN C.

iii. MARY b. in 1829, md. FRANCIS COPE YARNALL, of Philadelphia, Pa., and has issue: MARGARET CHESTON, CAROLINE COPE and EDWARD.

iv. WILLIAM ELLIS, Jr. b. in 1831, md. LOUISA SMITH, and has issue WILLIAM E., MARY YARNALL, THOMAS E. and LULU.

v.   THOMAS ELLICOTT b. in 1835, md. CECILIA HARVEY, and has issue WILLIAM, HARVEY, ISAAC, THOMAS E. Jr., NELLIE and CAREY.

vi.   MARTHA CAREY d. in infancy.

vii.   HANNAH ELLICOTT b. in 1837, md. DAVID SCULL, Jr., of Philadelphia, Pa., and has issue: WILLIAM E.

WILLIAM ELLIS COALE md. 2d **CASSANDRA WEBSTER**, dau. of Surgeon Joseph Brevitt, of the British Army, and had further issue: MARGARET CHESTON md. BARTHOLOMEW W. BEESLY, of Philadelphia; SKIPWITH HOLLAND; ELEANORA md. ALEXANDER G. CAREY, (q. v.;) and EDWIN BREVITT.

COWMAN.

JOSEPH COWMAN, of the City of London, and a seaman by profession, md. Mch. 5th, 1723-4, **Mrs. SARAH HILL**, widow, and had with other issue two sons: JOHN, of whom presently, and JOSEPH, who engaged in the Iron business with his father-in-law, Richard Snowden, and md Apl. 4th, 1754, ELIZABETH, youngest dau. of Richard and Elizabeth (Thomas) Snowden, and had issue: RICHARD b. Sept. 12th, 1777, md. ANN DARE, and d. in Mch. 1784, leaving three daus., Ann, Elizabeth, and Mary; JOSEPH md. ELEANOR HALL; ELIZABETH; SAMUEL; SARAH md. RICHARD HALL; and THOMAS md. HENRIETTA HARWOOD.

JOHN, eldest son of Joseph and Sarah Cowman, b. in 1737 md. Sept. 27th, 1757, SARAH, dau. of Gerard Hopkins, and d. Sept. 15th, 1808, having had issue:

i.   JOSEPH b. Sept. 8th, 1758, of whom presently.

ii.   MARY b. Apl. 18th, 1760, md. SAMUEL THOMAS. (q. v.)

iii.   GERARD b. May 6th, 1762, d. Dec. 31st, 1789.

iv.   JOHN b. Mch. 10th, 1764, d. Aug. 10th, 1826.

v.   SARAH b. Feb. 9th, 1766, md. Dec. 28th, 1786, WILLIAM GOVER, and had issue: SARAH b. Nov. 2d, 1787; MARY COWMAN b. Feby. 24th, 1789; WILLIAM ALEXANDER b. Feb. 16th, 1791; AUGUSTUS FREDERICK b. Jany. 18th, 1793; ELIZABETH b. Dec. 22d, 1794; MARGARET b. Sept. 10th, 1796; JOHN b. March 17th, 1798; ELIZA b. May 31st, 1800; ANN MARIA b. Aug. 1st, 1802; CAROLINE b. Sept. 4th, 1804; and ROBERT b. Nov. 1st, 1806.

vi.   **MARGARET** b. May 22d, 1769.

vii   **ANN** b. July 24th, 1771.

viii   **ELIZABETH** b. March 12th, 1774.

ix.   **RICHARD** b. Sept. 12th, 1777.

JOSEPH, eldest son of **John** and **Sarah** (**Hopkins**) **Cowman,** b. Sept. 8th, 1758, md. Feby. 3d, 1786. **MARY,** third dau. of **Samuel** and **Eiizabeth** (**Thomas**) **Snowden,** and d. in Aug. 1825. his wife d. Aug. 15th, 1834, having had issue: **ELIZABETH** b. Dec. 29th, 1786, d. in Aug. 1822; **SARAH** b. May 28th, 1789: **GERARD** b. Nov. 9th, 1791: **SAMUEL SNOWDEN** b. Feby. 9th, 1794. md. and had a son **THOMAS W.** b. in 1827, d. Aug. 5th, 1829; **JOHN G.** b. April 22d, 1796: **MARY** b. in 1798, d. Aug. 9th, 1817. unmarried: and **JOSEPH** b. May 22d, 1801.

ARMS FROM N. Y. GEN. & BIOG. RECORD.

De ZENG.

Baron **De ZENG,** of Rücherswalde—Wolkenstein near Marienburg in Saxony, Lord Chamberlain to the Duchess of Saxe-Weissenfels, and High Forest Officer to the King of Saxony, md. **Lady JOHANNA PHILLIPINA VON PONICKAU,** of Altenberg. and had issue:

i. **JOHN GEORGE FREDERICK ADOLF** md. the Countess of **SOLMS ZEKLENBURG**, who d. in 1800, and her husband in 1829, leaving issue: **HENRY LOUIS** killed by a fall from his horse in 1832; and **LOUISE** md. the **Baron Von OEHLSCHLAGEL**, of the Saxon Army, and d. s. p. in 1858.

ii. **FREDERIC AUGUSTUS** b. in 1756, at Dresden, entered the service of the Landgrave of Hesse Cassel, served in his army and was a Hof-Juncker to his Serene Highness. Came to America in 1781, as an officer in the Hessian Contingent of the British Army, and was stationed at New York. With difficulty obtained a discharge in November 1783, and settled in New York. November 3d, 1789, was made a citizen of New York under the Naturalization Act, and dropped the use of his title, though usually addressed by it. In 1796 established in connection with Jeremiah Van Rensselaer and Abraham Ten Eyck, the first Glass Works in New York. Was largely interested in the internal navigation of the State; md. in 1784, at Trinity Church, **MARY**, dau. of Caleb and Sarah Lawrence, who d. at Otsego in 1836, and her husband at Clyde, in Wayne County, New York, April 26th, 1838, having had issue: **GEORGE SCRIBA** md. **ELIZA SMITH**, and d. s. p.; **ERNESTINE** md. **JAMES HOUGHTALING**, M. D., of Kingston, N. Y.; **RICHARD LAWRENCE** md. his cousin **SARAH**, dau. of Richard and Mary Lawrence; **PHILIP MARK** md. **LUCRETIA SEARS**, of Bainbridge, New York; **WILLIAM STEUBEN** md. **CAROLINE C.** dau. of Maj. James Rees, of Philadelphia; **ARTHUR NOBLE**, d. s. p.; **SARAH** md her cousin **RICHARD L. LAWRENCE**; **AMELIA CLARISSA** md. **ADDISON GRISWOLD**, of Syracuse; and **MARIA** md. **WILLIAM S. STOW**, of Clyde, New York.

ARMS FROM A FAMILY TREE.

ELLICOTT.

ANDREW ELLICOTT md. **MARY FOX**, descended from Francis Fox, of St. Germans, Cornwall, England, and connected with the Lords Holland of that family: removed to America and settled in Bucks County, Pennsylvania, about 1700. He had a son **ANDREW** who md. **ANN BYE**, and had issue: three sons, JOSEPH b. in 1732, ANDREW and JOHN. They removed to Maryland in 1772, and settled on the Patapsco

River about 10 miles west of Baltimore, where Ellicott City now stands. By 1774 they had completed their first flour mill, which was burnt in 1809. In 1783 their trade increasing they bought their first water lot in the town of Baltimore, and built a wharf at the corner of Pratt and Light Streets, in order to export their flour to England.

They and their family after them, carried on an extensive milling business for a number of years, and were largely interested in the early progress of the Baltimore and Ohio R. R., and other works of public utility.

i.   **JOSEPH**, the eldest brother md. **JUDITH BLATER**, and d. in 1785, having had issue with others: **JOSEPH** d. in New York in 1826; **ANDREW** b. Jany. 24th, 1754, the celebrated surveyor, in 1790, appointed to lay out the City of Washington, in 1792 Surveyor-General of the United States, d. Aug. 28th, 1826, at West Point Military Academy where he was Professor of Mathematics; and a dau. **LETITIA** md. **JOHN EVANS**, and had issue: **David Ellicott** and **Charles W.**

ii.   **ANDREW**, of whom presently.

iii.   **JOHN** md. **CASSANDRA HOPKINSON**, and d. leaving an only son **JOHN** and three daus. **ELIZABETH; MARTHA** b. Nov. 7th, 1761, md. **JAMES CAREY**, (q. v.;) and **HANNAH.**

ANDREW, second son of **Andrew** and **Ann (Bye) Ellicott**, md. 1st **ELIZABETH BROWN**, and after her death, 2d **ESTHER BROWN**. He had issue:

i.   **JONATHAN** b. Nov. 9th, 1756, of whom presently.

ii.   **ELIAS** d. in infancy.

iii.   **ELIAS** b. Jany. 5th, 1759. (q. v.)

iv.   **GEORGE** b. March 28th, 1760, md. Dec. 29th, 1790, **ELIZABETH**, dau. of James and Deborah Brooke, and d. in 1832, having had issue: **ELIZABETH** b. Dec. 5th, 1793; **MARTHA** b. Sept. 13th, 1795, md. **NATHAN TYSON**, (q. v.;) **GEORGE** b. July 16th, 1798, md. —— **IGLEHART; MARY** and **ANNA B.** twins, b. May 14th, 1801, the former md. Oct. 19th, 1825, **THOMAS TYSON**; the latter md. **THOMAS TYSON** as his second wife and d. July 16th, 1839; and **SARAH** b. Nov. 3d, 1803, d. Aug. 31st, 1804.

v.   **BENJAMIN.**

vi. vii. viii.   **ANDREW, ELIZABETH** and **JOSEPH** d. unmarried.

ix.   **NATHANIEL** md. **ELIZABETH ELLICOTT**, and had issue **JOHN, HANNAH, NATHANIEL, CASSANDRA, MARY, JONATHAN** and **ANDREW.**

x.   TACY md. ISAAC McPHERSON, and had issue : ESTHER, MARY and ANN.

xi.   JAMES md. HENRIETTA, dau of Philip William and Mary Thomas, and had an only son CHARLES d. s. p.

xii. ANDREW md. HANNAH TUNIS, and had issue : JAMES ; ELIZA md. BENJAMIN POULTNEY, (q. v.) ; and JANE TUNIS md. THOMAS POULTNEY. (q. v.)

xiii. THOMAS. (q. v.)

xiv. JOHN md. MARY MITCHELL, and had issue : RACHEL b. April 6th, 1804 ; ANN b. Oct. 16th, 1805 ; MARY and JOHN.

JONATHAN, eldest son of **Andrew** and **Elizabeth (Brown) Ellicott**, b. Nov. 9th, 1756, was a man of stalwart frame, strongly marked Roman features, keen gray eyes, plain in speech and manners, and with a decided genius for mechanical invention. He was the projector and first President of the Frederick Turnpike leading from the town of Baltimore by the flour mills of his family to Frederick City ; and was the first President of the Baltimore Water Company. He md. **SARAH HARVEY**, of Bucks County, Pa., and d. in 1826. His wife was b. May 20th, 1764, was petite and delicate in figure, and remarkable for the fineness of her complexion at an advanced age, the great kindness of her disposition and profuse hospitality combined with economy and careful housewifery. She d. in 1840, having had issue :

i.   NATHANIEL b. in 1782, d. in 1786.

ii.   SAMUEL b. Dec. 13th, 1783, d. unmarried in 1842.

iii. ELIZABETH b. Dec. 5th, 1785, md. WILLIAM TYSON. (q. v.)

iv.   FRANCES b. Dec. 5th, 1785, d. in 1790.

v.   NATHANIEL H. b. April 26th, 1791, md. in 1826, THOMASINE R. TRIMBLE, of New York, and d. in 1860, having had issue : JANE T. md. JOSEPH WILLSON, and has issue : Cornelia, Mary and Henry.

vi.   WILLIAM b. Oct. 15th, 1793, md. in 1833, MARY ELEONORA NORRIS, and d. in 1836.

vii. SARAH b. Feby. 27th, 1796, md. WILLIAM E. GEORGE. (q. v.)

viii. FRANCES b. July 24th, 1798, d. in 1814.

ix.   JONATHAN H. b. Jany. 20th, 1801.

x.   LETITIA H. b. July 27th, 1803, md. in 1830, THOMAS R. FISHER, and has had issue : WILLIAM LOGAN ; GEORGE ; SARAH ; ELLICOTT ; MARY md. in 1862, GEORGE W. CARPENTER, and has issue : Lettie and Bessie ; and HARVEY.

xi.   MARY ANN b. Feby. 10th, 1806, d. unmarried in 1843.

xii.   BENJAMIN H. b. in 1809, md. in 1835, MARY WARFORD, and had issue: RACHEL,
       WARFORD and GEORGE.

ELIAS, third son of Andrew and Elizabeth (Brown) Ellicott, b. Jany.
   4th, 1759, md. April 26th, 1786, MARY, dau. of Evan and Rachel
   Thomas, of Mt. Radnor, and had issue:

i.   ELIZABETH b. Feby. 17th, 1787, md. LEWIN WETHERED. (q. v.)

ii.   EVAN THOMAS b. Sept. 17th, 1788, d. Aug. 10th, 1791.

iii.   RACHEL b. Feby. 17th, 1791, md. Jany. 15th, 1812, JOHN, son of Edward and Mary
       Hewes, and had issue: EDWARD b. Oct. 9th, 1812; ELIAS ELLICOTT b. March
       9th, 1814; HENRY b. Feby. 20th, 1816; MARY ELLICOTT b. April 9th, 1818;
       JAMES ELLICOTT b. Aug. 10th, 1820; BENJAMIN ELLICOTT b. Jany. 16th, 1823;
       and JOHN Jr. b. March 10th, 1827.

iv.   EVAN THOMAS b. Dec. 6th, 1793, the well known engineer, md. HARVEY M. BOND,
       and d. s. p.

v.   TACY b. Jany. 14th, 1795, md. JOSEPH KING. (q. v.)

vi.   BENJAMIN b. Nov. 13th, 1796, md. MARY CARROLL, and had issue: EUGENE md.
       in 1876, MAGGIE TYSON; and HENRIETTA.

vii.   ANN b. Aug. 24th, 1798, d. Jany. 15th, 1799.

viii. THOMAS b. Dec. 11th, 1799, md. LOUISA McFADON, and had issue MARY, PRISCILLA,
       JOHN and JAMES.

ix.   ANDREW b. Dec. 23d, 1801, of whom presently.

x.   JAMES b. Jany. 3d, 1804.

xi.   JOHN b. Jany. 18th, 1805.

xii.   SAMUEL b. Aug. 11th, 1806, md. MARY ANN, dau. of Joseph E. Todhunter, and
       d. leaving issue: ELIZA TODHUNTER, MARION, JOSEPH, FRANCIS FOX, and
       NANNIE POULTNEY.

xiii. ELIAS.

xiv.   HENRY.

xv.   PHILIP.

ANDREW, fifth son of Elias and Mary (Thomas) Ellicott, b. Dec. 23d, 1801, md. in 1823, EMILY A. McFADON. They both d. in 1866, having had issue: HENRY WILLIAM b. in 1824, of whom presently; JAMES P. b. in 1826, d. s. p. in 1873; EVAN THOMAS b. in 1828, d. s. p. in 1867; JOHN E. b. in 1832, d. in 1833; HARVEY BOND md. ROBERT T. MACCOUN; EMILY d. in 1848; and CAROLINE.

HENRY WILLIAM, eldest son of Andrew and Emily A. (McFadon) Ellicott, b. in 1824, md. in 1849, ELIZABETH Y. BARNEY, and has had issue: EMILY b. in 1851, d. in 1853; ADELE E. b. in 1854; HENRY WILLIAM, Jr. b. in 1856; ELIZABETH B. b. in 1862; MARY b. in 1864; and CHARLES RIDGELY b. in 1867.

THOMAS, eleventh son of the 3d Andrew Ellicott, md. MARY MILLER, and had issue: WILLIAM MILLER b. Sept. 30th, 1807, of whom presently; SARAH ANN; HANNAH who md. JACOB LINDLEY; LYDIA; REBECCA; CATHERINE; ESTHER; and ELIZABETH who md., as his first wife, JACOB LINDLEY, and had issue: THOMAS ELLICOTT, HAVARD E., and JACOB.

WILLIAM MILLER, eldest son of Thomas and Mary (Miller) Ellicott, b. Sept. 30th, 1807, md. Nov. 11th, 1830, SARAH, dau. of Thomas and Ann Poultney, and has had issue:

i. THOMAS POULTNEY md. CAROLINE ALLEN, and has had issue: THOMAS, SUSAN ALLEN, FRANCIS ALLEN, WILLIAM M., SARAH POULTNEY; PHILIP d. in infancy; RACHEL POULTNEY; and NANCY POULTNEY.

ii. THOMAS d. in infancy.

iii. WILLIAM MILLER, Jr. md. Nov 15th, 1860, NANCY MORRIS, dau. of Charles and Mary Ellis, of Philadelphia, and resides in that city; having had issue: CHARLES ELLIS b. Nov. 3d, 1861; WILLIAM MILLER 3d b. May 5th, 1863; LINDLEY b. Aug. 20th, 1864, d. May 7th, 1876; MARY MORRIS b. Feby. 1st, 1867; EDITH b. Aug. 8th, 1871; and LYDIA b. Oct. 12th, 1872.

iv. MARY MILLER md. June 20th, 1871, JOHN B. ROBERTS, and has issue: WILLIAM MILLER.

v. NANNIE POULTNEY d. in childhood.

vi. DAVID B.

vii. SARAH POULTNEY d. in childhood.

viii. CHARLES LEWIS.

ARMS FROM SHARPE'S PEERAGE.

FAIRFAX.

This family was seated at Towcester, in Northumberland, at the Conquest. and is supposed to be of Saxon stock. Mr. Charles Fairfax, uncle of the great Lord Fairfax, compiled a pedigree of the family still extant among his MSS. collections. According to that the family descends from Richard de Fairfax, who in 1204 possessed the Manor of Askham, and other lands in the vicinity of the City of York. Sir Guy Fairfax, one of the Judges of the Court of King's Bench in 1478, was his lineal descendant. He built a castle in the Manor of Steeton, Yorkshire, and made that his principal seat. He md. a Ryder, of Ryder, and had a son and heir, Sir William, who was a Judge of the Common Pleas, md. a sister of Lord Manners of Roos, and had with four daus. a son and heir Sir William who was High Sheriff of York in the reign of Henry VIII., md. in 1518, Isabel Thwaites who brought him the Manor of Denton and Askwith in Wharfedale, and Bishop Hill and Davy Hall within the walls of York. He joined the Pilgrimage of Grace, but appears to have been pardoned for his share in that outbreak.

By his will he divided his estates so as to found two families, leaving his paternal inheritance to his third son Gabriel, ancestor of the Fairfaxes of Steeton. His eldest son d. s. p. and Thomas the second son inherited his mother's property at Denton, Nun Appleton, Askwith, Acaster, and in the City of York. He was knighted by Elizabeth in 1576, md. Dorothy, dau. of George Gale of Asham Grange. and d. in 1599, having had issue: Thomas, of whom presently: Charles who was a Colonel in the army, a pupil of Sir Horace Vere, and was killed at the siege of Ostend; Edward of Newhall, the poet and translator of Tasso who d. in 1632: and two daus. Ursula and Christiana.

THOMAS, the eldest son b. in 1560, fought in the Low Country wars, and was knighted by Lord Essex for gallant conduct before Rouen. He served Elizabeth as a Diplomatist, was one of the Council of the North, under the Presidency of Lord Sheffield, from 1602 to 1619, and in Oct. 1627 was created Baron Fairfax of Cameron, in the Peerage of Scotland. He md. in 1582, **ELLEN,** dau. of **Robert Aske,** of Aughton, and d. May 1st, 1640, having had issue: **FERDINANDO** of whom presently; **HENRY** a clergyman, (q. v.;) **CHARLES** a lawyer, the antiquary who compiled the pedigree and left a large collection of MSS.; **JOHN** a soldier in the Low Country wars, killed at the seige of Frankenthal in 1621; **WILLIAM** also a soldier, and killed with his brother John; **PEREGRINE** Secretary to the Ambassador at Paris, and killed at the seige of Montaban in 1621; **THOMAS** a merchant adventurer, d. at Scanderoon in the same fatal year 1621; and three daus. **DOROTHY** md. **Sir WILLIAM CONSTABLE; ANNE** md. **Sir GODFREY WENTWORTH;** and **MARY** b. in 1588, and d. unmarried.

FERDINANDO succeeded his father as second Lord Fairfax, was b. Mch. 29th, 1584, fought on the side of the Parliament in the civil war, md. 1st in 1607, **Lady MARY SHEFFIELD,** dau. of the first **Earl Mulgrave,** and 2d in Sept. 1646, **RHODA,** dau. of **Mr. Chapman,** of London, and widow of Thomas Hussey, by whom he had a dau. **URSULA** md. —— **CARTWRIGHT,** of Aynho. Lord Fairfax d. March 14th, 1647–8, having had issue by his first wife: **THOMAS** 3d Lord, of whom presently; **CHARLES** a Colonel in the Parliamentary Army, mortally wounded at the battle of Marston Moor in 1644, and d. s. p. a few days afterwards; another son who d. in infancy; and six daus. **URSULA** b. in 1609; **ELLEN** b. in 1610, md. **Sir WILLAM SELBY,** of Twizell; **FRANCES** b. in 1612, md. **THOMAS WIDDRINGTON,** of York; **ELIZABETH** b. in 1614, md. **Sir WILLIAM CRAVEN,** of Lenchwicke; **MARY** b. in 1616, md. **HENRY ARTHINGTON;** and **DOROTHY** b. in 1617, md. **EDWARD HUTTON.** of Poppleton.

THOMAS, the eldest son, b. Jany. 16th, 1611–12, succeeded as 3d Lord Fairfax, and was the great Parliamentary General of the civil war, he was also largely instrumental in effecting the restoration of King Charles II. For the incidents of his life see the Biography by C. R.

Markham, published at London in 1870. He md. June 20th, 1637, ANNE, dau. and co-heir of **Lord Vere**, of Tilbury, who d. Oct. 16th, 1665. Lord Fairfax d. Nov. 12th, 1671, leaving an only dau. MARY b. July 30th, 1638, md. Sept. 15th, 1657, GEORGE VILLIERS, second Duke of Buckingham. She d. s. p. Oct. 20th, 1704, and the estates of the family were inherited by the heir of line for whom we must return to **HENRY**, brother of the 2d Lord Fairfax. He was b in 1587, was in holy orders, and the Rector of Bolton Percy. He md. **MARY**, dau. of **Sir Henry Cholmley**, and d. April 6th, 1665, having had issue: HENRY 4th Lord; and BRYAN b. Oct. 6th, 1633, d. leaving a son BRYAN, d. s. p.

HENRY, 4th Lord Fairfax, b. Dec. 30th, 1631, md. **FRANCES**, dau. of **Sir Robert Barwicke**, of Tolston, and d. in April 1688, leaving issue: THOMAS 5th Lord; and **HENRY**, of whom presently. THOMAS, 5th Lord Fairfax, took an active part in promoting the Revolution of 1688, md. CATHERINE, dau. and heir of Thomas Lord Colepepper, of Thoresway, by Margaret, dau. of Jean de Hesse, with whom he obtained the estate of Leeds Castle in Kent, and over five million acres of land in Virginia. Lord Fairfax d. in Jany. 1709-10, leaving issue:

i. THOMAS, 6th Lord Fairfax, b. in 1690. He was obliged to alienate Denton Hall and the Yorkshire property in order to save Leeds Castle, and the Kentshire estates. In 1747 he removed to America, alienated his English estates in favour of his brother Robert, and built "Belvoir" and "Greenway Court" in Virginia He is said to have met with a disappointment in love which prevented his ever marrying, was one of the writers of the Spectator, and the friend and patron of Washington. He d. s. p. at Greenway Court, in Feby. 1782.

ii. ROBERT succeeded his brother as 7th Lord Fairfax, md. twice but d. s. p. July 15th, 1793. leaving his English estates to his nephew Rev. Denny Martin.

iii. FRANCES who md. —— MARTIN, and had issue: Rev. Denny who inherited his uncle Robert's English estates.

HENRY, second son of the 4th **Baron Fairfax**, Sheriff of Yorkshire, in 1691 md. ANNE, dau. and co-heir of **Richard Harrison**, and d. in 1708, having had issue: HENRY who d. s. p. in 1759: THOMAS d. in infancy: RICHARD d. in infancy: and WILLIAM b. in 1691, who was Virginia Agent of his cousin, the 6th Lord Fairfax. He md. 1st SARAH,

dau. of Major Walker, of the Bahamas, and had issue by her: GEORGE
WILLIAM md. SARAH CARY, and d. s. p. in 1787; THOMAS entered the
Royal Navy and was killed at a sea-fight in the West Indies. June
26th, 1746; SARAH md. JOHN CARLISLE, (q. v.;) and ANNE md. 1st LAWRENCE,
brother of George Washington, and had a dau. d. at the age of seven;
md. 2d GEORGE LEE, by whom she had three sons.

WILLIAM FAIRFAX md. 2d DEBORAH CLARKE, of Salem, Mass.,
and d. Sept. 3d, 1757, having had further issue: WILLIAM an officer in
the British army, d. s p. of wounds received at the seige of Quebec
in 1759; HANNAH md. WARNER WASHINGTON, and BRYAN who succeeded
as 8th Lord Fairfax.

BRYAN, Lord Fairfax, was a clergyman of the Church of England. md.
ELIZABETH, youngest dau. of Wilson Cary, and had issue:

i.   THOMAS, of whom presently.

ii.   FERDINANDO md. ELIZABETH CARY, and had issue: GEORGE WILLIAM md.
       ISABELLA McNEILL; WILSON MILES CARY md. LUCY GRIFFITH; FERDINANDO
       md. two Misses JETT FARINDA md. PERRIN WASHINGTON; WILLIAM HENRY;
       MARY MUNRO; ARCHIBALD a Captain in the U. S. Navy, md. 1st SARAH, second
       dau. of Hon. John C. Herbert, of Alexandria, and 2d ELIZA NORRIS; EDWIN d.
       at sea; CHRISTINE md. THOMAS RAGLAND; LOUISA md. ——— TAPSCOTT;
       OCTAVIUS; FLORETTA; HERBERT; and WASHINGTON; all four at present deceased.

iii.   ELIZABETH md. DAVID GRIFFITH.

THOMAS, eldest son of the eighth Lord, b. in 1762, succeeded his father
in the title, resided at Vaucluse, Fairfax County, Virginia: he md. 1st
MARY AYLETT, 2d LOUISA WASHINGTON, and 3d MAR-
GARET, dau. of William Herbert, and d. April 21st, 1846, leaving
issue only by his third wife as follows:

i.   ALBERT md. April 8th, 1825, CAROLINE ELIZA, dau. of Richard and Eliza
       Snowden, and d. in the lifetime of his father. His widow md. March 1st, 1838,
       Capt. SANDERS, but has issue only by her first husband: CHARLES SNOWDEN
       succeeded as 10th Lord, md. ADA BENHAM, and d. s. p. in 1869; and JOHN
       CONTEE b. in 1830, md. in 1857, a dau. of Col. Edward Kirby, U. S. A., succeeded
       his brother, and is the present and eleventh Baron Fairfax, of Cameron.

ii.   HENRY md. ANN CAROLINE, 2d dau. of John C. Herbert.

iii.   ORLANDO md. MARY R. CARY.

iv.   RAYMOND d. in 1813.

v.   EUGENIA md. 1st EDGAR MASON, and 2d CHARLES K. HYDE.

vi. ETHELBERT d. in 1827.

vii. AURELIA md. JAMES W. IRWIN.

viii. LAVINIA d. in 1822.

ix. MONIMIA md. ARCHIBALD CARY.

x. REGINALD d. in 1862.

FARQUHAR.

CHARLES FARQUHARD md. SARAH, eldest dau. of **Roger** and **Mary P. Brooke,** and had issue:

i **ROGER BROOKE** b. Oct. 4th, 1837, md. **CAROLINE MILLER,** and has issue: **GEORGE BROOKE** b. Oct. 5th, 1868; **ANNA MILLER** b. Jany. 30th, 1871; **SARAH B.** b. Sept. 4th, 1872; and **ROBERT MILLER** b. May 2d, 1874.

ii. **MARY EDITH** b. April 3d, 1839.

iii. **CHARLES HENRY** b. May 24th, 1841.

iv. **GRANVILLE** b. March 22d, 1843.

v **ELIZA E.** b. March 20th, 1845.

GALLOWAY.

RICHARD GALLOWAY, of London, England, was the father of **RICHARD** who md. **Mrs. ELIZABETH LAWRENCE,** December 10th, 1686, and of **SAMUEL** who md. 1st **SARAH,** by whom he had four children, one of whom **SARAH.** md. March 9th, 1720, **HENRY HILL,** who d. before 1722, and another, **HANNAH** md. a **FORD.** By his 2d wife **ANNE PARDOE.** who d. in April 1723. (**SAMUEL GALLOWAY** d in Jany. 1720-1,) he had issue:

i.   **RICHARD** b. at London, Jany. 5th, 1689-90, called of Cumberstone, md. **MARY**, dau. of **Aquila Paca**, who afterwards md. **Dr. SAMUEL CHEW. RICHARD GALLOWAY** d. in Feby. 1731-2, leaving a dau. **SUSANNAH**.

ii.   **PETER** b. at West River, July 12th, 1690, md. Jany. 19th, 1715-16, **ELIZABETH**, dau. of **John** and **Elizabeth Rigbie**, and had issue: **JOSEPH** the celebrated Loyalist, b. in 1730.

iii.   **JOHN** b. Jany. 14th, 1692-3, and d. in 11 months.

iv.   **JOHN** b. Feby. 6th, 1693-4, md. 1st, July 31st, 1718, **MARY**, dau. of Samuel and Mary **Thomas**, and had issue:

    i.   **SAMUEL**, of whom presently.

    ii.   **MARY** md. June 13th, 1747, **BENJ. CHEW.** (q. v.)

    iii.   **JOSEPH** md. **ANN COOKSON.**

    JOHN GALLOWAY md. 2d **Mrs. JANE FISHBOURNE**, widow of William Fishbourne, by whom she had two children, **SAMUEL** and **SARAH**. She d. in June 1748, having had by her 2d husband who d. about Oct. 18th, 1747, a daughter, **JANE**, md. **JOSEPH SHIPPEN**, of Philadelphia.

v.   **ANN** b. April 12th, 1695, md. Dec. 25th, 1712, **ISAAC JOHNS.**

vi.   **PETER BINDS** b. April 25th, 1696.

vii.   **MARY** b. July 15th, 1697, md. Oct. 22d, 1715, **Dr. SAMUEL CHEW.** (q. v.)

viii.   Unnamed, b. in Oct. 1698, and d. an infant.

ix.   **JOSEPH** b. Oct. 8th, 1699, md. Aug. 8th, 1749, **ANNE HARRIS**, and d. in Dec. 1752, leaving an only dau. **ANNE** who md. June 2d, 1767, **JOSEPH PEMBERTON**. Mrs. **GALLOWAY** afterwards md. **PHILIP THOMAS.** (q. v.)

x.   **RICHARD** b. Jany. 10th, 1701-2.

xi.   Nameless, b. Oct. 12th, 1702, d. an infant.

xii.   **SAMUEL** b. April 7th, 1705, d. an infant.

xiii.   **SAMUEL** b. Aug. 9th, 1707.

xiv.   An unnamed son, b. and d. Nov. in 1709.

SAMUEL, son of **John** and **Mary Galloway**, md. about 1745, **ANNE**, dau. of **Dr. Samuel Chew**. He d. in November 1785, having had issue:

    MARY md. **THOMAS RINGGOLD**, who d. Oct. 26th, 1776, his wife d. Feby. 21st, 1817, having had issue:

11

i.   THOMAS b. Sept. 4th, 1768, who md. Feby. 10th, 1795, MARY GITTINGS, and d. in 1813.

ii. Gen. SAMUEL b. Jany. 15th, 1770, md. May 3d, 1792, MARY, dau. of Gen. John Cadwallader.

iii. ANNA MARIA b. March 9th, 1772, md. March 24th, 1795, Col. FRISBY TILGHMAN, and d. Feby. 21st, 1817.

iv. BENJAMIN d. unmarried Aug. 24th, 1798.

v.   TENCH b. March 6th, 1776, md. April 10th, 1799, MARY CHRISTIAN LEE.

ii. ANNE md. JAMES CHESTON. (q. v.)

iii. BENJAMIN md. HENRIETTA, dau. of Benjamin and Sarah Chew, of Cecil County.

iv. JOHN md. SARAH, dau. of Benj. and Mary Chew, and d. in June 1810, leaving an only dau. MARY who md. VIRGIL MAXCY, and had issue: Mary md. Francis Markoe, and Sarah md. Col. George W. Hughes.

SAMUEL GALLOWAY, of Calvert County, appears to have belonged to the above family, possibly a cousin of Samuel of West River. He d. in April 1723, leaving issue: SAMUEL, RICHARD, JOSEPH, MARY, ELIZA, SARAH, ANN and SOPHIA.

RICHARD, his second son, md. July 30th, 1719. SARAH SPARROW, (who afterwards md. HENRY HILL,) and d. in December 1736, leaving issue: RICHARD md. Sept. 29th, 1715. SOPHIA, dau. of William and Margaret Richardson, and d. in Oct. 1741, leaving an only dau. Elizabeth, who md. Thomas Sprigg, and had issue: Elizabeth.

GARRIGUES.

ROBERT H. son of William and Hannah Garrigues, of Philadelphia, md. May 22d, 1816, MARGARET E. dau. of Richard and Deborah (Brooke) Thomas, and d. Dec. 12th, 1876, at Green Hill, Ohio, having had issue:

i.   HELEN M. b. April 28th, 1817, md. June 27th, 1835, E. C. HALL, of Ohio.

ii. DEBORAH THOMAS b. March 11th, 1819, d. unmarried April 6th, 1862.

iii. EDWARD THOMAS b. Aug. 31st, 1820.

iv. CHARLES b. July 21st, 1821, md. March 13th, 1843, MARTHA STACKHOUSE, and d. June 24th, 1864.

v. SALLY ANN b. Aug. 24th, 1823.

vi. RICHARD THOMAS b. June 22d, 1825, md. Jany. 29th, 1850, SARAH WERT.

vii. ELIZA T. b. April 8th, 1827, md. March 29th, 1846, JESSE STACKHOUSE, of Ohio.

viii. WILLIAM P. b. Nov. 19th, 1828, md. Dec. 30th, 1852, RUTH BURT.

ix. HANNAH B. b. Dec. 13th, 1830, in Ohio, and d. March 1st, 1848.

x. MARY ANNA b. Dec. 1st, 1832, md. Sept. 29th, 1853, JOHN K. BURT, of Ohio.

xi. SUSAN H. b. Oct. 2d, 1835, d. Dec. 8th, 1836.

xii. EMILY T. b. Aug. 19th, 1837, d. the next day.

xiii. MARGARET B. b. Sept. 11th, 1838, d. Oct. 12th, 1842.

ARMS FROM BURKE'S GEN. ARMORY.

GEORGE.

ROBERT and ANN GEORGE, of Kent County, Md., of whom the former was descended originally from the George family of Scotland, and in the female line from William Edmundson, the well known Quaker Preacher of the seventeenth century; had issue: twelve children of whom only three lived to maturity; they were WILLIAM EDMUNDSON, of whom presently: **ELIZA** who md. **PHILIP E. THOMAS**, (q. v.:) and **SARAH**. **WILLIAM EDMUNDSON GEORGE** the only surviving son removed to Baltimore with his sister, and resided mainly with her until his own marriage. At the age of 21 he was taken into partnership by his brother-in-law, and continued in business with him or his sons until within a few years of his death. He was distinguished for urbanity, courtesy, strict adherence to principle, and a generous hospitality. He md. in 1812. **SARAH**, dau. of Jonathan and Sarah Ellicott, and d. in 1839, having had issue:

i.   **SARAH** d. in infancy.

ii.   **ELIZA** md. in 1839, **JOHN D. EARLY**, who d. having had issue: **JOHN D.** Cashier of the Commercial and Farmers Bank of Baltimore, md. April 27th, 1865, **MAUD G. RIEMAN**, and has three children, Eliza G., Evaline and Alexander Rieman; **WILLIAM GEORGE**; and **JOSEPH D.** who d. in 1850, aged 4 years.

iii.   **PHILIP THOMAS** md. in 1847, **ELLEN JENKINS**, and has had issue: **MARY ELLEN** d. in infancy; **SAMUEL ELLICOTT**; **SARAH**; and **JOSIAH**.

iv.   **ANNE** md. in 1843, **HENRY M. FITZHUGH**, and has issue: **SARAH, MARY, ANNE, DANIEL** and **WILLIAM**.

v.   **JONATHAN ELLICOTT**.

vi.   **ROBERT** md. n 1857, **JOSEPHINE BOSTON**, and has issue **JONATHAN ELLICOTT, ROBERT HARVEY, CECILIA** and **MARTHA**.

vii. **SARAH HARVEY**.

viii. **FRANCES** md. in 1854, **HENRY LATIMER**.

ix.   **MARY ANN** md. in 1851, **MARK W. JENKINS**, and has had issue: **JULIA**; and **BASIL** d. in infancy.

x.   **WILLIAM E.** md. in 1866, **MARGARET HAMILTON**, and had issue: **ANNE** d. in infancy.

ARMS FROM AN OLD ENGRAVING.

GILPIN.

BERNARD, son of **Gideon** and **Sarah Gilpin**, md. Aug. 21st, 1793, at Sandy Spring Meeting House, in Montgomery County, Maryland. **SARAH**, third dau. of **Richard** and **Sarah** (**Coale**) **Thomas**, who d. April 29th, 1805. having had issue:

i.   **SARAH** b. May 30th, 1794, md. **ROGER BROOKE**. (q. v.)

ii.   **ELIZABETH** b. Nov. 21st, 1795, md. **JAMES P. STABLER**. (q. v.)

iii. **ANN ROBINSON** b. July 1st, 1797, md. **EDWARD STABLER**. (q. v.)

iv.   **THOMAS** b. Feby. 10th, 1799.

v.   **SAMUEL** b. March 28th, 1801, of whom presently.

vi.   **HANNAH** b. May 20th, 1803, md. Feby. 5th, 1835. **ANDREW**, son of **Whitson** and **Rachel Birdsall**, of Loudoun County, Va.

vii. **LYDIA S.** b. April 16th, 1805, md. **WILLIAM BROOKE**. (q. v.)

BERNARD GILPIN md. 2dly Aug. 26th, 1807, **LETITIA GILBERT**, dau. of **Whitson Canby**, and had further issue: **WILLIAM HENRY** b. Aug. 10th, 1808; **JOSHUA CANBY** b. April 12th, 1810; **MARY B.** b. June 24th, 1812; **GIDEON EDWARD** b. Dec. 21st, 1814; **GEORGE FOX** b. April 4th, 1817; **CHARLES CANBY** b. Nov. 11th, 1819, d. Aug. 9th, 1820; **JAMES STABLER** b. April 12th, 1821; **CANBY** b. Dec. 1st, 1823; and **BERNARD** b. March 5th, 1826

SAMUEL, second son of **Bernard** and **Sarah** (**Thomas**) Gilpin, b. March 28th, 1801, md. **RACHEL GOVER,** and had issue:

i.   **EDWARD CANBY** md. Feby. 23d, 1854, in Philadelphia, **ANNIE FEAST,** and has had issue: **LIZZIE FEAST** b. Dec. 30th, 1854; **WILLIAM H.** b. April 4th, 1856; **SAMUEL** b. Sept. 1st, 1858, d. Sept. 4th, 1859; **JOSEPH** b. Oct. 21st, 1860, d. April 22d, 1862; **EDWARD** b. Nov. 4th, 1863, d. Aug. 1st, 1865; **MARY A.** b. Sept. 16th, 1865; and **CLARENCE LEA** b. July 21st, 1870.

ii.   **FRANCES A.** md. Oct. 19th, 1865, **EDWARD J.** son of **Edward** and **Deborah A. Lea,** and had issue: **EDWARD S.** b. Sept. 16th, 1867; **FRANK T.** b. June 6th, 1869; and **ALBERT G.** b. Aug. 13th, 1872.

GODEY.

WALTER GODEY md. in 1818, **CHARLOTTE,** eldest dau. of **John** and ——— (**Berry**) **Thomas,** and had issue:

i.   **THOMAS,** of whom presently.

ii.   **HENRY.**

Mrs. **GODEY** md. 2d Dr. **JOHN WOLFENDEN,** and had issue: **SARAH** d. unmarried in 1858.

THOMAS, her eldest son by her first marriage, md. June 29th, 1846, **SARAH ANN NORRIS,** and has had issue: **MARY CHARLOTTE** md. Oct. 10th, 1867, **HENRY W. WARNER,** and has two children, **MARY GODEY** and **ANNIE W.;** **HENRY** md. in 1876, **LOUISE WILSON;** and **THOMAS ARTHUR; FRANKLIN; THOMAS WALTER; EDWARD NEEDLES; CHARLES;** and **ROBERT W.** who all d. in infancy.

JAMES AP GRIFFITH.

A sister of Sir Rhys ap Thomas, K. G., md. Griffith ap Howell and had issue: James, who in his exile assumed the name of Robert Brampton or Brancetour. In 1516 we find him, through the influence of his uncle, a Gentleman Usher of the Royal Household.

After the death of Sir Rhys he seems to have returned to Wales and resided there, probably in some office under his cousin Rice ap Griffith. After the arrest of Rice, James ap Griffith held out for some time against the King's officers, and we find Henry addressing a special warrant to Lord Ferrars as Justice in South Wales, dated October 7th, 1531, directing the arrest of James ap Griffith ap Howell, who had fortified himself in the Castle of Emlyn. This was accordingly done and he was imprisoned in the Tower of London. From this he escaped some time in 1533, and going to Wales, collected a few of the old servants of his House, and taking his wife and daughter and young Thomas ap Rice went to Scotland. July 2nd, 1533, Lord Dacre writes to the King that a gentleman of Wailes, his wife and eight persons with them, were landed at St. Ninian's, in Scotland, and that he was uncle to Ryse of Wailes. In reply Dacre and Wharton, Henry's agents were ordered to watch him. A later letter says he had a daughter with him, and one who named himself Ryse, and that the party was well favoredly arrayed and appointed. He was ordered to a Castle S. W. of Edinburgh, and visited there by King James. Afterwards he came to Edinburgh and was much resorted to by the Courtiers, but had no audience of the King. Finally went to the Emperor, and is noticed as being at Antwerp in December 1533, and at Lubeck in the following May. After this we hear nothing of him until in 1539 when he appears in Paris in the train of Charles V. Henry at once instructed his Ambassador, Sir Thomas Wyatt, to demand his arrest. Wyatt informed the Constable Montmorency that he was an English subject who had robbed his Master and afterwards conspired against the King, had him watched to his lodgings by a spy, and in December 1539, taking with him a Provost Marshal's guard, surrounded the house at night. Wyatt entered Griffith's room where he sat writing at a table. He says in his report to the King that "Brancetour's colour changed as soon as he heard my voice; and with that came in the Provost and set hand on him. I reached to the letters he was writing, but he caught them afore me and flung them backwards into the fire. I overthrew him and cracked them out; but the Provost got them." Upon this Brancetour declared himself the Emperor's servant, and taking other papers from his pocket placed them in the Provost's hands. The Provost leaving a guard with Wyatt and Brancetour, went to the Chancellor for instructions. Wyatt then attempted to persuade the prisoner to submit to him, but he made the Emperor his master and refused. "Once he told me" says Wyatt, "that he had heard me oft times say that kings have long hands; but God, quoth he, hath longer." The Provost returning took charge of Brancetour till the morning. After breakfast the next day, Wyatt saw Cardinal Granvelle and the Chancellor, and finally the matter was referred to the Emperor. He was extremely angry. The man he said "was his servant, and had been in Perse, and had followed him in all his viages in Affrica, in Province, in Italy and France these ten or twelve years past." Wyatt answered that Brancetour was his master's subject, and had of his own knowledge, committed treason in Spain, and insisted that he should be surrendered in accordance with previous treaties in regard to persons guilty of treason. The Emperor cared nothing for treaties. Brancetour was his servant and should go free, and Wyatt was compelled to let him do so. Griffith returned to Germany in the train of the Emperor, and we next hear of him in a letter written by Sir Thomas Seymour at the siege of Buda, August 8th, 1542, who says "there lately came to Vienna James Griffith up Powell, who calls himself Robert Brampton, and hath a letter from the Pope to the King of Hungary, to be captain of two hundred howshereres or light horse of Hungary." May 6th, 1549, Cardinal Pole writes to Bishop Ceneda, Papal Envoy in France, recommending Captain Griffith who with Dr. Hilliard, were the Cardinal's Envoys to the Protector of England. With this letter closes the record of his eventful life.

HANDY.

SAMUEL HANDY came to America from England about 1635, and d. in Somerset County, Maryland, in 1721. He was the father of Col. ISAAC HANDY; whose son HENRY md. JANE, dau. of Capt. William Winder, and sister of Levin Winder, Governor of Maryland.

Their son Dr. WILLIAM WINDER HANDY md. Feby. 24th, 1842, MARY ANN, dau. of Thomas and Ann (Thomas) Poultney, and d. Jany. 27th, 1864, having had issue: THOMAS POULTNEY md. Oct. 31st, 1865, and d. in 1876, leaving issue: WILLIAM WINDER b. April 3d, 1871: and MARY ANN b. April 14th, 1872.

HARRIS.

WILLIAM HARRIS, of Anne Arundel Co., md. MARGARET —— and d. in Jany. 1732, leaving issue: ROBERT; STEPHEN; WILLIAM, of whom presently: PRUDENCE; SARAH; and MARGARET.

WILLIAM, third son of William and Margaret Harris, md. after 1735, MARGARET, fifth dau. of Samuel and Mary (Hutchins) Thomas, and had issue:

i. MARGARET md. HENRY WILSON. (q. v.)

ii. SAMUEL md. April 2d, 1771, RACHEL, dau. of Henry Willson, and had issue: WILLIAM md. MARY CONSTABLE; and SAMUEL md. ELIZA CONKLING.

iii. MARY md. May 29th, 1770, RICHARD ROBERTS, and had issue: RICHARD md. —— KENT; and MARGARET.

iv. ELIZABETH md. JOHNS HOPKINS. (q. v.)

HERBERT.

WILLIAM HERBERT, of Muckross, on the Lakes of Killarney, in Ireland, came to America, and was President of the Bank and Mayor of Alexandria: md. a dau. of John and Sarah (Fairfax) Carlisle, of Virginia, and had issue: JOHN CARLISLE, of whom presently: WILLIAM who md. a sister of John P. Dulany, of Virginia; MARGARET md. THOMAS, 9th Lord Fairfax: SARAH md. Rev. OLIVER NORRIS, of Philadelphia: ANN d. unmarried: ELIZA P. d. unmarried in 1865: and LUCINDA d. in youth.

12

JOHN CARLISLE, eldest son of **William Herbert**, md. **MARY**, dau. of Major **Thomas Snowden**, and had issue:

i. Dr. **THOMAS SNOWDEN**, of whom presently.

ii. **ANN CAROLINE** md. Hon. **HENRY FAIRFAX**. (q. v.)

iii. **ALFRED** a graduate of West Point, brevetted first Lieutenant July 27th, 1836, for gallantry in the Florida War; resigned his commission June 30th, 1837; Civil Engineer from 1837 to 1842; Superintending Engineer of several Southern Railroads; Professor in State Military Academy, S. C., 1843-46; in U. S. Ordnance Bureau 1846-53; U. S. Assistant or Principal Examiner of Patents 1853-57.

iv. **SARAH** md. Capt. **ARCHIBALD FAIRFAX**, U. S. N. (q. v.)

v. **WILLIAM FAIRFAX**.

vi. **EMMA** md. Rev. **W. BRYANT**, of Virginia.

vii. **MARY VIRGINIA** md. Capt. **THOMAS T. HUNTER**, U. S. N., who resigned his commission at the beginning of the Civil War, and entered the Confederate Navy; both d. having had issue: Dr. **FREDERICK** md. —— **LIPSCOMB**; **THOMAS** in the Confederate Navy during the Civil War; **MADELINE** md. Major **EDMONDSTONE** of South Carolina; **JULIA** md. Lieut. Col. **FRANKLIN HARWOOD**, U. S. A.; **WILLIAM**; **CHARLES**; **SARAH**; and **MINNIE**.

viii. **JULIA**.

ix. **EUGENIA**.

x. **LUCINDA** md. **JOHN EVERSFIELD**.

xi. **ELIZA**.

xii. **EDWARD** md. **MARY H. BARRETT**, and has issue: **WILLIAM PINKNEY** md. **REBECCA**, dau. of Robert Beverly.

Dr. **THOMAS SNOWDEN**, eldest son of **John C.** and **Mary** (Snowden) **Herbert**, md. 1st **CAMILLA HAMMOND**, and 2d **ELIZABETH DUER**, by whom he had no issue. By his first wife he had issue:

i. **JOHN CARLISLE**.

ii. **JAMES R.** served as a Confederate Colonel of Infantry during the Civil War, is a Brigadier General in the Maryland Militia, and one of the Police Commissioners of Baltimore City; md. **ELIZABETH COLEMAN**, dau. of Mark Alexander, of Mecklenburg County, Va., and has issue: **ANN GORDON**; **CAMILLA HAMMOND**; **MARK ALEXANDER**; and **MARY COLEMAN** who d. in 1877.

iii. **MATTHIAS HAMMOND**.

HOPKINS AND JOHNS.

RICHARD JOHNS, b. at Bristol, England, settled at the Cliffs, in Calvert Co., Md., in 1675, md. **ELIZABETH** (**Kinsey**) widow of Thomas Sparrow, and had issue: **RICHARD**; **AQUILA**; **ISAAC**; **ABRAHAM**; **PRIS-CILLA**; **ELIZABETH**; and **MARGARET** who md. in 1700, **GERARD HOPKINS**, of Anne Arundel County.

GERARD HOPKINS who md. **MARGARET JOHNS** d. in Jany. 1743-4, and his wife in March 1749-50, having had issue the following sons:

i. **JOSEPH** b. Nov. 2d, 1706, md. Aug. 17th, 1727, **ANN**, dau. of John and Eliza Chew.

ii. **GERARD** b. March 7th, 1709, of whom presently.

iii. **PHILIP** b. Aug. 9th, 1711, settled on the Eastern Shore of Maryland.

iv. **SAMUEL** b. Jany. 16th, 1713-14, md. Sept. 2d, 1740, **SARAH**, dau. of Jacob and Elizabeth (Arnold) Giles, and had issue: **GERARD** b. April 6th, 1742, md. Dec. 19th, 1778, Mrs. **RACHEL HARRIS**, widow; **SAMUEL** b. Dec. 9th, 1743; and **JOHN** b. Jany. 4th, 1745-6.

v. **RICHARD** b. Dec. 15th, 1715, md. **KATHERINE** ——— and had issue: **NICHOLAS** b. May 12th, 1747; **RACHEL** b. Jany. 31st, 1749-50; **RICHARD** b. Feby. 17th, 1750-1; **SARAH** b. Sept. 20th, 1751; **KATHERINE** b. Jany. 20th, 1753, d. Sept. 27th, 1763; **GERARD** b. Feby. 21st, 1754, d. Dec. 2d, 1757; **SAMUEL** b. Sept. 25th, 1756; **ELIZABETH** b. Sept. 17th, 1758; and **JOSEPH** b. April 9th, 1761.

vi. **WILLIAM** b. Aug. 8th, 1717.

vii. **JOHNS** b. Dec. 30th, 1720. (q. v.)

Besides these sons, **GERARD** and **MARGARET HOPKINS** had two daughters, **ELIZABETH** b. June 13th, 1703, md. Jany. 10th, 1723-4, **LEVIN HILL**, and had issue: **PRISCILLA** and **MARY**: and **MARGARET** md. **AQUILA JOHNS**.

GERARD, second son of **Gerard** and **Margaret** (**Johns**) Hopkins, b. March 17th, 1709, settled at South River, and md. **MARY HALL**, a Roman Catholic, who joined Friends about 1733. He d. July 3d, 1777, having had issue:

i. **MARGARET** b. Jany. 11th, 1730-1, md. **JOHN**, son of John and Elizabeth Thomas. (q. v.)

ii.　　　GERARD b. Aug. 6th, 1732.

iii.　　MARY b. Nov. 11th, 1734.

iv.　　SARAH b. Nov. 7th, 1737, md. JOHN COWMAN. (q. v.)

v.　　　RICHARD b. Feby. 7th, 1739-40, d. in infancy.

vi.　　ELIZABETH b. Nov. 3d, 1741, md. BASIL BROOKE. (q. v.)

vii.　　RACHEL b. Dec 3d, 1742, md. EVAN THOMAS. (q. v.)

viii.　JOSEPH b. Jany. 11th, 1744-5, of whom presently.

ix.　　RICHARD b. March 20th, 1747. (q. v.)

x.　　　HANNAH b. Aug. 29th, 1749.

xi.　　ELISHA b. Oct. 15th, 1752, practiced medicine, md. 1st HANNAH HOWELL, of Philadelphia, and had issue: DEBORAH ISAAC HOWELL; PATIENCE HOWELL md.
GERARD R. HOPKINS. (q. v.;) ELIZABETH HOWELL; and HANNAH HOWELL
both of whom md. JOSEPH JANNEY. (q. v.)

Dr. ELISHA HOPKINS md. 2d SARAH, dau. of Samuel and Elizabeth (Thomas)
Snowden, and d. Sept 30th, 1809, having had further issue: SAMUEL SNOWDEN
b. Nov. 6th, 1797; BASIL BROOKE b. Nov. 6th, 1799; HENRIETTA ANN b. July
30th, 1801; THOMAS SNOWDEN b. June 18th, 1803; JOHN SNOWDEN b. May
16th, 1805; and RICHARD SNOWDEN b. Sept. 1st, 1807.

JOSEPH, third son of Gerard and Mary (Hall) Hopkins, b. Jany. 11th,
1744-5, md. ELIZABETH HOWELL, who d. Nov. 4th, 1810, and
her husband Sept. 11th, 1825, having had issue: ISAAC HOWELL b.
Dec. 19th, 1770; PATIENCE b. Nov. 5th, 1771, md. PHILIP SNOWDEN,
(q. v.); GERARD b. Jany. 22d, 1775, md. Oct. 14th, 1804, HENRIETTA,
dau. of Samuel and Elizabeth (Thomas) Snowden; HANNAH and MARY twins,
b. April 12th, 1777; ISAAC GRAY b. June 16th, 1783; PRISCILLA b.
Oct. 24th, 1785; MARY b. April 9th, 1788; SAMUEL b. April 9th, 1790;
and SARAH b. Sept. 3d, 1792.

RICHARD, fourth son of Gerard and Mary (Hall) Hopkins, b. March
20th, 1747, md. Dec. 23d, 1774, ANN, dau. of Samuel and Elizabeth
(Thomas) Snowden, who d. March 16th, 1818, and her husband Sept.
20th, 1823, having had issue: ELIZABETH b. Nov. 20th, 1775, md.
——— PLUMMER, and d. June 25th, 1806; GERARD R. b. Aug. 10th,
1777, of whom presently; MARY b. Sept. 1st, 1779; SAMUEL SNOWDEN

b. July 15th, 1783; HENRIETTA SNOWDEN b. Jany. 20th, 1786, md. —— PLUMMER, and d. Dec. 19th, 1862; ANN b. June 29th, 1789, d. unmarried Oct. 8th, 1864; RICHARD b. Dec. 26th, 1791, d. unmarried Aug. 2d. 1872; SARAH b. April 16th, 1793, d. unmarried in 1874; and MARY JANET b. Oct. 6th, 1796.

GERARD R. eldest son of Richard and Ann (Snowden) Hopkins, b. Aug. 10th, 1777, md. PATIENCE HOWELL, dau. of Dr. Elisha and Hannah (Howell) Hopkins, and had issue:

i.　LOUISA MARIA.

ii.　EMMELINE PATIENCE.

iii.　ROBERT BARCLAY living in Louisville, Kentucky, md. CATHERINE MOORE EWING, and has issue: ROBERT, KATIE md. —— THOMPSON; THOMAS BUTLER; SALLIE; and MARSHALL EWING.

iv.　ALFRED THOMAS also living in Louisville, Kentucky, md. LOUISA XAVIER ROBINSON, and has issue: MARGARET HOWELL; NANNIE; SUSAN; ROBINSON; and LOUISA.

JOHNS, youngest son of Gerard and Margaret (Johns) Hopkins, b. Oct. 30th, 1720, md. in 1744, ELIZABETH GILLISS, and had one son EZEKIEL. After his first wife's death JOHNS HOPKINS md. 2d in 1749, MARY (Richardson,) widow of Col. Crockett, of the British Army, and had a son JOHNS who md. CATHERINE HOWELL, Feby. 16th, 1758. JOHNS HOPKINS, Sr. md. 3d. ELIZABETH, dau. of Samuel and Mary Thomas, and had issue by her:

i.　SAMUEL b. in 1759. (q. v.)

ii.　PHILIP b. in 1761, md. March 21st, 1787. MARY, dau. of Isaiah Boone, and d. July 25th, 1814, his wife d. Sept. 15th, 1816, aged 46 years, having had issue: HANNAH b. April 10th, 1788, md. July 2d, 1807, JACOB JANNEY, and d. Nov. 1st, 1819, having had issue: Philip Hopkins b. June 20th, 1808; Lewis b. April 14th, 1810; Mary b. Jany. 27th, 1812; and Henry b. April 27th, 1814; JOHNS b. May 28th, 1790; ELIZABETH b. June 3d, 1791; ISAIAH BOONE b. July 25th, 1793; SUSANNAH b. Oct. 2d, 1795, d. April 2d, 1817; EZEKIEL b. Dec. 7th, 1797; HESTHER b. April 4th, 1800; MARY b. Dec. 10th, 1800, d. unmarried Sept. 14th, 1824; ANN b. May 10th, 1805; RACHEL b. May 2d, 1808; RICHARD b. July 28th, 1810; and SARAH b. July 20th, 1812.

iii. **RICHARD** md. **HANNAH HAMMOND**.

iv. **MARY** md. **SAMUEL PEACH**.

v. **MARGARET** md. **JESSE TYSON**. (q. v.)

vi. **GERARD T.** of whom presently.

vii. **ELIZABETH** md. March 26th, 1825, **JOHN**, son of Joseph and Hannah Janney.

viii. **EVAN** md. Jany. 25th, 1810. **ELIZABETH**, dau. of Joseph and Elizabeth Hopkins, and had issue: **ELIZABETH** b. Oct. 26th, 1810; and **JOSEPH** b. Nov. 26th, 1812.

ix. **ANN** md. Nov. 5th, 1801, **THOMAS**, son of Caleb and Grace Shrieves. Their descendants now live in California.

x. **RACHEL** md. March 29th, 1804, **ROBERT**, son of Joseph and Mary Hough, of Pennsylvania, and had issue: **SAMUEL** b. June 21st, 1806.

xi. **WILLIAM**.

GERARD T., third son of **Johns** and **Elizabeth (Thomas) Hopkins**, md. April 6th, 1796, **DOROTHY**, dau. of **Roger** and **Mary Brooke**, and d. in 1834, having had issue:

i. **MARY** b. Aug. 12th, 1797, md. May 12th, 1817, **BENJAMIN P. MOORE**, and had issue: **ELIZABETH** md. **SAMUEL B. WALTON**, of Omaha City, Neb.; **ROBERT** d. s. p.; **DEBORAH**, **BENJAMIN P.** md. in 1876 **FLORENCE**, dau. of Jared Sparks the historian; **REBECCA**, **WILLIAM** and **GERARD**, who all d. s. p.

ii. **EDWARD** b. Dec. 9th, 1798, d. Mch. 9th, 1800.

iii. **DEBORAH** b. Nov. 27th, 1800, d. s. p. in 1830.

iv. **ELIZABETH** b. Mch. 31st, 1802.

v. **SARAH** b. Dec. 8th, 1805, d. s. p.

vi. **THOMAS** b. May 19th, 1811.

vii. **WILLIAM** b. July 5th, 1813.

viii. **GERARD T.** b. Oct. 5th, 1815, md. **ELIZABETH COATES**, and has issue: **FRANK N.** md. **FANNY MONROE**. **ANNIE** md. **EVAN POULTNEY**, (q. v.;) **BESSIE**; **JOHNS**; **GERARD** and **ROGER BROOKE**.

ix. **MARGARET** b. Aug. 26th, 1817, md. **THOMAS JOLLIFFE**, who d. leaving issue: **THOMAS HOPKINS**, **WILLIAM HOPKINS** md. **LUCY MATTHEWS**; **ELIZABETH** md. **NATHANIEL B. CRENSHAW**, of Virginia, and has had issue: Margaret b. in 1873, and John Meredith, and Nathaniel d. in infancy; and **FANNIE**.

SAMUEL, eldest son of **Johns** and **Elizabeth** (**Thomas**) **Hopkins**, b. in 1759, md. **HANNAH**, dau. of **Joseph** and **Hannah** (**Jones**) **Janney**, and d. Feby. 9th, 1814, having had issue:

i. **JOSEPH JANNEY** b. Aug. 28th, 1793, md. **E. SCHOFIELD**, and had issue: **LEWIS N.**; **GERARD** md. Oct. 6th, 1874, **EMILY R.** eldest dau. of Nicholas and Henrietta Snowden, and has issue: Joseph Waverly b. July 15th, 1875; and Blanche b. Sept. 23rd, 1876; **SAMUEL** md. in 1877, **MARTHA**, dau. of John M. and Elizabeth Smith, of Baltimore; and **JOSEPH**.

ii. **JOHNS** b. May 19th, 1795, the celebrated merchant and millionaire, founder of the Johns Hopkins University, Hospital, and Orphanage for Colored children, at Baltimore, Md.; d. unmarried in 1873.

iii. **ELIZA** b. May 19th, 1797, md. **NATHANIEL CRENSHAW**, of Virginia.

iv. **SARAH** b. Feby. 27th, 1799, md. **RICHARD M.** son of Abijah and Jane (McPherson) Janney, who d. leaving issue: **JOHNS HOPKINS** md. **CAROLINE SYMINGTON**, and has issue: Lena, Richard and Johns; **SAMUEL M.** md. **E. HALL**, and has issue: Mary, John, and Sarah; **JANE** md. **FRANCIS WHITE**, (q. v.;) **HANNAH**; and **MARGARET** md. **JOSEPH ELLIOTT**.

v. **HANNAH** b. Nov. 19th, 1801.

vi. **SAMUEL** b. Nov. 20th, 1803, md. **LAVINIA JOLLIFFE**, and had issue. **JOHN**; **ELLA** md. **MONROE MERCER**; **Dr. ARUNDEL**; and **MAHLON**.

vii. **MAHLON JANNEY** b. June 18th, 1805.

viii. **PHILIP** b. May 31st, 1807.

ix. **MARGARET** md. **MILES WHITE**, of North Carolina, who d. in March 1876, having had issue: **Dr. ELIAS**, d. s. p.; and **FRANCIS** md. **JANE**, dau. of Richard M. and Sarah Janney, and has had issue: Miles, Sarah, Francis d. in infancy, and Richard.

x. **GERARD** b. Nov. 26th, 1809.

xi. **MARY** b. Oct. 8th, 1811.

ARMS FROM SHARPE'S PEERAGE.

HOWARD,

OF NORFOLK.

THOMAS PLANTAGENET, surnamed "De Brotherton," eldest son of
King Edward I., of England, by his second wife, Margaret, dau. of
Philip III., of France, b. in 1301, was created Earl of Norfolk, Dec.
16th, 1312, and Earl Marshal, Feby. 10th, 1335-6, being the first so
designated. He md. 1st, ALICE, dau. of Sir Roger Halys, Knt., by
whom he had issue: MARGARET, of whom presently; and ALICE md.
EDWARD de MONTACUTE, and had a dau. JOAN md. WILLIAM UFFORD, Earl
of Suffolk, and d. s. p.

THOMAS PLANTAGENET md. 2d, MARY, dau. of William Lord
Roos, and widow of William Le Brus, and d. in 1338, having had a
son, who became a monk at the Abbey of Ely.

MARGARET, eldest dau. and eventually heir of Thomas Plantagenet,
was created Duchess of Norfolk for life Sept. 29th, 1397, and md. 1st,
JOHN LORD SEGRAVE, who d. in 1353, having had issue: ANNE,
a nun, Abbess of Barking; and ELIZABETH, of whom presently.

MARGARET, Duchess of Norfolk, md. 2d Sir WILLIAM MANNY,
K. G., and had a dau. ANNE md. JOHN HASTINGS, Earl of Pembroke.

ELIZABETH, second dau. and co-heir of **Margaret**, Duchess of Norfolk, md. **JOHN**, 10th Baron Mowbray, who d. in 1360, having had issue, with others: JOHN, 11th Baron, created in 1377 Earl of Nottingham, d. s. p. in 1379: and **THOMAS**, 12th Baron, created Earl of Nottingham in 1383, and Duke of Norfolk, Sept. 29th, 1397, Earl Marshal and K. G., md. ELIZABETH, dau. and co-heir of Richard Fitz-Alan, Earl of Arundel, and d. in 1413, having had issue: MARGARET, eventually one of the co-heirs of her cousin John Mowbray, 4th Duke of Norfolk, md. JOHN, son and heir of Sir Robert Howard, Knt., who was elder surviving son and heir of Sir John Howard, by his second wife, Alice, dau. and heir of Sir William Tendring, of Tendring: which Sir John was only surviving son of Sir Robert Howard, by Margaret, dau. of Robert Lord Scales; said Sir Robert being son of Sir John Howard, Knt. of Wigenhall, by Joan, sister of Richard de Cornwall, and grandson of William Howard, Chief Justice of the Common Pleas, 1297 to 1308, by Alice, dau. and heir of Sir Edward Fitton, Knt.

Sir **ROBERT HOWARD**, who md. **MARGARET de MOWBRAY**, had issue by her, a son Sir JOHN, summoned as Baron Howard, Oct. 15th, 1470, created Earl Marshal and Duke of Norfolk, June 28th, 1483, K. G. Slain at Bosworth Field in 1485, and being attainted, all his honors were forfeited. He had issue by his first wife, **CATHERINE**, dau. of William Lord Molines, with several daughters, an only son and heir THOMAS, created Earl of Surrey, June 28th, 1483, attainted with his father, but restored to the Earldom of Surrey in 1489, and created Duke of Norfolk and Earl Marshal, Feby. 1st, 1514, Lord Treasurer and K. G., and d. May 21st, 1524, having had issue by his 2d wife, AGNES, sister and heir of Sir Philip Tilney, Knt., of Boston, with others, a sixth dau. CATHERINE md. RICE AP GRIFFITH. (q. v.)

13

HOWARD,

OF WASHINGTON.

Sir **HENRY HOWARD**, of England, had three sons **EPHRAIM**; Dr. **JOHN**; and **JOSHUA** who md. 1st **REBECCA OWINGS**, and 2d a Mrs. **WARFIELD**. By his first wife he had issue: **SARAH** md. ―――― **WINCHESTER**, **MARY** md. **SAMUEL THOMAS**, (q. v.) **RACHEAL** md. **SAMUEL ROBERTSON**; **SAMUEL** md. ―――― **D'ARCEY**, and was father of Eli Howard of Baltimore, and grandfather of Mrs. John Leary, Mrs. Fannie Saltzer, and Emma Howard; **JOSEPH**, (q. v.); **BEALE**, **DEBORAH** md. ―――― **D'ARCEY**; **JOSHUA**; and **HENRY**, of whom presently.

HENRY HOWARD, fifth son of **Joshua** and **Rebecca (Owings) Howard**, b. May 28th, 1791, an M. D., and Professor of Medicine, md. 1st, **HANNAH**, dau. of **James Snowden Pleasants**, who d. leaving issue:

i. **VIRGINIA PLEASANTS** md. Professor **COURTENAY**, and d. leaving issue **HENRY HOWARD**; **DAVID** d. s. p.; and **ALEXANDER DALLAS BACHE**.

ii. Dr. **MARSHALL PLEASANTS** md. **ANNA NORMAN McCENEY**, and d. leaving issue: **MARGARET V.** md. **ELISHUA RIGGS**; **LAURA V.** md. **SAMUEL RIGGS**; **HENRY PLEASANTS**, and **MARSHALL PLEASANTS**.

iii. **LAURA PLEASANTS** md. Prof. **WILLIAM H. McGUFFEY**, L. L. D., of the University of Virginia, and has had issue: **ANNA** d. s. p.

iv. Dr. **HAMILTON PLEASANTS** md. **MARIA E.** dau. of Thomas Gibbs, and d. Dec. 20th, 1863, having had issue: **IDA** d. s. p.; and **HAMILTON**.

Prof. **HENRY HOWARD** md. 2nd **ELIZA**, dau. of Joseph Elgar, since deceased, and d. March 2d, 1874, leaving further issue: **ELIZA ELGAR**; and **ANNA ELGAR**.

JOSEPH, second son of **Joshua** and **Rebecca (Owings) Howard**, md. **MARY**, fouth dau. of **Samuel** and **Mary (Cowman) Thomas**, and had issue: **SAMUEL** d. s. p.; **MARIA** md. ―――― **IRVINGS**; **MARY** md.

JAMES THORNTON; Dr. FLODOARDO, of whom presently; SARAH ANN md. ——— TIBBALS; and d. leaving issue: Dr. WILLIAM F. of Cincinnati, Ohio, and ANNIE; HENRIETTA md. ——— McKENZIE; ELIZABETH md. ——— THORNTON; and LAWRENCE.

FLODOARDO, second son of **Joseph** and **Mary** (Thomas) Howard, b. May 11th, 1811, md. June 11th, 1833, **LYDIA MARIA**, dau. of **Samuel Robertson**, and has had issue:

i. FLODOARD WILLIAM b. May 14th, 1834, md. 1st Oct. 23d, 1860, SARAH ROSANNA, dau. of Robert Henning, who d. leaving issue: WILLIAM ROBERT b. Aug. 31st, 1861; FLODOARDO BENNETT b. May 27th, 1866, d. June 9th, 1871; and LYDIA MARY b. July 2d, 1873. FLODOARD W. HOWARD md. 2d Nov. 14th, 1876, ANNA M., dau. of Alexander Brown.

ii. SAMUEL ROBERTSON b. March 24th, 1837, d. Sept. 29th, 1838.

iii. LYDIA MARY b. March 6th, and d. Oct. 16th, 1838.

iv. GEORGE ROBERTSON b. Aug. 22d, 1839, d. Sept. 13th, 1840.

v. LAURA ROBERTSON b. Oct. 11th, 1841, md. May 28th, 1873, G. HERBERT, and has issue: MILDRED b. April 30th, 1874; and LYDIA ROSE b. May 14th, 1876.

vi. JOSEPH LAWRENCE b. Aug. 19th, 1844, d. July 26th, 1850.

vii. ROBERTSON A. M., M. D., L. L. B., &c., b. Dec. 12th, 1847, a member of the Maryland and District of Columbia Bar; md. June 8th, 1875, ISOLINA, dau. of Samuel Carusi, and has had issue: JOSEPH THORNTON b. April 10th, and d. June 11th, 1876.

viii. EDWIN b. Oct. 5th, 1850.

JANNEY.

JOSEPH, son of Joseph and Hannah (Jones) Janney, md. 1st. ELIZABETH HOWELL, dau. of Dr. Elisha and Hannah (Howell) Hopkins, and had issue: HANNAH ANN md. ROBERT HULL, of Baltimore, and had a son, WILLIAM JANNEY.

JOSEPH JANNEY md. 2d. **HANNAH HOWELL HOPKINS,** a sister of his first wife, and d. leaving further issue:

i.   **ELIZABETH** md. **J. M. SEWELL.**

ii.   **REBECCA** md. **JOSEPH MERREFIELD.** and has issue **JOSEPH JANNEY; WILLIAM JANNEY; ELIZABETH** md. **HENRY COX;** and **REBECCA JANNEY.**

iii.   **WILLIAM JANNEY.**

ARMS FROM BERRY'S ENC. HERALDICA.

JOHNSON.

THOMAS JOHNSON, a lawyer of Poole, near Garmouth, in England, md. **MARY,** dau. of **Roger Baker,** of Liverpool, and a ward in Chancery, and is said to have emigrated to Maryland about 1660. This date is evidently incorrect; it was about thirty years later that he settled in Calvert County in that State, and trafficked in furs with the Indians.

Early in the following century he attempted to return to England, and appears to have set sail in a vessel whose cargo represented his hard earned fortune. The vessel was captured by the Spaniards, and he lost his all. After a long imprisonment he escaped and returned to America in a Canadian vessel. From Canada he travelled on foot to his home in Maryland. The fatigue and hardships of the journey seriously injured his health, and in 1714, shortly after his return, he died. His wife died in a few months, leaving an only child, **THOMAS** b. Feby. 19th, 1701-2.

THOMAS, son of **Thomas** and **Mary** (Baker) **Johnson,** was md. Mch. 30th, 1725, by Rev. Jonathan Ray to **DORCAS,** dau. of **Joshua** and **Elizabeth Sedgewick,** of Connecticut, who d. Dec. 11th, 1770, and her husband Apl. 12th, 1777, having had issue:

i.   **THOMAS** b. Dec. 13th, 1725, d. in infancy.

ii. **BENJAMIN** b. July 6th, 1727, d. in May, 1786.

iii. **MARY** b. Aug. 5th, 1729, md. **WALTER HELLEN,** and d. in 1801.

iv. **REBECCA** b. Nov. 8th, 1730, md. **THOMAS McKENZIE,** and d. s. p. Mch. 11th, 1767.

v.   **THOMAS** b. Nov. 4th, 1732, elected to the Congress of 1774, and re-elected till 1777, when he was elected first Governor of the State of Maryland. Jany. 6th, 1776, elected a Brigadier-General, and commanded the "Flying Camps." June 15th, 1775, on his motion Washington was elected Commander-in-Chief of the Continental forces. Being absent on account of illness did not sign the Declaration of Independence. Aug. 5th, 1791, appointed a Justice of the U. S. Supreme Court. He md. Feby. 16th, 1766, **ANN,** only dau. of **Thomas Jennings,** of Annapolis, and d. Oct. 26th, 1819, leaving issue: **THOMAS; ANN** md. **Maj. JOHN GRAHAM; REBECCA** md. **THOMAS JOHNSON; DORCAS;** and **JOSHUA.**

vi. **JAMES** b. Sept. 30th, 1736, a Colonel in the Continental Army, md. **MARGARET SKINNER,** and had issue: **JAMES; THOMAS;** and **REBECCA.**

vii. **ELIZABETH** b. Sept. 17th, 1739, md. **Capt. GEORGE COOK,** of the Maryland Navy.

viii. **JOSHUA** b. June 25th, 1742, of whom presently.

ix. **Dr. JOHN** b. Aug. 9th, 1745.

x.   **BAKER** b. Sept. 30th, 1747. (q. v.)

xi. **ROGER,** of whom presently.

ROGER, eleventh child of **Thomas** and **Dorcas** (Sedgewick) **Johnson,** b. March 18th, 1749, was md. Feby. 4th, 1781, by Rev. Francis Lander to **ELIZABETH,** eldest dau. of **Richard** and **Sarah** (Coale) **Thomas,** who d. Sept. 7th, 1837, her husband having d. Mch. 3d, 1831. They had issue:

i.   **RICHARD** b. Nov. 9th, 1781, md. **JULIANNA DORSEY,** and d. July 14th, 1839, having had issue, with others: **RICHARD DORSEY** who md. **NANNIE SIMMS,** and has issue: Richard; **MARION** md. **Dr. DUVALL. FLORA** md. —— **WILLIAMS; EDITH MAY** md. **THOMAS MORGAN,** and another dau. unmarried.

ii.   **GEORGE** b. July 25th, 1783, md. **ELIZABETH DUNLOP**, and had ten children, of whom are living **ELIZABETH DORCAS** md. **GEORGE LOWRY**: **THOMAS** md **HENRIETTA JOHNSON**, and has issue: William and Roberta; and **ROBERTA** md. **ROBERT**, eldest son of Maj. George Peter, of Montgomery County, Md.

iii. iv.   **SAMUEL** and **HENRIETTA** b. in November, 1784, d. unmarried. .

v.   **WILLIAM THOMAS** b. Oct. 4th, 1787, md. **DOLLY MACTIER**, and d. s. p.

vi.   **SARAH** b. Dec. 26th, 1788, md. **ELI DORSEY**, and d. Aug. 25th, 1834, leaving five children.

vii.   **JOSEPH** b. Oct. 30th, 1790, md. **ELEANOR HILLEARY**, and d. Mch. 4th, 1835, leaving issue: **THOMAS ROGER**. Dr. **WILLIAM HILLEARY**, and three daughters.

viii.   **CHARLES** b. Feby. 18th, 1792, d. Oct. 16th, 1867, unmarried.

ix.   **DORCAS** b. May 14th, 1793, md. **HENRY MACTIER**, and d. s. p. Dec. 4th, 1815.

x.   Dr. **JAMES THOMAS** b. Nov. 12th, 1794, md. **EMILY NEWMAN**, and d. Sept. 4th, 1867, having had issue: Dr. **JAMES T.**; **OTIS**; **ELIZABETH R.** md. **WILLIAM RICHARDSON**; and **SUSAN BIRD** md. **JOHN V. WHITE**.

xi.   **ELIZA** b. Aug. 8th, 1796, md. Rev. **WILLIAM ARMSTRONG**, and has had issue: **WILLIAM J.** d. leaving issue: William I., Eliza, and Nettie; **ANNA TOWNSEND** md. Dr. **READ**, of Accomac County, Va.; and **HENRIETTA** md. **THOMAS PARRAMORE**, of the same State.

JOSHUA, second son of **Thomas** and **Dorcas (Sedgewick) Johnson**, b. in 1742, removed to France, and engaged in mercantile life at Nantes. He afterwards removed to London, and was appointed Consular Agent of the United States. He md. **CATHERINE NUTH**, and had issue: eight children, among whom were **THOMAS BAKER**, d. unmarried, and **LOUISA CATHERINE** b. Feby. 12th, 1775, md. July 27th, 1797, at London, **JOHN QUINCY**, son of President John Adams, and removed with him in the Autumn of that year to Berlin; Mr. Adams having been appointed Minister to that Court. In 1824 he was elected President of the United States, and served one term. He d. Feby. 23d, 1848, leaving issue surviving: CHARLES FRANCIS b. Aug. 18th, 1807, at Boston, was graduated at Harvard College in 1825, admitted to the Boston Bar in 1828, a member of the Massachusetts Legislature 1831-6, Member of Congress from Massachusetts 1859-61, Minister to England from 1861-68, and acted with consummate ability in that position, especially during the critical period of the Civil War. He md. in 1829, the youngest dau. of Peter C. Brooks, of Boston, and has had issue: John Quincy b.

Sept. 22d, 1833, a prominent politician of Massachusetts, resides at Quincy; Charles Francis, Jr., b. May 27th, 1835, admitted to the bar in 1858, served through the Civil War, mustered out with the Brevet rank of Brigadier General; Henry Brooks b. Feby. 16th, 1838, private Secretary to his father while Minister to England, in 1870 Assistant Professor of History at Harvard College, and Editor of the North American Review.

BAKER, seventh son of **Thomas** and **Dorcas** (**Sedgewick**) **Johnson,** b. Sept. 30th, 1747, was a Colonel in the Continental Army, md. Dec. 9th, 1784, **CATHERINE,** dau. of Colonel **Nicholas Worthington,** and d. June 18th, 1811, leaving issue: **BAKER; CATHERINE WORTHINGTON** md. March 4th, 1806, **WILLIAM ROSS,** of Fredericktown, Md.; **WILLIAM; JULIANNA** md. Rt. Rev. Bishop **JOHN JOHNS,** of Virginia; **MATILDA CHASE; CAROLINE WORTHINGTON GOLDSBOROUGH; WORTHINGTON** md. May 14th, 1822, **MARY JANE FITZHUGH,** dau. of Judge Richard Potts; and **CHARLES WORTHINGTON** b. Sept. 28th, 1805, md. **ELEANOR MURDOCK,** dau. of Dr. Bradley and Harriet (Murdock) Tyler, and had issue: **HARRIET** md. in 1849, **CHARLES SCHLEY;** and Gen. **BRADLEY TYLER** md. June 25th, 1851, **JANE CLAUDIA,** dau. of Hon. Romulus M. and Anna Hayes (Johnson) Saunders, and has issue: Bradley Saunders.

JONES,

DAVID JONES, who was a nephew of Nicholas Sluby, of Sweden, md. **MARIA,** dau. of **Richard S.** and **Mary Thomas,** and had issue:

i.   **DEBORAH** md. Feby. 29th, 1838, Col. **EDWARD WILKINS,** of Kent, and had issue: **JULIANA** md. Capt. **ROBERT S. EMORY,** and has issue: Edward Wilkins, Maria Ella, Julia, Isabelle, and Robert Julienne; **EDWARD MIFFLIN** md. **MARY ANNA MERRITT,** and has issue: Susan Carter, Fanny Louise, and Jenny; and **MARIA DEBORAH** md. **JAMES RUSSELL,** of Baltimore City, and has issue: James, Olive, and Maria.

ii.   **ANN MARIA** md. **JAMES WHITAKER**, who d. leaving issue **HARRIET, FRANK,
       JAMES, ANNIE,** and **MIFFLIN.**

iii.   **MARY** md. **A. W. SPARKS**, and has issue **HENRY** and **ELLA.**

iv.   **OLIVER PERRY** md. **MARY BROWN**, and d. in 1868, leaving issue **EDWARD,
       HIRAM, DAVID PAUL,** and two daughters.

v.   **RICHARD.**

iv.   **THOMAS** md. Sept. 10th, 1840, **FANNIE ISABELLE**, dau. of **R. T. Jones**, and has
       issue: **MARIA THOMAS**, (now Lilly T. Armstrong); **THOMAS BROWN** b. Feby.
       7th, 1845; **JAMES ARMSTRONG** b. Aug. 20th, 1851; **MARY BROWN;** and
       NICHOLAS SLUBY b. Apl. 16th, 1853.

JONES,

OF NORFOLK.

Lieutenant-General Sir **JOHN THOMAS JONES**, Bart., of Cranmer Hall,
Norfolk. a K. C. B. and Aide-de-Camp to her Majesty, Queen Victoria,
md. April 20th, 1816, **CATHERINE MARY**, only dau. of **Effingham
Lawrence**, of London, and d. Feby. 26th, 1843, leaving issue:

i.   **LAWRENCE** second Bart., killed by Greek Brigands, and d. s. p. Nov. 7th, 1845, and
       was succeeded by

ii.   **WILLOUGHBY** b. Nov. 24th, 1820, third Bart., md. April 15, 1856, his cousin **EMILY**,
       dau. of **Henry T. Jones**, and his wife **Lady Hardinge**, and has issue: **LAW-
       RENCE JOHN**, b. Aug. 15th, 1857, and **MARY FLORENCE.**

iii.   **HERBERT WALSINGHAM** b. Oct. 10th, 1826, md. April 23d, 1850, **CATHERINE
       RACHEL**, dau. of **Daniel Gurney**, of North Runcton, Norfolk, and **Lady Harriet
       Hay**, second dau. of **William**, 15th Earl of Erroll.

iv.   **EMILY FLORENCE** md. Dec. 27th, 1849, **WILLIAM FRANKS**, Jr., of Woodhill,
       Hertfordshire.

KANE.

JOHN K. KANE, Judge of Admiralty of the U. S. District Court for the Eastern District of Pennsylvania, md. **JANE,** dau. of **Thomas Leiper,** and d. Feby. 21st, 1858, having had issue: Dr. **JOHN K.;** **ROBERT PATTERSON,** of the Philadelphia Bar; Gen. **THOMAS LEIPER,** Col. of the 42d Pennsylvania Volunteers in the Civil War; **ELIZABETH;** and Dr. **ELISHA KENT** the celebrated Arctic Explorer, b. Feby. 3rd, 1820.

Dr. Kane was educated at the University of Virginia for the profession of a Civil Engineer, but was compelled to leave that Institution in 1838, owing to a disease of the heart, from which he never fully recovered. The next year he began the study of Medicine at the University of Pennsylvania, and October 19th, 1840, while still an undergraduate, and not of age, he was elected Resident Physician to the Pennsylvania Hospital. In May 1843, having obtained the post of Surgeon in the U. S. Navy, he sailed in the Frigate Brandywine with Commodore Parker, as Physician to the Embassy to China. After the Embassy left, he remained six months in Whampoa, practicing his profession. Between 1843 and 1846, he travelled extensively in the Philippines, Borneo, Sumatra and India, passed through Persia, Egypt and Syria, crossed Greece on foot, travelled on the Continent, and in England, and returned to the United States in 1847. In May of that year, he visited Africa, and afterwards took part in the Mexican War. In these travels he met with numerous adventures, and displayed undaunted courage, and persistence in his plans despite of all obstacles. In 1850 he accompanied Lieut. De Haven's Arctic Expedition as its Surgeon and Naturalist, publishing an account of the Expedition in 1854. In 1853, Mr. Henry Grinnell and Mr. George Peabody were instrumental in fitting out another Arctic Expedition, to which Dr. Kane contributed his pay (about $3,000,) and the proceeds of Lectures which he delivered in 1852-3. He was appointed the Commander of the Expedition which sailed from New York, May 30th, 1853, in the Advance. The surviving officers and men returned October 11th, 1855, having been compelled to abandon their vessel in the ice, and to travel with sledges and dogs for 84 days to the Danish settlements on the coast of Greenland, where they met Capt. Hartstene, who had been sent to their relief. The story of the Expedition was most graphically told by Dr. Kane in two volumes published by Childs & Peterson, of Philadelphia, in 1856. Gold medals were awarded him by Congress, the Legislature of New York, and the Royal Geographical Society of London. His health again gave way, and after a visit to London, he sailed for the West Indies, Feby. 17th, 1856. On the voyage he suffered a paralytic stroke, and d. at Havana, December 25th, of the same year.

KING.

JOSEPH KING, Jr., md. Dec. 17th, 1817. TACY, dau. of Elias and Mary Ellicott, and d. leaving issue:

i.   FRANCIS THOMPSON b. Feby. 25th, 1819, md. Jany. 8th, 1846. ELIZABETH TABER, who d. in Mch. 1856, having had issue: MARY b. Dec. 8th, 1847; ANNIE b. in 1848; BESSIE b. in 1855; and two other children who d. in infancy.

ii.   THOMAS b. July 19th, 1820.

iii.   MARY ELLICOTT b. Sept. 2nd, 1823, md. GEORGE WARDOUR, and has a dau. MARY.

iv.   JOSEPH b. July 17th, 1825, md. June 1st, 1869, JANE GILMOR, dau. of Hon. Benjamin C. and Jane Grant (Gilmor) Howard.

v.   ELIAS d. unmarried.

KNIGHT AND CANBY.

An account of this family will be found in Martindale's History of Byberry and Moreland, published in 1867. From that we find that the earliest known ancestor was Giles Knight, of Gloucestershire, England, who was born in 1653, was an Elder of the Society of Friends, and came to

America in 1682, leaving England in the ship "Welcome," with William Penn, August 30th of that year, and landing at Newcastle on the Delaware some time in October. He md. Mary English, was frequently a member of the Provincial Assemby, and d. August 20th, 1726. His only son Joseph b. in 1680, md. Abigail Antill, and d. April 26th, 1762, his wife d. November 19th, 1764, aged 82 years. Giles, their son was b. November 17th, 1719, md. Elizabeth James, February 24th, 1738, and d. July 13th, 1799, at Bensalem, Pa.

Israel, their tenth child was b. March 4th, 1760, md. November 26th, 1782, Sarah, dau. of Isaac and Esther Tyson, of Baltimore, and d. January 31st, 1810, his wife d. April 8th, 1824, aged 66 years.

Isaac, their second son was b. September 14th, 1785, md. September 24th, 1811, at Sandy Spring Meeting House, Julianna Maria, dau. of Samuel and Anna (Warfield) Thomas. He was a man of considerable engineering ability, and the inventor of Knight's Box for the wheels of Railroad Cars. He d. April 1st, 1855, and his wife February 20th, 1868, leaving issue: Sarah d. in infancy; Charles Alexander b. November 11th, 1812, d. July 12th, 1848; Eliza Snowden; Dr. Samuel Thomas, of whom presently; William Henry b. January 20th, 1820, d. October 31st, 1847; Ann Rebecca; Maria Louisa, of whom presently; Mary Virginia: and Granville Sharp b. July 18th, 1828, d. October 2d, 1851.

Dr. SAMUEL THOMAS, fourth child of Isaac Knight, b. December 20th, 1817, was graduated in Medicine at the University of Maryland in 1835, and has since practiced in Baltimore. He md. first November 12th, 1839. REBECCA JANE, dau. of Joseph E. and Lucretia Moore. She d. August 22d, 1851, leaving issue: JULIA; LUCY GIBBONS md. JAMES ATTLEE; Dr. LOUIS WILLIAM b. October 21st, 1844; EMMA; MARTHA THOMAS; Dr. SAMUEL THOMAS, Jr. b. April 7th, 1850, at the age of 17 was graduated in Medicine at the University of Maryland, and obtained the position of Clinical Recorder in the University Hospital. He d. February 12th, 1870, from disease contracted there.

Dr. SAMUEL T. KNIGHT md. 2dly September 2d, 1852. MARY, dau. of William and Tabitha McConkey.

MARIA LOUISA, seventh child of Isaac Knight, md. May 11th, 1848, Samuel Canby, and has issue:

i.   **WILLIAM THOMAS** b. April 13th, 1849, md. May 28th, 1870, **IDA L. FISH**, of
       Boston, a niece of Hon. Hamilton Fish, Secretary of State of the United States, and
       has one child, **CLARENCE S.**

ii.   **EDWIN KNIGHT** b. December 6th, 1853

iii. **ALBERT HENRY** b. October 7th, 1856.

KNOWLES.

Dr. **WILLIAM G. KNOWLES** md. October 27th, 1835, at Longwood,
MARTHA ANN, dau. of **Dr. Gustavus Warfield** and **Mary Thomas**,
his wife, and had issue:

i.   **GEORGE GRAY** b. March 12th, 1837, at Darby, near Philadelphia, md. April 28th,
       1864, by the Rev. Halsey Dunning, to **MARY ELIZABETH WHITE**, she d. in
       March, 1865.

ii.   **MARY WARFIELD** b. April 15th, 1839, md. December 31st, 1863, **WILLIAM H.
       HORNER**, and d. leaving issue: **MARTHA THOMAS** b. April 1st, 1865; **MARY
       WARFIELD** b. March 5th, 1867; **WILLIAM** b. Oct. 25th, 1873, d. June 14th, 1874;
       and **EMMA CROZER** b. February 25th, 1876, d. June 9th, 1876.

iii. **GUSTAVUS WARFIELD** b. March 12th, 1841, md. March 29th, 1870, by Rev. Dr.
       Benjamin Griffith, to **EMMA**, dau. of **John P. Crozer**, of Upland, and had issue:
       WILLIAM b. Dec. 14th, 1870; **HENRY CROZER** b. April 22d, 1872, d. Jany. 13th,
       1874; and **SALLY** d. in infancy.

iv.   **LOUISA VICTORIA** b. August 19th, 1843, md. Oct. 27th, 1868, at her father's residence
       in Baltimore, by Rev. Dr. Thos. J. Shepherd, to **CLARENCE ALBERTUS
       EVANS**, and has issue: **WILLIAM KNOWLES** b. August 10th, 1869; and **EMMA
       CROZER** b. June 12th, 1874.

LARGE.

JAMES LARGE, of Philadelphia, md. Jany. 15th, 1817, **ELIZABETH**,
dau. of **Thomas** and **Ann (Thomas) Poultney**, who d. Apl. 12th,
1833, having had issue:

IN CRUCE SALUS.

Lawrence

i. **THOMAS POULTNEY** b. Feby. 12th, 1819, md. June 26th, 1857, **MARY STRICK-LAND**, and d. July 27th, 1852, having had issue: **ELIZABETH POULTNEY** d. unmarried in Dec. 1872.

ii. **MARY** b. Oct. 7th, 1820, md. Oct. 31st, 1839, **ROBERT H. LARGE**, and has had issue: **SALLIE** b. Oct. 15th, 1840, md. Mch. 1st, 1870, **Dr. THEODORE FASSITT**; **JAMES** b. Aug. 23d, 1842; and **JOHN B.** b. Mch. 7th, 1846, md. Apl. 10th, 1872, **SARAH W. MEADE**, and has issue: **George Gordon Meade** b. Aug. 26th, 1873; and **Robert H.** b. Oct. 31st, 1875.

iii. **ANN POULTNEY** b. Oct. 31st, 1822, md. Feby. 4th, 1839, **WILLIAM MIFFLIN**, and has issue: **JAMES** b. in Aug. 1840, md. Nov. 29th, 1871, **LILY WIGHT**, of New York.

iv. **SARAH M.** b. May 24th, 1847, md. **SAMUEL H. TAGART**, Attorney-at-Law, of Baltimore.

ARMS OF JOHN LAWRENCE, OF WASHINGTON

LAWRENCE,

OF LANCASHIRE.

The earliest ancestor of this family of whom there is any record was Robertus Laurentius or Robert Laurens of Ashton Hall, Lancashire, who accompanied Richard Cœur de Lion in his Crusade, and distinguishing himself at the siege of Ptolemais or St. Jean D'Acre in 1191, by being the first to mount the walls in the final assault, was created a Knight Banneret by the King, and received a grant of the coat of arms still borne by his descendants, viz.: Argent, a cross raguly gules. His son Sir Robert married a daughter of James Trafford of Trafford, in Lancashire, and left

by her a son and heir James, living in the thirty-seventh year of the reign
of Henry the Third, who married Matilda, daughter and heiress of John
Washington of Washington, in 1252, having with her, besides others, the
Manors of Washington and Sedgewick, in Lancashire.   Their son John who
bore Lawrence and Washington Quarterly on his shield of arms, levied a
fine of Washington and Sedgewick in 1283, was a Burgess for Lancaster in
1301, and married in 1283, Margaret, daughter of Walter Chesford, of Lancashire.   Their son John presented to the Church at Washington in 1328,
and d. about 1360, leaving by his wife, Elizabeth Holte, of Stubley, in
Lancashire, a son and heir Sir Robert, whose son of the same name was
of the private retinue of Henry the Fifth in his French wars in 1417, and
married Margaret Holden, of Lancashire, by whom he had issue: Sir
Robert, living in 1454; William, who served in France, and afterwards
fought on the Lancastrian side in the Wars of the Roses, dying at the
battle of St. Albans in 1455, and being buried in the Abbey Church;
Thomas, who was ancestor of Sir Thomas Lawrence of Chelsea Baronet,
who was Secretary of the Province of Maryland; and Edward, of whom
presently.

Sir Robert, the oldest son and heir married Amphilbus, daughter of
Edward Longford of Longford, Lancashire, and had two sons, Sir James,
knighted by Lord Stanley, at Hutton Field, in Scotland; and Sir Thomas,
who married Eleanor, daughter of Lionel, Lord Welles, and was ancestor
of Lancelot Lawrence, of Yeland Hall.   Sir James married a lady whose
name is unknown, and had two sons James and Robert.   The elder had
only one son and heir Sir John, who with Sir Edward Stanley commanded
the left wing of the English Army at the battle of Flodden, where he was
killed in 1513.   Dying without issue, the greater part of his estate was
divided between the four daughters of his Uncle Robert   The remainder
went to Lancelot Lawrence, of Yeland Hall, and Yeland Redmain Manor
as heir male.   He was the son of an Edmund Lawrence, who died in the
sixth year of the reign of Henry the Eighth, and grandson of Thomas Lawrence who married Eleanor Welles.   He died twenty years afterwards, leaving
two sons, Thomas, and Sir Oliver who was knighted by the Duke of
Somerset at Musselburgh Battle, in 1547.   Thomas died in the thirty-fifth
year of the reign of Henry the Eighth, leaving an only son and heir,
Robert, who died in the second year of the reign of Philip and Mary, possessed of lands at Yeland Redmain, Dylake, Heysham, Myddleton, Bolton,
Warton, Skirton Hutton, Flokborow and Sylverdale, in Lancashire.   The
main line of the Lawrences of Ashton became extinct in his person, as he
left no issue by his wife Anne Bradley, of Bradley.

We now return to Edward, youngest son of Sir Robert Lawrence and Margaret Holden. His son Nicholas called of Agercroft, under the will of his uncle William, inherited estates at Shurdington, which are still in the possession of his descendants. Robert his son married Margaret, daughter of John Lawrence, of Rixton, in Lancashire, and Mary, daughter of Eudo, eldest son of Richard, Lord Welles, and had issue: Sir Robert, who married a daughter of Thomas Stanley, and died without issue in 1511; John; and William who was living in 1509, when he purchased landed property to the amount of £2000 sterling per annum, including the estates of Sevenhampton in Gloucester, Seahouse in Somerset, Blackley Park and Norton in Worcestershire. He married Isabel, daughter of John Molyneux, of Shorely, in Lancashire, and had issue, with others: a third son William, whose son John born in 1538, died and was buried in the Abbey of Ramsay, in Huntingdonshire, leaving a son William who was High Sheriff of Cambridge and Huntingdon Shires at the death of Queen Mary. He married first Frances Houston, and settled at St. Ives, in Buckinghamshire, and for his second wife, Margaret, daughter of Edward Kaye, of Woodson, in Yorkshire. By his first wife he had issue: Henry who married Elizabeth, daughter of John Hagar, of Bourne Castle; and William, ancestor of the Lawrences of Chichester and Aldingbourne. By his second wife he had Robert, ancestor of the Lawrences of Norfolk. Henry Lawrence who married Elizabeth Hagar, was buried at St. Ives, February 25th, 1580, leaving issue: John, his heir; and William who is said to have married Joan ———, who afterwards married John Tuttell, a Mercer of Great St. Albans, Hertfordshire, whither William Lawrence had removed about 1580.

John Lawrence was knighted by James the First in 1603. He married Elizabeth, daughter and heiress of Ralph Waller, of Clerkenwell, Middlesex, and died in February 1604. His son was the celebrated Sir Henry Lawrence, the father of Milton's friend.

He was born in 1600, entered Emanuel College, Cambridge, in 1622, and was graduated M. A. in 1627. He was the author of several theological works, in 1641 returned a member of Parliament for Westmoreland, and afterwards sat for Hertfordshire and for Colchester in Essex. He married Amy, daughter of Sir Edward Peyton, of Iselham, in Cambridgeshire. Was appointed by Cromwell, Lord President of his Council in 1654, and gazetted as a Lord of the Other House in December 1657.

He was a man of character and distinction, and was so highly esteemed by Cromwell, who was his second cousin, that although he refused to take any part in the King's trial and execution, he retained him in his high offices, and at the Protector's death, as Lord President, he proclaimed Oliver's son Richard as his successor.

His monument may yet be seen in the Chapel of St. Margaret's, in Hertfordshire.

His son Henry was an intimate friend of the Poet Milton, who addressed a sonnet to him, and was a member of Parliament for Carnarvonshire in 1656.

ST. ALBANS.

LAWRENCE,

OF NEW YORK.

April 2d, 1635, old style, the ship "Planter," Nicholas Trarice, Master, bound for New England, had among its passengers John Lawrence, aged 17; William, aged 12; Marie their sister, aged 9; and their mother Joan and her second husband John Tuttell, a Mercer, and four small children, all from Great St. Albans, Hertfordshire. Joan Tuttell is said to have married as her first husband William Lawrence (q. v.), uncle of Sir Henry Lawrence, President of Cromwell's Council, by whom she had issue: John, William, and Marie Lawrence. John Lawrence was born at St. Albans in

1618, he first landed at Plymouth Colony, but afterwards removed to Ipswich and finally to Long Island, where in 1644 he became one of the patentees of Hempstead, under grant from the Dutch Governor Wilhelmus Kieft. In the following year, with his brother William and sixteen others, he obtained the patent of Flushing from the same Governor and they were among those to whom the confirmatory patent was issued by the English Governor Nicoll, February 16th, 1666. In 1658 he had removed from Long Island to New Amsterdam, which place became his permanent home. In 1665 he was appointed one of its first Aldermen, on its incorporation by the English under the name of New York, and in 1672 its Mayor. In 1674 he was appointed a member of the Governor's Council, and continued in that position until 1698. In the following year he died leaving six children; for whose descendants and some particulars of those branches of the Lawrence family not mentioned in these Notes, the reader is referred to the Lawrence Genealogy, compiled by Thomas Lawrence, of Rhode Island, in 1858. William, younger brother of John Lawrence, was born at Great St. Albans, in 1623. Joining with John in the patent of Flushing in 1645, he made that place his residence; was a Magistrate there under the Dutch Rule, and afterwards held a military commission under the English. At his death he was the largest landed proprietor at Flushing, and his sword, plate and personals, were valued at £4,430 sterling. He was twice married and left issue by both wives. In 1664 he married his second wife, Elizabeth Smith, who afterwards became the wife of Philip Carteret, Governor of New Jersey, who named Elizabethtown after her. Joseph Lawrence, her eldest son by her first marriage, married Mary, daughter of Col. Richard Townley, an intimate friend of his father, and a member of the Provincial Council of New York. Mr. Lawrence died in 1759, leaving an eldest son Richard, of whom presently.

RICHARD, eldest son of **Joseph** and **Mary Lawrence**, b. in 1691, md. Feby. 6th, 1717, by Friends' ceremony, in their Meeting House, at Flushing, **HANNAH**, dau. of **Samuel** and **Mary (Beckett) Bowne**, of that place, and had issue:

i. **MARY** b. April 2d, 1718, md. **EDWARD BURLING.**

ii. **ELIZABETH** b. June 15th, 1719, md. **JOHN EMBREE.**

iii. **JOSEPH** b. September 10th, 1721.

iv.   CALEB b. Feby. 10th, 1723-4, md. **SARAH BURLING**, and had a dau. **MARY** md. in 1784, Baron **FREDERICK AUGUSTUS De ZENG**, (q. v.;) and a son **RICHARD** md. **MARY LAWRENCE**, and had issue: William; Caleb; Mary Anne Colden; Richard L. md. Sarah, dau. of Baron Frederic De Zeng; and Sarah md. Richard De Zeng.

v.   **HANNAH** b. April 2d, 1726.

vi.   **LIDDYA** b. Sept. 29th, 1728.

vii.   **JOHN** b. Jany. 31st, 1730-1, lived 9 days.

viii. **JOHN** b. Jany. 22d, 1731-2, of whom presently.

ix.   **EFFINGHAM** b. Feby. 11th, 1734-5, removed to London, England, and engaged in business there. Md. a Miss **FARMER**, and had issue **WILLIAM EFFINGHAM**; **EFFINGHAM**; **EDWARD BILLOPP**; and **CATHERINE MARY** md. Lieut. Gen. Sir **JOHN THOMAS JONES**, Bart. (q. v.)

x.   **NORRIS** b. Jany. 6th, 1737-8, md. **ANN PELL**, and d. in early manhood, having had issue: **MARY** b. Oct. 10th, 1765; **HANNAH** b. Oct. 21st, 1767; and **NORRIS** b. Feby. 15th, 1769.

xi.   **JOSEPH** b. Aug. 23d, 1741, inherited under his father's will the old Family Mansion at Bayside, and md. **PHŒBE TOWNSEND**.

JOHN, fifth son of **Richard** and **Hannah Lawrence**, b. Jany. 22d, 1731-2, md. Aug. 13th, 1755, **ANN**, dau. of **John** and **Ann Burling**, and d. in New York City, July 26th, 1794, his wife d. at the same place Feby. 14th, 1821, having had issue:

i.   **EDWARD BURLING** b. June 13th, 1756, md. **ZIPPORAH**, dau. of Dr. **William Lawrence**, of Oyster Bay, and d. Apl. 16th, 1832, having had issue: **EDWARD L.** b. June 13th, 1780, md. **MATILDA WHITING**, and had three children, Robert lost at sea, Ann Maria md. Martin Baker, and Sarah md. Joshua Baker; **PHŒBE** md. **THOMAS WHITING**; **JOHN L.** md. **ADELINE TUPPER**; **WALTER** md. **MALVINA DANIELS**; **CORNELIA** md. **THOMAS TREADWAY**; and **JANE** md. **HENRY B. FOWLER**.

ii.   **HANNAH** b. July 6th, 1758, md. **JACOB SCHIEFFELIN**. (q. v.)

iii.   **EFFINGHAM** b. June 6th, 1760, of whom presently.

iv.   **MARY** b. Sept. 11th, and d. Nov. 13th, 1762.

v.   **MARY** b. Oct. 17th, 1763, md. Dec. 26th, 1780, her cousin **EFFINGHAM**, son of John and Elizabeth Embree, and d. Sept. 16th, 1831, having had issue: **JOHN LAW-RENCE**; **EFFINGHAM LAWRENCE** md. **ELIZA HARTMAN**; **LAWRENCE EFFING-HAM** md. **SARAH FRANKLIN**; **JANE** md. **JOHN WINES**; **MARY ANNE** md. **GILBERT HICKS**; and **HANNAH** md. **JOHN WRIGHT**, and after his death ———— **MERCEREAU**.

vi. **CATHERINE** b. May 15th, 1765, d. unmarried May 9th, 1834.

vii. **JANE** b. Sept. 2d, 1768, md. **ISAAC LIVESAY,** and d. s. p. Aug. 24th, 1854

viii. **PHEBE** b. Dec. 24th, 1770, d. July 2d, 1771.

ix. **ANNA** b. May 22d, 1772, md. **THOMAS BUCKLEY.** (q. v.)

x. **JOHN BURLING,** of whom presently.

xi. xii. **PHEBE** and **CORNELIA,** twins, b. Mch. 17th, 1778, the latter d. Mch. 27th, of the same year, and her sister Aug. 8th, 1780.

JOHN BURLING, tenth son of **John** and **Ann** (Burling) **Lawrence,** b. Oct. 21st, 1774, was a merchant and druggist of New York City; his business being still carried on by his grandsons, Emlen and John B. Lawrence, Jr. He md. Feby. 15th, 1804, **HANNAH,** dau. of **Caleb Newbold,** of Philadelphia, and his wife **Sarah Haines,** of New Jersey, and d. Oct. 8th, 1844, having had issue:

i. **EDWARD NEWBOLD** b. Feby. 12th, 1805, md. **LYDIA ANNA,** dau. of **Hon. Effingham** and **Anna** (Townsend) Lawrence, of Flushing, and dying at Liverpool, England, Oct. 21st, 1839, was buried at Bayside, Long Island, leaving issue: **FREDERIC NEWBOLD** b. Feby. 28th, 1834, md. **ELIZABETH,** dau. of **Kerr Boyce,** of South Carolina.

ii. **GEORGE NEWBOLD** b. Oct. 20th, 1806, md. Oct. 23d, 1834, **MARY ANN,** dau. of George Newbold, and has issue: **EMLEN NEWBOLD** b. Dec. 24th, 1836; and **JOHN BURLING,** Jr. b. in 1844, md. **KATHERINE D.** dau. of **Gabriel Wisner,** of New York City.

iii. **MARY NEWBOLD** b. Oct. 31st, and d. Nov. 15th, 1808.

iv. **NEWBOLD** b. Oct. 23d, 1809, md. Oct. 21st, 1851, at Philadelphia, **ANNA H.** dau. of Joseph Trotter, of that city, and has issue: **CAROLINE TROTTER** b. Aug. 25th, 1852; **ANNIE TROTTER** b. Dec. 10th, 1853; **NEWBOLD TROTTER** b. May 6th, 1855; **SUSAN NEWBOLD** b. July 27th, 1856; and **MARY GERTRUDE** b. March 27th, 1860.

v. **ALFRED NEWBOLD** b. July 10th, 1813, md. June 30th, 1837, **ELIZABETH,** dau. of Hon. John L. Lawrence, of New York City, and has had issue: **WOODHULL** b. April 19th, 1850, d. July 7th, 1870; **HANNAH NEWBOLD** b. April 9th, 1852; and **JOHN L.** b. June 22d, 1857.

iv. **CAROLINE AUGUSTA** b. Aug. 18th, 1815, md. **WILLIAM EFFINGHAM LAW-RENCE,** of Bayside, L. I., and d. April 20th, 1841, leaving one son **EDWARD N.** b. April 15th, 1841, d. at Madeira, of Consumption.

vii. **JOHN B.** b. Dec. 30th, 1817, md. **MARY ADELINE FURMAN,** of Maspeth, L. I.

viii. **THOMAS NEWBOLD** b. Jany. 15th, 1820.

EFFINGHAM, second son of **John** and **Ann** (Burling) **Lawrence**, b. June 6th, 1760, began mercantile life for himself in 1781, and retiring with an ample competency thirteen years afterwards, purchased a house in Flushing, L. I., and resided there until his death. He md. about 1785 **ELIZABETH WATSON MERRITT**, widow of Lieut. Merritt, and dau. of **Thomas Watson**, of New Jersey, and d. Dec. 13th, 1800, having had issue:

i.   **WATSON EFFINGHAM**, of whom presently.

ii. **EFFINGHAM WATSON** was in business about 1830 with Gideon Freeborn, as Freeborn & Lawrence, but subsequently removed to Flushing, L. I. He md. **REBECCA**, dau. of **Benjamin Prince**, and has issue: **WILLIAM HENRY** b. July 25th, 1824; **Rev. FRANCIS EFFINGHAM, D. D.**, b. May 12th, 1827, now Rector of the Protestant Episcopal Church of the Holy Communion, New York City; and **FREDERIC** b. Nov. 12th, 1830.

iii. **MARY WATSON** b. in Mch. 1787, md. in 1808 **JAMES T. TALLMAN**.

iv. **ANNA WATSON** b. in 1792, d. in June, 1868.

v.   **JOHN WATSON** b. in 1798. (q. v.)

WATSON EFFINGHAM, eldest son of **Effingham** and **Elizabeth Lawrence**, was born Aug. 13th, 1788, went into business in New York in 1808. In 1819 removed to Flushing, where he resided for several years. Between 1825 and 1827 he was engaged in the banking business in New York with Charles Lawton. After the dissolution of their partnership Mr. Lawrence had an intimation from his friend Judge Wright, engineer of the Delaware and Hudson Canal Company, that he had in his survey of the route of the Canal discovered large beds of Hydraulic Limestone in Ulster County. Mr. Lawrence having some knowledge of mineralogy examined the stone, and satisfied of its quality, made large investments in the manufacture of cement from it, and removing to that district became the founder of Lawrenceville. Through his friends, Gen. Jos. G. Totten and Col. De Russey, he succeeded in introducing his Rosendale Cement into general use, and most of the Government works have been constructed with it. Mr. Lawrence furnished numerous articles in genealogical or antiquarian subjects to Thompson's Long Island and similar works, and was a prominent member of the Protestant Episcopal Church. He md. 3d Jany. 1810. **AUGUSTA MARIA**, dau. of **John Nicoll**, of New Haven, Conn., and a lineal descendant of the first English Governor of New York, and d. Sept. 16th, 1872, having had issue:

i.   JANE NICOLL b. Nov. 14th, 1810, md. Sept. 13th, 1831, JOHN GEORGE ANDER-SON, of Florida, and has issue: JAMES EFFINGHAM b. Oct. 24th, 1838; LAW-RENCE MEL b. July 21st, 1841, d. Apl. 6th, 1862; AUGUSTA LAWRENCE b. Oct. 6th, 1845, md. 1st, EDWARD HOUSETOWN, who d. without issue, and 2d, Sept. 20th, 1870, WILLIAM G. POOLE, and had issue: Lawrence Anderson b. Dec. 17th, 1871.

ii.   EFFINGHAM NICOLL b. Aug. 30th, 1812, of whom presently.

iii.   ELIZABETH WATSON b April 3d, 1814, md. LAWRENCE P. HILL, and d. s. p. Oct. 10th, 1867.

iv.   JOHN NICOLL b. Nov. 17th, 1816, d. March 27th, 1817.

v.   AUGUSTA NICOLL b. May 8th, 1818, d. Nov. 16th, 1820.

vi.   ANNA WATSON md. June 18th, 1839, MANDELBERT CANFIELD, but has had no issue.

vii.   CHARLOTTE AUGUSTA b. April 3d, 1823, d. May 16th, 1858, unmarried.

viii.   WATSON AUGUSTUS b. Dec. 31st, 1825, d. July 13th, 1841.

ix.   MARY TALLMAN b. July 2d, 1828, md. Feby. 5th, 1861, RICHARD MANSFIELD EVERIT, and has had issue: RICHARD LAWRENCE b. Dec. 19th, 1861; EMMA AUGUSTA b. Oct. 27th, 1863, d. July 27th, 1864; ANNIE COLEY b. May 14th, 1867; and EDWARD HOTCHKISS b. Aug. 5th, 1870.

x.   EMMA AUGUSTA b. April 27th, 1832.

xi.   CHARLES EDWARD b Nov. 30th, 1836, md. April 17th, 1860, LEILA HOMEYARD, and has issue: ASHTON CLEVELAND b. Oct. 7th, 1861; LEILA HOMEYARD b. Feby. 23d, 1863; ERNEST MINTURN b. May 10th, 1869; and LAURA EFFING-HAM b. May 16th, 1875.

EFFINGHAM NICOLL, eldest son of Watson E. and Augusta Maria (Nicoll) Lawrence, b. Aug. 30th, 1812, md. 1st Feby. 6th, 1837, MARGARET CLENDINNING, dau. of Horace W. and Margaret Bulkley, and 2d Nov. 30th, 1853, MARGARET, dau. of William and Sarah Hogan, by whom he had no issue; by his first marriage he has had issue:

i.   CLENDENNING NICOLL b. Jany. 19th, 1838, d. March 15th, 1843.

ii.   THEODORE b. Sept. 1st, 1839, d. Dec. 21st, 1861.

iii.   GEORGE ANDERSON b. March 24th, 1841, md. Nov. 28th, 1866, CHARLOTTE L., dau. of Randolph M. and Louisa Cooley, and has issue: RANDOLPH MORGAN b. Nov. 23d, 1867; MARGARET CLENDINNING b. Sept. 20th, 1869; KATE CHESTER b. Oct. 26th, 1870; and BERTHA EFFINGHAM b. July 29th, 1875.

iv.   **WATSON EFFINGHAM** b. Sept. 26th, 1842, d. Sept. 9th, 1844.

v.   **EFFINGHAM BULKLEY** b. March 30th. 1844, d. Oct. 13th, 1844.

vi.   **CHESTER BULKLEY** b. Sept. 15th, 1845, md. Jany. 9th, 1867. **CATHERINE**
        COVELL, dau. of George C. and Kate Peters, and has had issue: **KATE**
        EFFINGHAM b. Oct. 9th, 1867, d. June 7th, 1868; **GEORGE COVELL** b. May 10th,
        1869; and **CHESTER BULKLEY**, Jr. b. June 13th, 1872.

vii.   **MARGARET CLENDINNING** b. Sept 3d. 1847, d. Jany. 16th, 1849.

viii.   **AUGUSTUS MARIA** b. Nov. 29th. 1849, d. Dec. 2d, 1849.

ix.   **EDWIN** b. Oct. 19th, 1850, d. Oct. 22d, 1850.

x.   **ALBERT EFFINGHAM** b. Nov. 12th, 1851.

JOHN WATSON, third son of **Effingham Lawrence** and **Elizabeth**
Watson, was born in 1800, and served a clerkship in the office of
Samuel Hicks. When of age he associated himself with William Howland in the shipping and commission business as Howland & Lawrence.
He has been a director of the old U. S. Branch Bank of New York,
was a member of the State Legislature in 1840 and '41, a member of
Congress from the first district in 1846 and '47, and President of the
Seventh Ward Bank of New York 1847 to 1854, when he resigned that
position, and retired from business. In 1826 he md. **MARY KING**,
dau. of **Walter** and **Eliza (Southgate) Bowne**. Through her father
she was descended from one of the original patentees of Flushing. She
d. in 1873, having had issue:

i.   **CAROLINE** md. in October, 1847. **Hon. HENRY BEDINGER**, of Virginia. He was
        a member of Congress from that State, and afterwards U. S. Minister to Denmark,
        where he resided several years. He died in 1859 and his wife ten years afterward,
        leaving issue: MARY md. June 29th, 1871, Capt. JOHN MITCHELL, who had been
        an officer in the Union Army during the Civil War; Rev. HENRY b. in 1853, a
        clergyman of the Protestant Episcopal Church, md. April 18th, 1876, ADA, dau. of
        W. N. Doughty, of Flushing; CAROLINE DANSKE b. in Denmark, md. May 3d,
        1877, A. STEPHEN DANDRIDGE.

ii.   **ELIZA SOUTHGATE** md. in 1849 Gen. ARMISTEAD T. M. RUST, of Virginia.
        Mrs. RUST d. in 1858, leaving issue: LAWRENCE b. in 1851, now (1876) a
        M. A. and Professor of the Greek Language and Literature in Kenyon College,
        Ohio; and REBECCA md. in October, 1875, EDMUND LEE, of Virginia.

iii.   **MARY BOWNE** md. November 5th, 1853, **HENRY A. BOGERT**, and has had issue: **MARY LAWRENCE** b. Jan. 19th, 1855, md. June 3d, 1873, **WILLIAM ELLIMAN**, and has one son b. Sept. 11th, 1876; **HENRY LAWRENCE** b. Jan. 20th, 1857; **JOHN LAWRENCE** b. Oct. 27th, 1858; **EMILY ELOISE** b. Oct. 29th, 1860, d. Apl. 8th, 1864; **EDWARD LUDLOW** b. Dec. 19th, 1862, d. Oct. 21st, 1863; **WALTER LAWRENCE** b. Dec. 7th, 1864; **JAMES LAWRENCE** b. Mch. 31st, and d. July 21st, 1867; **MARSTON TAYLOR** b. Apl. 18th, 1868; **FRANCIS LAWRENCE** b. July 11th, 1869, d. July 19th, 1870; **FANNY LAWRENCE** b. Sept. 8th, 1870; and **THEODORE LAWRENCE** b. June 24th, 1875.

iv.   **EMILY** md. in December 1874, **CHARLES H. SHEPARD**.

v.   **ANNA LOUISA** md. in 1862, Rev. **THOMAS JAGGAR**, now Protestant Episcopal Bishop of Southern Ohio.

vi.   **WALTER BOWNE** b. in 1839. md. in October 1866, **ANNA TOWNSEND**.

vii.   **REBECCA** d. in childhood.

viii. **ISABELLA.**

ix.   **FANNY** md. in July 1873, Rev. **FREDERICK B. CARTER**, a clergyman of the Protestant Episcopal Church.

x.   **ROBERT** b. Dec. 1st, 1852.

LEIPER.

The first of this name in America were James and Thomas Leiper. The former of these was a surgeon and resident of London, in England. It is not known at what date he removed to America, but in 1771 he was in Prince George's County, Maryland; and in the autumn of that year, being about to voyage to Lisbon for his health, he made his will, dated November 15th, in which he mentions his mother Helen Scott, his wife Elizabeth, his children George Robert Leiper, and Lucy Ann Hebbard, his brother Thomas Leiper, and Sisters Nancy and Janet. Before taking the expected voyage, Dr. James Leiper seems to have died, as his will was proved December 2d, 1771.

THOMAS LEIPER, his brother, came to this country from Scotland in 1764, at the age of nineteen, and accumulated a large fortune as a Tobacconist in Philadelphia. He was Orderly Sergeant, Treasurer and

Secretary of the first City Troop, and at one time President of the Common Councils of the City. He afterwards engaged in the Milling business, and in quarrying stone in Delaware County; md. **ELIZABETH**, the eldest dau. of **George Gray**, of Gray's Ferry, and d. in 1825, having had issue:

i.   **ELIZABETH** md. **ROBERT TAYLOR**, and had issue: **Dr. GEORGE GRAY, JAMES LEIPER; SAMUEL LEIPER**, and **THOMAS LEIPER**.

ii.   **MARTHA** md. Rev. Dr. **JACOB J. JANEWAY.**

iii.   **HELEN HAMILTON** b April 20th, 1792, md. April 20th, 1814, Dr. **ROBERT M. PATTERSON**, and d. Dec. 17th. 1871, leaving issue.

iv.   **ANN GRAY** md. **GEORGE GRAY THOMAS.** (q. v.)

v.   **JANE** md. Judge **JOHN K. KANE.** (q. v.)

vi.   **JULIA** md. Col. **HENRY TAYLOR**, of Va.

vii.   **GEORGE GRAY**, of whom presently.

viii.   **WILLIAM J.** d. unmarried.

ix.   **SAMUEL M.** md. **MARY**, dau. of Dr. **Charles S. Lewis**, and granddaughter of Gen. William Irvine

x.   **JAMES** md. **ANN**, dau. of Pierce and **Christiana Crosby**, and had issue. an only dau. **ELIZABETH GRAY** who md. **JOHN HOLMES**, of Philadelphia, and d. Feby. 1st, 1873, leaving several children.

GEORGE GRAY, seventh child of **Thomas** and **Elizabeth** (Gray) **Leiper**, lived at Lapidea, near Leiperville, Delaware County, Pennsylvania, md. May 3d, 1810, **ELIZA SNOWDEN**, dau. of **John Chew Thomas**, and d. November 17th, 1868 having celebrated his Golden Wedding-day eight years previously. His wife d. September 28th, 1868. Their children were:

i.   **ELIZABETH**, of whom presently.

ii.   **THOMAS GRAY.**

iii.   **ANNE** md. Dr. **JESSE BONSALL**, and d. s. p. June 6th, 1847.

iv.   **JOHN CHEW** md. Mch. 24th, 1852, **MARY LEWIS FAYSSOUX**, of Philadelphia, and has issue: **GEORGE GRAY** b. Jany 23d, 1853; **MARTHA F.** d. in infancy; **REBECCA FAYSSOUX; EDWARD FAYSSOUX** b. October 29th, 1858, Cadet Midshipman, U. S. N.; **ELIZA SNOWDEN; BARNARD BEE** b. April 21st, 1863; and **JOHN HENRY THOMAS** b. December 23d, 1867.

v. **MARY THOMAS** md. Nov. 12th, 1851, **JOHN HENRY THOMAS**, Attorney-at-Law, of Baltimore, Md., son of **Dr. William Thomas**, of St. Mary's County, Md. and his wife, **Eliza Sotheron Tubman**, and has issue: **GEORGE LEIPER** b. Sept. 19th, 1852. Attorney-at-Law; **WILLIE** d. in infancy; and **ELIZA SNOWDEN**.

vi. **MARTHA GRAY** md. July 15th, 1852, **THOMAS IRWIN CAREY**. (q. v.)

vii. **GEORGE GRAY** md. **SALLIE HAMILTON**, and d. leaving issue: **ELIZA SNOWDEN**.

ELIZABETH, eldest child of **Judge Leiper**, md. **THOMAS SMITH**, who d. in 1856, leaving issue:

i. **MARY THOMAS** md. Dec. 7th, 1871, **ARCHER N. MARTIN**, and has issue: **AUBREY HENRY** b. Mch. 30th, 1873; **ROBERT NEVINS** and **CHARLES LAWRENCE** b. May 31st, 1875.

ii. **ELIZA LEIPER** md. Sept. 28th, 1865, **JAMES EDWARD FARNUM**, of Media, Pa., and has issue: **PAUL** b. Aug. 15th, 1867; **EDWARD** b. May 2d, 1869; **GEORGE LEIPER** b. May 10th, 1872; and **ELIZABETH** b. Apl. 1st, 1875.

iii. **ANNE LEIPER** md. June 7th, 1868, **ROBERT MARTIN**, and has issue: **LILLY LEIPER**, and **ADELAIDE NEVINS**.

iv. **GEORGE LEIPER** d. in youth.

v. **JOHN MILLER**.

vi. **HARRIET J.**

LEWIN.

JOHN LEWIN b. in 1538 md. **SYBIL**, dau. of **Sir William Allen**, Knt., of London, and had issue: **WILLIAM**, who md. ———, and had a son **SAMUEL** who resided in London and engaged in mercantile life. His son **William**, b. in 1664, was Sheriff of London City in 1713, and a Knight. He md. **Lady Susanna Champion**, and d. in 1737, having had issue: Dolly md. Samuel Wethered, (q. v.); Richard, Sheriff of Kent in 1726; Sarah md. Lord Colchester, and Catherine md. Sergeant Maynard, M. P.

LEACH.

THOMAS LEACH was the son of **Thomas** and **Ann Leach**, of Chertsey, in the County of Surrey, England, and was b. July 16th, 1682. After serving an apprenticeship in London, he sailed for Newport, R. I., arriving there Nov. 28th, 1706. His wife **SARAH** d. at Philadelphia, Pa., Mch. 31st, 1755, aged 70 years.

LUDLOW.

ROBERT C. LUDLOW, U. S. N. md. **ANN CATHERINE**, dau. of John and **Mary (Sykes) Wethered**, and had issue:

i. **BAINBRIDGE**, U. S. N.

ii. **AUGUSTUS**, of whom presently.

iii. **MARY WETHERED** md. Oct. 5th, 1837, Hon. **JAMES CARROLL**, and has had issue: **ACHSAH RIDGELY**; **SARAH WETHERED**; **JAMES** d. in infancy; **JAMES** d. in infancy; **MARY LUDLOW**; **SOPHIA GOUGH**; **HARRY DORSEY GOUGH**, and **CATHERINE LUDLOW**.

iv. **CATHERINE**.

AUGUSTUS, second son of **Robert C.** and **Ann Catherine (Wethered) Ludlow**, md. **AUGUSTA CROOK**, and d. leaving issue: **MARY CLARE** md. **SAMUEL G. B. COOK**; **SARAH WETHERED** md. **TATLOW JACKSON**; **CHARLOTTE SELLMAN** md. **J. SETH HOPKINS**; **KATE** md. **ALONZO LILLY**, Jr.; and **ROSE**, her twin sister, unmarried.

    Mrs. **AUGUSTUS LUDLOW** md. 2d **HANS P. MOWINCKEL**, and has further issue: **AUGUSTA** and **NETTIE**.

MORRIS.

SAMUEL MORRIS, of Philadelphia, md. **REBECCA WISTAR**, of the same city, and had issue; BENJAMIN; ANTHONY; CASPAR; SARAH md. RICHARD WISTAR; LUKE, of whom presently; ISAAC; CATHERINE; and ISRAEL WISTAR md. MARY, dau. of Levi Hollingsworth, and had with other issue: CASPAR, a practicing physician in the City of Philadelphia; connected with numerous charitable institutions; and a prominent member of the Protestant Episcopal Church in the Diocese of Pennsylvania.

Dr. CASPAR MORRIS md. **ANN**, eldest dau. of James and Mary (Hollingsworth) Cheston, and has had issue:

i. **JAMES CHESTON**, M. D., md. 1st **H. A. TYSON**, and had issue by her: ISAAC TYSON; CASPAR; J. CHESTON; and HENRY V. D. JOHNS. He md. 2d **MARY ELLA JOHNSON**, and had further issue: LAWRENCE; WILLIAM STEWART; MARY; and ISRAEL WISTAR.

ii. **ISRAEL WISTAR** md. Dec. 3d, 1855, **ANNE MORRIS**, dau. of Effingham L. and Hannah Ann Buckley, and has issue: EFFINGHAM BUCKLEY b. Aug. 23d, 1856.

iii. **GALLOWAY CHESTON** md. **HANNAH**, dau. of Joseph and Sarah Perot, and has issue: ELLISTON PEROT; and HERBERT.

iv. **MARY H.** md. **HENRY M. MURRAY**, of West River, and has had issue: CORNELIA; MARY DORSEY; ROBERT; EMILY HOLLINGSWORTH; SALLY CHESTON; ANN CHESTON; and HENRY M. Jr. who d. in infancy.

LUKE, fourth son of Samuel and Rebecca (Wistar) Morris, md. 1st **ELIZABETH**, dau. of William and Sarah (Morris) Buckley, and had issue by her: SAMUEL BUCKLEY. He md. 2d **ANN PANCOAST**, and had further issue:

i. **ELIZABETH** md. THOMAS WISTAR.

ii. **MARY** md. **CHARLES ELLIS**, see "Tyson Pedigree."

iii. **SARAH** md. **JOSEPH PEROT**, of Philadelphia. He d. in 1875, having had issue: JOSEPH md. a Miss LEE; ELLISTON md. JULIA ——; HANNAH md. GALLOWAY C. MORRIS; and EFFINGHAM BUCKLEY md. MARY BURROUGHS.

iv. **HANNAH ANN** md. EFFINGHAM L. BUCKLEY. (q. v.)

ARMS FROM BURKE'S GEN. ARMORY

POULTNEY.

THOMAS POULTNEY, md. April 21st, 1790, **ANN**, second dau. of Evan and Rachel (Hopkins) Thomas, who d. Feby. 4th, 1858, having had issue:

i.   **ELIZABETH** b. Dec. 2d, 1792, md. **JAMES LARGE.** (q. v.)

ii.   **EVAN THOMAS** b. March 22d, 1795, md. **JANE TUNIS**, and d. having had issue: ANN md. **WILLIAM T. RIGGS** THOMAS md. **SUSAN CARROLL**, and has issue: Carroll, Evan and Thomas; and JANE md. Hon. **JOHN BIGELOW**, Associate Editor of the N. Y. *Evening Post*, and in 1865 and 1866, Minister at the Court of France. They have had issue: Grace Poultney d. in infancy; John; Poultney Jennie; Annie; Ernest d. in infancy; and Flora.

iii.   **SAMUEL THOMAS** b. June 16th, 1797, of whom presently.

iv.   **PHILIP** b. May 18th, 1799, md. April 23d, 1847, **ANN ELIZABETH McNEIR**, of Annapolis, and d. Sept. 10th, 1860, leaving issue: EVAN b. in 1848, md. Nov. 25th, 1873, **ANNA**, dau. of Gerard T. and Elizabeth Hopkins.

v.   **RACHEL THOMAS** b. July 14th, 1801, md. **DAVID U. BROWN.** (q. v.)

vi.   **MARY ANN** b. June 16th, 1804, md. **Dr. WILLIAM W. HANDY.** (q. v.)

vii.   **SARAH CRESSON** b. July 8th, 1806, md. **WILLIAM M. ELLICOTT.** (q. v.)

viii.   **THOMAS** b. Dec. 7th, 1808, md. Nov. 24th, 1830, **JANE T.** dau. of Andrew and Hannah (Tunis) Ellicott, and had issue: THOMAS; and HANNAH md. HENRY D. FARNANDIS, and has issue: Annie and Bessie.

ix.   **LYDIA** b. Sept. 25th, 1810, md. Dr. **WILLIAM H. DAVIS**, and d. s. p.

x.   **LUCY** b. Oct. 18th, 1812, md. Dr. **DORSEY**, and had issue: **NANNIE** md. **CHARLES D. FISHER**, and has issue: Lucy, Sallie and Nannie. **WILLIAM** and **LYDIA** both d. s. p.

xi.   **BENJAMIN** b. Sept. 18th, 1815, md. **ELIZA**, dau. of Andrew and Hannah Ellicott, and d. leaving issue: **MARIA** md. **THOMAS P. HANDY**. (q. v.)

SAMUEL THOMAS, fourth son of Thomas and Ann (Thomas) Poultney, b. June 16th, 1797, md. Sept. 30th, 1828, ELLIN MOALE CURZON, and d. leaving issue:

i.   **ELIZABETH MOALE** b. June 29th, 1829, md. Nov. 26th, 1856, **RICHARD HALL PLEASANTS**, and has had issue: **JOHN PEMBERTON** b. Sept. 4th, 1857; **RICHARD CURZON** b. Dec. 14th, 1859, d. in infancy: **ELLIN CURZON**; **WILLIAM ARMISTEAD**; **RICHARD HALL** **SAMUEL POULTNEY** d. in infancy; **ELIZABETH**; and **JACOB HALL**.

ii.   **THOMAS** b. Oct. 23d, 1832, md. 1st May 8th, 1859, **GEORGIANNA VIRGINIA McCLELLAN**, who d. having had issue: **RICHARD CURZON** b. Jany. 25th, 1861; **ARTHUR EMITT** b. Aug. 2d, 1863; and **JOHN McCLELLAN** d. in infancy. **THOMAS POULTNEY** md. 2d Jany. 3d, 1867, **SUSAN MEADE WARD**, of Virginia, and has further issue: **HARRIET FITZHUGH** b. Jany. 26th, 1868; **ELLIN CURZON** b. Sept. 23d, 1870; **WILLIAM DAVIS** b. Sept. 21st, 1873; and **ANNIE WARD** b. Nov. 17th, 1874.

iii.   **RICHARD CURZON** b. Feby. 8th, 1835, d. Feby. 10th, 1855.

iv.   **NANCY THOMAS** b. April 27th, 1837, md. Nov. 12th, 1863, **A. SMITH FALCONAR**.

v.   **SAMUEL EUGENE** b. Dec. 22d, 1839, md. Nov. 4th, 1869, **LEILA LIVINGSTON MINIS**, and has issue: **EUGENE** b. Oct. 23d, 1871; and **JOHN LIVINGSTON** b. Jany. 25th, 1875.

vi.   **WALTER De CURZON** b. Nov. 4th, 1845.

REESE.

THOMAS L. REESE md. Nov. 24th, 1813. **MARY MOORE**, and had issue :

i.   **MARY BROOKE** b. Aug. 12th, 1814, d. in childhood.

ii.   **ANN** b. May 21st, 1816, md. Sept. 23d, 1840, **CALEB S. HALLOWELL**, and has had issue: **MARY JANE** d. in youth; **CHARLES** md. **FANNY FERRIS**, and has had issue: William Ferris, Charles, Benjamin Shoemaker d. in infancy, and Lewis Bush; **AMELIA BIRD**; **EMMA ROBERT SHOEMAKER THOMAS REESE** and **ELIZABETH MOORE**, all five of whom d. in infancy or youth.

iii.   **GERARD HOPKINS** b. Sept. 8th, 1818, md. Sept. 18th, 1845, **SARAH JANE JAN-NEY**, and has had issue: **THOMAS LACEY**, Jr. **ELIZABETH MOORE**, **MARY ANNA** d. s. p.; and **CORNELIA STABLER**.

iv.   **THOMAS MOORE** b. July 18th, 1820, md. Sept. 8th, 1840, **MARTHA**, dau. of William and **Deborah Stabler**, and has had issue: **FRANK** d. s. p.; **HENRY STABLER** md. Jany. 19th, 1876, **BELLE LIPPINCOTT**, and has one child, Gordon Lippincott. **WALTER** md. Apl. 17th, 1877, **JANET D. BARRETT** and **LAWRENCE MOORE**.

v.   **CHARLES** b. June 16th, 1823, md. May 12th, 1847, **SUSAN WETHERALD**, and has had issue: **PERCY MEREDITH** md. **ELIZABETH McCORMICK**. **MARY WALTON** md. **W. BURR**, and has one child, Agnes. **ANNE HALLOWELL**. **ESTELLE EVAN-GELINE**. **WARREN HASTINGS**; **ALICE MAUD MURIELLE**; **FREDERICK HER-MANN**; the last five d. in childhood.

vi.   **EDWARD** b. June 16th, 1825, md. in May, 1854, **MARY A. GILPIN**, and has issue: **JULIET CANBY**; **FANNY GILPIN**; **CATHERINE STABLER**; and **JAMES STONE**.

ARMS FROM SHARPE'S PEERAGE.

RICE.

Griffith ap Rice, claiming to be the eldest son of Rice ap Griffith (q. v.) and Lady Katherine Howard, his wife, md. Eleanor, dau. of Sir Thomas Jones, Knt., and was restored in blood in the reign of Philip and Mary. He had issue: Walter, of whom presently; Barbara md. David Fludd; and Mary md. Walter Vaughan, of Grove.

Sir Walter, son and heir of Griffith ap Rice, called himself Walter Rice, and was living in 1600. He md. Elizabeth, eldest dau. of Sir Edward Mansel, Knt., of Margam, and had four sons: Henry, of whom presently; Thomas; Anthony; and Edward; and seven daughters: Jane md. John Fludd, of Llanvair, Cledoga; Eleanor; Barbara; Mary; Elizabeth; Joan and Lettice.

Henry, eldest son of Sir Walter Rice, Knt., had issue a son Henry who lived at Newton, md. Mary, dau. of Sir Thomas Lewys, Knt., of Penmark, and had issue: Sir Edward d. unmarried; and Walter md. Elizabeth Deer, widow of Richard Games, of Llanelly, and had issue: Griffith, of whom presently; Henry and Walter d. in infancy; and Elizabeth md. Richard Middleton, of Middleton Hall.

Griffith, second son and heir of Henry Rice, of Newton, was a member of Parliament in the reigns of King William III. and Queen Anne, md. Sept. 6th, 1722, Katherine, second dau. and co-heir of Philip Hoby, of Neath Abbey, and d. Sept. 26th, 1729, having had issue: Edward, of whom presently; Philip d. in infancy; Elizabeth md. Thomas Lloyd, of Altecadnoe; Katherine md. William Brydges, of Tyberton; Maria d. unmarried; Albinia d. unmarried; and Arabella d. in infancy.

Edward, only son of Griffith and Katherine (Hoby) Rice, md. Sept. 6th, 1722, Lucy, dau. of John Morley Trevor and his wife, Lucy, sister of Charles, first Earl of Halifax, and d. Apl. 5th, 1727, leaving issue: George, of whom presently; Lucy d. unmarried; and Katherine d. in infancy.

GEORGE, only son of **Edward** and **Lucy (Trevor) Rice,** and heir to his grandfather Griffith Rice, was a member of Parliament, a Privy Councellor, and Lord Lieutenant of the County of Caermarthen. He md. Aug. 16th, 1756, **Lady CECIL TALBOT,** only dau. and heir of **William,** first Earl Talbot, who had been created Oct. 17th, 1780, Baron Dynevor, with remainder to her, which title she inherited at his decease, becoming Baroness Dynevor in her own right. Her husband d. Aug. 3d, 1779, having had issue:

i.   **GEORGE TALBOT** b. Oct. 5th, 1756 (q. v.)

ii.   **HENRIETTA CECILIA** b. Sept. 28th, 1758, md. Dec. 16th, 1787, **MAGENS DORRIEN MAGENS,** who d. in 1849, having had issue **CECILIA GEORGE WILLIAM;** and **MARIA.**

iii.   **LUCY** b. May 29th, 1763, d. unmarried.

iv.   **WILLIAM** b. April 1st, 1760, d. April 20th, 1770.

v.   **MARIA** b. April 5th, 1773, md. Nov. 17th, 1796, **JOHN MARKHAM,** Rear Admiral of the White, and d. in 1810.

vi.   **EDWARD,** of whom presently.

EDWARD, third son of **George** and **Lady Cecil (Talbot) Rice,** b. Nov. 19th, 1776; in Holy Orders and Dean of Gloucester, md. July 9th, 1800, **CHARLOTTE,** dau. of **General Lascelles,** and d. Aug. 5th, 1862, having had issue five sons:

i.   **EDWARD** d. June 5th, 1820.

ii.   Rev. **FRANCIS WILLIAM** b. in 1804, Vicar of Fairford, in 1869 succeeded his cousin the 4th Lord, as 5th Baron Dynevor; md. 1st in 1830, **HARRIET IVES,** dau. of D Raymond Barker, and had issue **ARTHUR De CARDONNEL** b. in 1836, md. in 1869, **SELINA,** dau. of Hon. A. Lascelles; and **ELLEN** md. Rev. J. G. **JOYCE.** Rev. **F. W. RICE** md. 2d Nov. 18th, 1856, **ELIZA AMELIA,** dau. of Rev. H. Carnegie Knox, and has had further issue **FRANCIS CARNEGIE** b. July 15th, 1858; **WILLIAM TALBOT** b. March 24th, 1861; **CECIL MINA; ALICE;** and **MARY.**

III. **GEORGE ROBERT** d. s. p. May 12th, 1854.

iv. **Rev. HENRY**, Rector of Great Rissington, md. Dec. 12th, 1837, **EMMA**, dau. of W. F. Lowndes-Stone, of Brightwell Park, and has had issue two sons: **EDWARD** b. in 1855, and **HENRY** b. in 1862; and seven daughters, **FRANCES EMMA** md. April 23d, 1861, CECIL CHARLES, only son of Sir Peter Van Notten Pole, Bart.; **CATHERINE**; CECIL LOUISE; FLORENCE MARIA; GEORGIANNA; AMY AUGUSTA; and BEATRICE.

v. **JOHN TALBOT** md. 1st Oct. 13th, 1846. **CLARA LOUISA**, dau. of Sir John Chandos Reade, Bart., who d. Aug. 11th, 1853; and 2d Oct. 24th, 1855, **ELIZABETH LUCY**, dau. of Robert Boyd.

Dean EDWARD RICE had also seven daughters:

i. **CHARLOTTE** md. Sept. 1st, 1835, Rev. A. CAMERON.

ii. **CECIL** md. Jany. 4th, 1837, Col. **CHARLES AUGUSTUS ARNEY**, and d. June 2d, 1852.

iii. **MARIA** md. Sept. 3d, 1839, Rev. **CANON EDWARD BANKES**.

iv. **ELIZA** d. unmarried Oct. 7th, 1828.

v. **LUCY HORATIA** md. June 7th, 1832, Rev. **WILLIAM ESCOTT**.

vi. **FRANCES EMMA** md. March 20th, 1842, Rev. **WILLIAM WIGGIN**, and d. May 1st, 1860.

vii. **MARIA LOUISA** d. unmarried Feby. 21st, 1845.

GEORGE TALBOT, eldest son of **George Rice** and the **Baroness Dynevor**, b. Oct. 8th, 1756, succeeded his mother as 3d Baron Dynevor, md. Oct. 20th, 1794, **FRANCES**, dau. of **Thomas**, first Viscount Sidney, and d. April 9th, 1852, having had issue one son: GEORGE RICE b. Aug. 5th, 1795, of whom presently; and six daughters, FRANCES; CECIL; HARRIET LUCY; CAROLINE MARY; KATHERINE SARAH; and MARIA ELIZABETH.

GEORGE RICE, only son of the third **Baron Dynevor**, succeeded his father as fourth Baron, assumed the additional name of "TREVOR," on inheriting the estates of the Trevors, of Glynde, in Sussex, becoming **GEORGE RICE RICE-TREVOR**. He was Hon. Colonel of the Caermarthenshire Militia, md. Nov. 27th, 1824, **FRANCES**, dau. of **Lord Charles Fitzroy**, and d. in 1869, having had issue:

i.   **FRANCES EMILY** md. May 1st, 1848, **EDWARD FFOLLIOTT WINGFIELD**, and d. Nov. 26th, 1863.

ii.   **CAROLINE ELIZABETH ANNE** md. Feby. 24th, 1849, Sir **THOMAS BATESON**, Bart.

iii.   **EVA GWENTHAM** d. unmarried July 28th, 1842.

iv.   **SELINA** md. Nov. 12th, 1862, Sir **WILLIAM LYGON PAKENHAM**, third Earl of Longford.

v.   **ELEANOR MARY.**

RICHARDSON.

ROBERT RICHARDSON, of Somerset County, in Maryland, md. **SU-SANNA**, ———, and d. in Nov. 1682, leaving issue: **WILLIAM** of whom presently; **ELIZABETH**; **SUSANNA**; **ROBERT**; **TABITHA**; **SARAH**; and **CHARLES**. WILLIAM, the eldest son, was apparently a Minister of the Society of Friends, md. **ELIZABETH**, widow of Richard Talbot, and d. in May, 1698, having had issue:

i.   **WILLIAM**, who had a son **WILLIAM**

ii.   **DANIEL** md. Mrs. **ELIZABETH WATSON**, widow, who d. in April 1710, leaving issue by her first husband: **WILLIAM** and **JAMES**; and by her second **NATHANIEL**.

iii.   **SOPHIA** md. **RICHARD GALLOWAY**. (q. v.)

iv.   **JOSEPH** md. Oct. 25th, 1705, at West River Meeting House, **SARAH**, eldest dau. of Samuel and Mary (Hutchins) **Thomas**, and had issue:

    i.   **SAMUEL** md. ——— **CROWLEY.**

    ii.   **PHILIP** md. ——— **BEARD.**

    iii.   **JOHN** md. ——— **WILLIAMSON.**

    iv.   **ELIZABETH** md. Jany. 19th, 1737-8, **FRANCIS**, son of Charles and Sidney (Winn) **Pierpont**, and had a dau. Mary md. Jany. 24th, 1755, **Benjamin Powell.**

v.   WILLIAM md. ISABEL CALAMIES.

vi.   SARAH md. NEHEMIAH, Jr., son of Nehemiah Birkhead.

vii.   JOSEPH md. ——— BUCE.

Of the same family was **RICHARD RICHARDSON**, who d. in Apl. 1804, (although I am unable to say whose son he was). He md. Aug. 13th, 1754, **ELIZABETH**, dau. of **John** and **Elizabeth Thomas**, and had issue: **JOHN THOMAS** md. **JEMIMA SHECKELLS**; **WILLIAM** md. ——— **PLUMMER**; **ANN** md. **FREDERIC MILLS**; **DEBORAH** md. ——— **SHECK-ELLS**, removed from Maryland and settled in the Genesee country before 1804: **REBECCA** md. **GASSAWAY WATKINS**, who d. in July, 1817, leaving a son RICHARD GASSAWAY; and **SARAH** md. **RICHARD RICHARDSON**.

RUSSELL AND SEWALL.

THOMAS RUSSELL, of Greenhill, Cecil County, Maryland, md. **ANN**, dau. of **Samuel** and **Mary Thomas**, and had issue:

i.   MARIA d. unmarried.

ii.   FRANCES md. WILLIAM E. SEWALL, and had issue: ANN md. in 1819 THOMAS S. THOMAS; FRANCES; MARTHA S.; WILLIAM b. in 1805, md. a lady of New York in 1840, and had issue: William Russell and Fanny Jane; Dr. THOMAS b. in 1808 md. in 1848 REBECCA MAULDEN, and has issue: Thomas Russell, Mary Adelaide md. Sept. 3d, 1874, William H. Fisher, and Charles; BASIL b. in 1810, md. in 1845 ADELAIDE HUMBERT; and MARIA.

iii.   NANCY, who d. unmarried.

iv.   THOMAS, who d. in early manhood.

v.   WILLIAM, who also d. s. p.

ANN (THOMAS) RUSSELL afterwards md. **DANIEL**, only son of **Thomas** and **Ann Sheridine**, and d. without further issue.

ARMS FROM DOUGLAS' PEERAGE.

RUTHERFURD.

The earliest member of this family on record was Robertus Dominus de Rutherford, witness to a Charter given by David the 1st of Scotland in 1140. We next find Hugo de Rutherforde living in 1215, who was father of Sir Nicholas, living in 1261. His sons Nicholaus, and Aymer de Rutherford, were among the Barons of Scotland who swore fealty to Edward 1st of England in 1296. Sir Robert Rutherford, son of Sir Nicholaus, was a friend of King Robert Bruce. His son Sir Richard witnessed a Charter to the Abbacy of Coupar in 1328, and another to the Monastery of Dryburgh in 1338. He was father of William who was forfeited April 12th, 1357. His son Sir Richard Rutherford of that Ilk seems to have recovered his position and estates, for we find him in 1398 an Ambassador to the English Court, and in 1400 one of the Wardens of the Marches, on the Border. He married Jean Douglas and had three sons: James of Lethbertshiels, in Stirlingshire; John, ancestor of the family of Hunthill which eventually enjoyed the titles of Lord Rutherford and Earl of Teviot; and Nichol of Mackerston, who was ancestor of the Rutherfords of Hundalee. The eldest James had issue an only son James, who married before 1457, Margaret, daughter of Lord Erskine, and had a grant from James IV., in 1492 of the lands of Edgerston. He had issue: Philip and Thomas. The elder of whom married Elizabeth, daughter of Walter Ker of Cessford, ancestor of the present Duke of Roxburghe, and had Richard, d. s. p. Helen married twice but had no issue; and Christian married James Stewart, ancestor of the Earls of Traquair, to whom she carried the lands of Rutherford and Wells.

Thomas, younger son of James and Margaret Rutherford succeeded his nephew Richard in the lands and barony of Edgerston, and his son Robert obtained a confirmation of them in 1559. This Robert was succeeded by his son Thomas, called the Black Laird, and renowned for the exploits of himself and his nine sons on the Border. Richard his eldest son married a grand-daughter of the Laird of Buccleugh, and Robert their son married Margaret Riddell, daughter of the Baron of that Ilk. His eldest son John espoused the cause of King Charles the First, and was one of the leaders of his Scottish army, under the Marquis of Hamilton. He married Barbara Abernethy, daughter of the Episcopal Bishop of Caithness, and had issue twelve daughters; John and Andrew who both died without issue; Thomas, and Robert who was ancestor of Sir Walter Scott, Bart., of Abbotsford, in the female line. Thomas married Susanna, daughter and heiress of Riddell of Minto, and dying in 1720, had issue with five daughters, a son Sir John, who married in 1710, Elizabeth Cairncross, of Colmslie, and had nineteen children, of whom one son Robert was a Baron of the Russian Empire: Walter, another son removed to America, spelled his surname "Rutherfurd," was a Major in the British army and married Catherine, third daughter of James Alexander, and sister of Maj. Gen. William Alexander, of the American Revolutionary Army, who claimed and assumed the titles of Earl of Stirling and Viscount of Canada, as heir male of Henry, 5th Earl and Viscount, who died without issue December 4th, 1739. Walter and Catherine Rutherfurd had issue a son John b in 1760, graduated at the College of New Jersey in 1776; was one of the first Presidential Electors, and a Senator of the United States from New Jersey from 1791 to 1798. In 1807 he was the principal member of a Commission appointed to lay out the streets of New York. He md. Helena, dau. of Lewis Morris, the Signer, and niece of Staats Long Morris, who was an officer of the British Army, and md. the Dowager Duchess of Gordon, and of the celebrated Gouverneur Morris. John Rutherfurd d. Feby. 23d, 1860, having had issue: Robert Walter b. in May 1778, of whom presently; Mary b. in 1784, d. June 16th, 1863, unmarried; Anna md. Dr. John Watts; Helena md. Peter G. Stuyvesant, a descendant of the last Dutch Governor of New York; and two other daus. who d. unmarried.

ROBERT WALTER, only son of John and Helena (Morris) Rutherfurd, b. in May 1778, md. his cousin **SABINA,** dau. of Lewis Morris, Jr., and his wife **Ann Elliott,** of South Carolina, and d. leaving issue:

1. **WALTER** md. **ISABELLA BROOKS,** and d. in 1868, leaving issue:

    i.   **JOHN ALEXANDER.**

    ii   **WALTER** md. **LOUISE LIVINGSTON.** dau. of Oliver H. Jones.

    iii.   **FRANK MORRIS.**

    iv.   **WILLIAM WALTER.**

ii.   **JOHN** md. **CHARLOTTE LIVINGSTON**, and d. in 1871, leaving issue **HELEN MORRIS**; **LIVINGSTON**; and **ARTHUR.**

iii.   **LEWIS MORRIS**, a distinguished astronomer and scientist, md. **MARGARET STUYVE-SANT CHANLER**, and has issue:

    i.   **STUYVESANT**, who changed his name to **RUTHERFURD STUYVESANT**, in accordance with the will of his great uncle P. G. Stuyvesant, whose heir he was, and md. **MARY E.** dau. of H. E. Pierrepont.

    ii.   **MARGARET.**

    iii.   **LOUISA.**

    iv.   **LOUIS M.**

    v.   **WINTHOPE.**

iv.   **ROBERT WALTER** b. July 14th, 1819, md. Oct. 17th, 1848, **ANNA LAWRENCE**, dau. of Phineas Henry and Phœbe Buckley, and has had issue:

    i.   **ROBERT WALTER** b. Aug. 12th, 1849, at Morrisania, drowned in the Passaic River, Aug. 5th, 1852.

    ii.   **SABINA ELLIOTT** b. Aug. 4th, 1851, at Edgerston Cottage, New Jersey.

    iii.   **SARAH** b. July 29th, 1853, at Edgerston, d. in infancy.

    iv   **MARY** b. Dec. 18th, 1855, at Edgerston.

    v.   **ROBERT ALEXANDER** b. July 13th, 1860, at Edgerston.

    vi.   **HENRY LAWRENCE** b. June 4th, 1862, at Fairlawn Cottage, near Belleville, New Jersey.

    vii.   **ELIZABETH** d. in infancy.

RUTLAND.

Thomas Rutland, of South River, in Anne Arundel County, Md., whose will was proved Dec. 24th, 1731, mentions in it his son Thomas, his dau. Elizabeth Stuard, and his grand-children Thomas Sappington, and Jeane child of his dau. Ann Wayman.   Thomas, only son of Thomas Rutland, d. before

Feby. 1774; his wife Anne made her will Aug. 25th, 1773, (her husband then living) in which she mentions her aunt Hannah Norwood, gives a pair of gold sleeve buttons to Mary Snowden, dau. of Eliza Snowden, but leaves the bulk of her property to her nieces Ann Beall, Eliza Harrison, and Mary Dorsey, children of her sister Elizabeth Dorsey. This will was proved Jany. 23d, 1776, and some Elizabeth Rutland was one of the witnesses. Thomas Rutland who made his will in 1790, mentioning his wife Ann and his children, Thomas, Margaret and Elizabeth, was evidently of this family, and son of the second Thomas Rutland. Eliza Rutland who md. Richard Snowden. (q. v.) was a sister of this third Thomas Rutland.

ARMS FROM SHARPE'S PEERAGE.

ST. JOHN.

William de St. John, of St. John, near Rouen in Normandy, came to England with the Conqueror, as Grandmaster of his Artillery in 1066, and was a Baron by tenure; John, his second son, succeeded his brother who d. s. p., was Lord of Stanton St. John, Co. Oxon., and of Faumont Castle, Co. Glamorgan and living in 1140. Roger, his son and heir, living in 1175, md. Cicely, dau. and heiress of Robert de Haye, and had a dau. and heiress, Muriel de St. John md. Reginald de Aurevalle, and had a dau. and heiress Mabell md. Adam de Port, descended from Hugh de Port, of Basing, who held fifty-four Lordships at the general survey. Adam de Port after his marriage assumed the name of St. John. William, their son and heir, living in 1220, had a son and heir Robert, who md. Agnes, dau. of William de Cantelupe, and d. in 1266, leaving a son and heir John, who had two sons, John summoned by writ in the life of his father, as Baron St. John, the younger, and also in 1322 as Lord St. John of Basing; and William of Faumont Castle md. Isabel, dau. and heiress of William Combmartin, and had Sir John md. Beatrix — —, and had a son and heir Sir John md. Elizabeth, dau. and heiress of Sir Henry Umfreville of Penmark, Co. Glamorgan, and had a son and heir Sir John md. Isabel, dau. and co-heir of Sir John Pavely, of Paulers Pury, Co. Northampton, and had a son and heir Sir Oliver md. Elizabeth, dau. and heiress of Sir John Delabere, who brought him a very large estate. They had a son and heir Sir John, who was Mayor of Bordeaux 1414-21, md. Elizabeth Pawlett, and had a son and heir Sir Oliver of Penmark md. Margaret, sister and heiress of John (de jure) Baron Beauchamp, of Bletshoe, great grandson of Roger Baron Beauchamp, of Bletshoe, by writ June 1st, 1363, with whom he obtained the estates of Bletshoe and Lydiard Tregoze, and d. in 1437. His wife afterwards md. John Beaufort, Duke of Somerset, and was mother of Margaret, wife of Edmund Tudor, Earl of Richmond, and mother of King Henry VII. By her first husband she had two sons, Oliver ancestor of the celebrated Viscount Bolingbroke, and an elder Sir John of Bletshoe, K. B. md. Alice, dau. of Sir Robert Bradshaigh of Haigh, Co. Lancaster, and had a son and heir Sir John K. B. md. Sybil, dau. of Morgan ap Jenkins ap Philip and had with other issue: Sir John md. Margaret, dau. of Sir William Waldgrave K. B. of Smallbridge, Co. Suffolk, and had a son Oliver, created Baron St. John, of Bletshoe, in 1559; and Katherine md. Sir Griffith ap Rhys. (q. v.)

SCHIEFFELIN.

This family is of German origin, the name being originally spelled Schüffelin, the present spelling not obtaining until the middle of the last century.

One branch settled in Switzerland, Conrad Schüffelin, of Nörlingen in Germany, becoming a citizen of the Canton of Geneva, at the beginning of the sixteenth century. He and his descendants held the fief de la Molière and afterwards assumed the arms and title of de la Pâsle. The

Schieffelin.

first of the family in America was Jacob Schieffelin, who was born at Walhaim Underdeck, in Germany, February 4th, 1732. He came to America in 1735. His family Bible printed in 1560, is now in the possession of his lineal descendant, Mr. Eugene Schieffelin, of New York City.

JACOB SCHIEFFELIN md. Sept. 16th, 1756, **REGINA MARGARETTA KRAFTEN RITSCHAURIN**, who was b. in Milhaus Enderguse, Germany, and after her husband's death, md. a **Mr. GORDON**, and d. July 27th, 1816. **JACOB** and **REGINA SCHIEFFELIN** had issue:

i.   **JACOB**, of whom presently.
ii. **MELCHIOR** b. Aug. 16th, 1759.
iii. **JONATHAN** b. July 16th, 1762.
iv. **THOMAS**.

JACOB SCHIEFFELIN, Jr. was b. in Philadelphia, Aug. 24th, 1757, and baptised by the Rev. Mr. Muhlenberg of the Lutheran Church. When a young man he went to Detroit as private Secretary to Governor Hamilton. When of age he built two houses there, and owned considerable property in the town. He came to New York, holding a commission in the British Army early in 1780, and August 16th, 1780, md. **HANNAH**, oldest dau. of **John** and **Ann** (**Burling**) **Lawrence**, one of the handsomest women of her time, and a distinguished poetess. He afterwards removed to Montreal where his two eldest sons were born. Taking his wife back to New York he left her there, and spent some time in London. Returning to Montreal, his wife joined him and his other children were b. in that ancient city. About 1793 he returned to New York, and went in business with his brother-in-law John B. Lawrence. October 1st, 1794, he joined the German Society of New York. Four years afterwards his brother-in-law and he dissolved partnership, to allow Mr. Schieffelin to engage in ship owning, which Mr. Lawrence considered too hazardous a business. For many years he occupied the old Walton House on Pearl Street, New York. When he dissolved partnership with his brother-in-law he took his son Henry into the firm. Their first venture in the purchase of a ship was very successful, as on her first voyage she cleared about $25,000 above her original cost, with which money Mr. Schieffelin bought his country seat at Manhattanville, where he lived many years, and where he d. April 16th, 1835. He left issue by his wife **HANNAH LAWRENCE**, who d. Oct. 3d, 1838:

i.   **EDWARD LAWRENCE** b. Sept. 13th, 1787, d. Oct. 5th, 1850, at Lyme, Connecticut. He md. Jany. 1st, 1802, **SUSAN ANNA**, dau. of **Alexander Stewart**, and had issue: **EDWARD ANNA** b. in 1809, md. in 1830 **FRANK NICOLL SILL**, who d. in 1848. She then md. **Dr. JOHN NOYES**, who d. in 1854. After his death she md. **Captain S. CHADWICK**, of Lyme, who has since d. s. p.

ii.   **HENRY HAMILTON** b. June 20th, 1783, of whom presently.

iii. **ANNA MARIA** b. April 11th, 1788, md. April 4th, 1808, **BENJAMIN FERRIS**, and d. Oct. 24th, 1843, having had issue: **EMILY MATILDA** b. in 1810, md. **EDWARD RICHARDS**; **LAURA MARY** b. in 1812, md. 1st **CORNELIUS M. GAUL**, and 2d **REDFIELD A. WATKINSON**. **HANNAH M.** b. in 1814, md. **Dr. SAMUEL BLOIS**; **BENJAMIN CLINTON** b. in 1817; **CAROLINE EUDORA** b. in 1819, md. **HOMER MORGAN**. **JULIA** b. in 1823, md. **S. B. NOBLE**; **ADELAIDE** b. in 1825, md. **WM. HOWLAND PELL** and **ELLEN** b. in 1828, md. **COLUMBUS BEMENT ROGERS**.

iv.   **EFFINGHAM** b. Feby. 17th, 1791, md. Sept. 9th, 1813, **MARY**, dau. of **Caspar Lander**, and d. at East Chester, July 14th, 1863, leaving issue: one son, **EDGAR**, who has three daughters and two sons, and a grandchild by another son **CHARLES M. SCHIEFFELIN**, who md. **MARY**, dau. of William Chisolm, and niece of Rev. Dr. Wm. A. Muhlenberg, and has issue two daughters and a son.

v.   **JACOB** b. April 20th, 1793, md. and living in Tioga County, Pennsylvania, having issue: **CLINTON, HANNAH, CORNELIA, ALFRED,** and **EDWARD GERARD**.

vi.   **JOHN LAWRENCE** b. Feby. 25th, 1796, d. at New Haven, April 22d, 1866, leaving issue: **MARY** who md. **HENRY J. SAYERS**, of New York.

vii. **RICHARD LAWRENCE** b. Nov. 9th, 1801, md. Aug. 3d, 1833. **MARGARET HELEN**, dau. of George Knox McKay, U. S. A., and has issue: **SARAH SOPHIA** b. June 22d, 1834, md. Jany. 30th, 1858, Rev. **CUTHBERT C. BARCLAY**, who d. Feby. 7th, 1863; **GEORGE RICHARD** b. July 27th, 1836, md. May 10th, 1868, **JULIA**, dau. of Isaac C. Delaplaine, and has three children; **HELEN MARGARET** b. May 7th, 1841, md. June 21st, 1866, **WILLIAM IRVING GRAHAM**, and has issue: Helen M. b. April 26th, 1867, and Julia b. Sept. 18th, 1870. Mr. **GRAHAM** d. Aug. 25th, 1871, and his widow md. April 7th, 1875, **ALEXANDER ROBERT CHISOLM**, and has issue by him, one son b. Sept. 4th, 1876.

HENRY H. SCHIEFFELIN, second son of **Jacob** and Hannah (Lawrence) Schieffelin, b. June 20th, 1783, md. April 19th, 1806. **MARIA THERESA**, dau. of **Dr. Samuel Bradhurst**, and by her, who d. May 22d, 1872, had issue:

i.   **THERESA** b. in 1807, md. in 1827, **WILLIAM N. CLARK**, and has issue: **WILLIAM N.** md. **MATILDA ANDERSON**; **SAMUEL BRADHURST** md. **ELIZA TRACY**; **THERESA**; **EUPHEMIA**. and **LAWRENCE**.

ii. **HENRY MAUNSELL** b. Aug. 7th, 1808, md. in 1835, **SARAH LOUISA**, dau. of David Wagstaffe, and after her death **SARAH KENDALL**, of Maine, and has issue: **FANNY** and **MARY THERESA**.

iii. **SAMUEL BRADHURST** b. Feby. 24th, 1811, author of "Foundations of History," and other works. Md. in 1835 **LUCRETIA HAZARD**, and has issue: **WILLIAM HENRY** b. in 1836, md. in 1863 **MARY**, dau. of **Hon. John Jay**; **ALICE** b. in 1838, md. in 1859 **RUSSELL STEBBINS**; and **MARY THERESA** b. in 1840, md. in 1863 General **CHARLES E. DODGE**.

iv. **JOSEPH LAWRENCE** b. in 1813.

v. **PHILIP** b. in 1815, md. **ELIZABETH**, dau. of Richard Townley Haines, of Elizabethtown, New Jersey, and has issue: **THERESA** md. Rev. **WILLIAM T. SABINE**, and **ELLA**.

vi. **SIDNEY AUGUSTUS** b. in 1818, living at Geneva, md. **HARRIET SCHUYLER**, of Belleville, and has two sons and three daughters.

vii. **JULIA** b. in 1821, md. in 1840 **CLEMENT REMINGTON**, and d. Sept. 15th, 1871, leaving issue: **MARY THERESA** md. **WILLIAM CHAMBERLAIN**, and **JULIA** md. **CHARLES MORGAN**.

viii. **BRADHURST** md. twice, and has issue: **LAURA G.** md. in 1875 **DAVID BARTON CUSHING**; and **EMILY**.

ix. **EUGENE** b. in 1827, an artist of some distinction, though calling himself an amateur, md. **CATHERINE**, dau. of Valentine G. Hall.

SHIPLEY.

WM. SHIPLEY was b. in Leicestershire, England, in 1693, md. **MARY**, dau. of Robert and Ann Tatnal, he came alone to America, and was followed by his wife and her children, **THOMAS, ANN,** and **ELIZABETH,** in the Spring of 1725. She d. in 1726, and her husband in 1743, md. **MARY MARRIOTT**, and d. in 1789, leaving nine children, three d. in infancy: **MARY** their fourth child, md. **PHINEAS BUCKLEY**; **JOSEPH** md. **MARY LEWIS,** and d. in 1832, leaving a large family: **SARAH** md. **CYRUS NEWLIN,** and d. in 1834, leaving issue: **MARY** and **THOMAS**; **ANN** md. **JOHN JONES,** and d. in 1808, leaving issue: **CYRUS** and **LYDIA**; **ANNA** md. **WM. BYRNES,** and d. in 1805, leaving issue: **THOMAS** who md. his cousin **LYDIA JONES**.

SNOWDEN.

Richard Snowden, of Wales, who is said to have held a Major's commission under Oliver Cromwell, came to Maryland in the seventeenth century. His son Richard is mentioned as a well-known owner of land in Maryland, near South River, in a deed dated Oct. 13th, 1679. Aug. 1st, 1686, a tract of land called Robin Hood's Forest, and containing 10,500 acres, was granted to him. He was living Oct. 13th, 1688, when William Parker deeds to him certain land for a consideration of £306. In 1704 he was still living, but died soon after that date. His son Richard Snowden, Jr., md. before 1691 Mary ———; both of them were living as late as Dec. 19th, 1717, when they sign their son's marriage certificate.

Richard, apparently their only son, was born about 1790, and early in life began to take an active interest in affairs. His father probably was the builder of Birmingham Manor-house about 1690, but the son added very largely to the lands belonging to the Manor. From the fact that many of the tracts of land which he inherited from his father were re-surveyed in 1719, I am led to believe that the third Richard Snowden died in that year. His son added over 10,000 acres to the original tract in the same year. Before 1736 he engaged in the manufacture of Iron on the Patuxent River, near his residence, and Sept. 29th, 1736, certain land was granted to the "Patuxent Iron Work Company," in which were partners "Richard Snowden, owning 11-16, Edmund Jennings, of Annapolis, owning 2-16, and John Galloway and Joseph Cowman, of Annarrundel, and John Pritchard, mariner, then of London, each owning 1-16."

This business Richard Snowden continued until his death, at which time it appears by his will he was sole owner of the works, and was engaged in building a new forge. These Iron Works were the first ever operated in Maryland.

RICHARD SNOWDEN md. 1st, May 19th, 1709, **ELIZA**, dau. of **William** and **Eliza Coale**, and had issue by her:

i.   **DEBORAH** md. **JAMES BROOKE**. (q. v.)

ii.   **ELIZA** md. **JOHN THOMAS**. (q. v.)

iii. **MARY** b. in 1712, md. **SAMUEL THOMAS**. (q. v.)

SNOWDEN.

SNOWDEN.

Snowden

Mrs. ELIZA (COALE) SNOWDEN d. about 1713, and her husband md. 2d, Dec. 19th, 1717, ELIZABETH, dau. of Samuel and Mary (Hutchins) Thomas, and had further issue by her (who d. in Aug. 1775):

iv.   RICHARD b. in 1719-20, md. ELIZABETH, only dau. of John and Miriam Crowley, and d. s. p. Mch. 18th, 1753.

v.   THOMAS, of whom presently.

vi.   . ANN md. HENRY WRIGHT CRABB, and had issue: RICHARD; ELIZABETH md. Mch. 29th, 1771, WILLIAM, son of Samuel Robertson: JEREMIAH md. ELIZABETH GRIFFITH; RALPH; and JOHN.

vii. MARGARET md. JOHN CONTEE, and had issue: ELIZABETH md. JAMES KEITH, JEAN, RICHARD md. ELIZABETH SANDERS; and ANN md. DENIS MAGRUDER.

viii. SAMUEL b. in 1728. (q. v.)

ix.   ELIZABETH md. JOSEPH COWMAN. (q. v.)

x.   JOHN. (q. v.)

THOMAS, eldest surviving son of Richard and Elizabeth (Thomas) Snowden, b. about 1722. md. before 1744. MARY, dau. of Henry Wright. Henry Wright was b. in England, and sent to America when a boy. An annuity was regularly paid to the gentleman who had charge of his education, and after his death to Henry himself. At his marriage he received a handsome service of silver marked with the letter W. and soon after this event the annuity ceased. Once previously he attempted to discover his parentage, but immediately received a letter through the channel by which his annuity came, notifying him that it would cease unless he desisted from his attempt. He md. a Miss Sprigg, of Prince Georges County, and d. 1750, leaving two daus., Margaret, unmarried; and Mary who md. Thomas Snowden. He d. in May 1770, leaving issue:

i.   HENRY d. s. p. in April 1775.

ii.   RICHARD md. ELIZA, dau. of Thomas and Ann Rutland, and d. leaving an only dau. MARY who was left an orphan at an early age by the death of her mother, and was brought up at her uncle Major Thomas Snowden's residence, "Montpelier." She md. JOHN CHEW THOMAS. (q. v.)

iii.   **THOMAS** b. in 1751, usually known as **Major THOMAS**, presumably from his having seen service in the Revolutionary War. He lived at "Montpelier," which was on the great Northern and Southern Post-road, and entertained great numbers of people who were then continually passing upon it, and in accordance with the hospitable customs of the day, would not hesitate to stop at his residence for the night. Washington himself once spent a night there, and the bed in which he slept is still preserved. **Major SNOWDEN** md. **ANN RIDGELY**, a great heiress, and d. in 1803; his wife on Good Friday of 1834, having had issue:

i.   **RICHARD**, of whom presently.

ii.   **THOMAS** lived at Summerville, and d. unmarried.

iii.   **MARY** md. at "Montpelier," **JOHN C. HERBERT**, of Walnut Grange, Virginia. (q. v.)

iv   **NICHOLAS** b. Oct. 21st, 1786. (q. v.)

v.   **CAROLINE** d. at the age of 8 years.

RICHARD, eldest son of **Major Thomas** and **Ann (Ridgely) Snowden**, who inherited from his parents the estate of "Oakland," md. 1st Feby. 13th, 1798, at "Bushy Park" **ELIZA**, dau. of **Dr. Charles Alexander Warfield**, and was 2dly md. May 18th, 1818, by Rev. Oliver Norris, to **LOUISA VICTORIA WARFIELD**, sister of his first wife, by whom he had no issue. He d. having had issue by his first wife:

i.   **ANN LOUISA** md. **JOHN CONTEE**, who d. having had issue eight daus. now d. and two sons still living; **CHARLES SNOWDEN** md. **BETTY BOLLING**. and **RICHARD** md. **ANNA BOLLING**.

ii.   **THOMAS** b. March 7th, 1802, md. Nov. 30th, 1824, **ANN REBECCA NICHOLLS**, and had issue: **NICHOLAS** d.; **CHARLES A.**, **ELLA** md. Dr. **A. M. SNOWDEN**, (q. v.); **JONATHAN HUDSON** d.; **THOMAS** d.; **SARAH REBECCA** md. **CHARLES MARSHALL**, (q. v.); and **CAROLINE**.

iii.   **CAROLINE ELIZA** md. April 8th, 1828, the Hon. **ALBERT FAIRFAX**. (q. v.)

iv.   **EMILY ROSEVILLE** md. Oct. 21st, 1828, **Col. TIMOTHY P. ANDREWS**, U. S. A. (q. v.)

v.   **CHARLES ALEXANDER** b. April 6th, 1805, d. at "Oakland," in 1823.

vi.   **HARRIET** d. in infancy.

vii.   **RICHARD NICHOLAS** b. at "Oakland," July 19th, 1815, md. at "Longwood," January 1st, 1835, **ELIZABETH RIDGELY**, dau. of Dr. Gustavus Warfield, and d. in California, having had issue: **GUSTAVUS WARFIELD** b. July 27th, 1835; **RICHARD** b. Oct. 13th, 1837; **GEORGE THOMAS** b. Aug. 29th, 1840; **EVAN WARFIELD** b. Nov. 5th, 1842; **MARY THOMAS** b. Oct. 30th, 1844; and **ELIZABETH WARFIELD** b. Sept. 1st, 1849.

NICHOLAS, third son of **Major Thomas** and **Ann** (**Ridgely**) **Snowden,** b. at "Montpelier," Oct. 21st. 1786, md. at Roxbury Mills, Oct. 7th, 1806, **ELIZABETH WARFIELD,** dau. of **Samuel** and **Annie Thomas,** and d. Mch 8th, 1831, at "Montpelier." His wife d. at Avondale, June 16th, 1866, having had issue :

i.   **ANN ELIZABETH** b. at Roxbury Mills, July 31st, 1808, md. at "Montpelier," Sept. 23d, 1828, **FRANCIS M. HALL,** and had issue by him : **FRANCIS** b. in Aug. 1829, md. **EUGENIA CONTEE;** and **ELIZABETH SNOWDEN** b. Jany. 28th, 1831, md. **RICHARD HILL.**
    Mr. **HALL** d. at Collington Meadows, Sept. 3d, 1831, and his widow md. at "Montpelier," Oct. 4th, 1836, **CHARLES HILL,** and d. July 15th, 1847, having had issue by him : **LAURA BROOKE** b. in Aug. 1837 ; **NICHOLAS** b. in 1839 ; **EUGENE** b. in Feby. 1841 ; **AUGUSTINE** b. in Aug. 1842, d. in 1866 ; and **NORMAN** b. in 1847.

ii.   **THOMAS J.** b. at Roxbury, Feby. 12th, 1810, d. at Magnolia, Florida, July 3d, 1835.

iii.   **LOUISA** b. at "Montpelier," June 3d, 1811, md. there June 5th, 1834, **Col. HORACE CAPRON,** and d. at Laurel, Mch. 27th, 1849.

iv.   **JULIANNA MARIA** b. at Laurel, Jany. 28th, 1813, md. at "Montpelier," June 23d, 1835, **Dr. THEODORE JENKINS;** he d. at the same place Dec. 15th, 1866, having had issue : **THEODORE** b. Apl. 19th, 1838, killed at the battle of Cedar Mountain, Aug. 9th, 1862 ; **ELIZABETH SNOWDEN; LOUIS WILLIAM** b. June 16th, 1842 ; **FRANCIS XAVIER** b. Sept. 29th, 1844 ; **MARY ELIZA** b. Nov. 5th, 1846 ; **ANN LOUISA** d. in childhood ; and **ARTHUR** b. in 1852.

v.   **ADELINE** b. at Laurel, Oct. 9th, 1814, md. **W. W. W. BOWIE.** (q. v.)

vi.   **EDWARD** b. at Laurel, Oct. 29th, 1816, md. June 29th, 1841, at "Longwood," **MARY THOMAS,** dau. of Dr. Gustavus Warfield.

vii.   Dr. De **WILTON** b. Aug. 19th, 1818, of whom presently.

viii.   **HENRY** b. Sept. 29th, 1820, at Laurel, md. April 27th, 1847, at Alexandria, Va., **MARY C. COWMAN,** who d. s. p.

ix.   **ELIZA** b. Apl. 8th, 1822, at Laurel, entered the Georgetown Convent in 1847.

x.   **EMILY ROSEVILLE** b. June 24th, 1824, at "Montpelier," md. Apl. 29th, 1845, at Avondale, **CHARLES C. HILL,** and had issue : **ANN ELIZABETH** and **CHARLES,** twins, **ANN** d. July 15th, 1847 ; **IDA, EDWARD; SNOWDEN; EMILY ROSEVILLE; EDITH;** and **ALBERT.**

xi.   **NICHOLAS** b. Apl. 7th, 1828, at "Montpelier," md. May 28th, 1850, at Philadelphia, **HENRIETTA,** dau. of **William** and **Deborah Stabler,** and d. near Harrisonburg, Virginia, June 6th, 1862, having had issue : **EMILY ROSEVILLE** b. Apl. 7th, 1851, md. **GERARD HOPKINS,** (q. v.); **MARION** b. June 28th, 1853, d. Jany. 7th, 1857 ; **LUCY** b. Mch. 13th, 1855; **HELEN** b. Apl. 7th, 1857; **FRANCIS** b. Mch. 19th, 1859; and **MARY** b. June 3d, 1861.

xii.   Dr. **ARTHUR MONTEITH** b. Dec. 30th, 1830, at "Montpelier," md. May 19th, 1857, at Laurel, **ELLA**, dau. of **Thomas** and **Ann Rebecca** (Nicholls) **Snowden**. She d. in Greenbrier County, Va., April 11th, 1858, and her husband md. 2dly June 5th, 1866, **MARY VAUX**, of Northumberland County, Va. He was a Surgeon in the C. S. A., and falling overboard from the Steamer Wenonah on the Chesapeake Bay, was drowned Aug. 28th, 1869.

Dr. De WILTON SNOWDEN, seventh child of **Nicholas** and **Elizabeth** (**Warfield**) Snowden, b. Aug. 19th, 1818, at Laurel, md. March 8th, 1839, at Easton, Md., **EMMA C. CAPRON**, and has had issue: **NICHOLAS** b. Feby. 20th, 1842, at Avondale, d. in Sept. 1849, at Upper Marlboro; **JOHN C.** b. June 29th, 1843, at Bacon Hall, md Oct. 24th, 1867, **MARIA GRIFFITH**; **ELIZABETH THOMAS** b. June 22d, 1844, at Avondale, d. April 29th, 1845, at Laurel; **HENRY** b. June 17th, 1846, at Laurel, d. Aug. 29th, 1846, at the same place; De **WILTON BOWIE** b. June 12th, 1848, in Chesterfield County, Va., md. July 30th, 1873, **ALMIRA HEATH**, and has one child, **STANLEY HEATH** b. July 28th, 1875, d. in July, 1877; **ELIZABETH** b. March 29th, 1851, at Upper Marlboro, and d. there Oct. 29th, 1855; **ARTHUR** b. July 8th, 1853, at the same place, and d. there July 28th, 1853; **AMELIA CHEW** b. May 7th, 1855, at Laurel; **ADELINE** b. May 28th, 1858, at Washington, d. there the same year; **MARY THOMAS** b. Aug. 11th, 1860, at the same place.

SAMUEL, third son of **Richard** and **Elizabeth** (**Thomas**) Snowden, b. Nov. 2d, 1728, md. **ELIZABETH**, dau. of **Philip** and **Ann** (**Chew**) **Thomas**, and d. June 27th, 1801, his wife had d. Jany. 30th, 1790, having had issue:

i.   **RICHARD** md. **HANNAH HOPKINS**.

ii.   **ANN** md. **RICHARD HOPKINS** (q. v.)

iii.   **ELIZABETH** b. in 1732, d. Aug. 25th, 1703.

iv.   **PHILIP**, of whom presently

v.   **MARY** md. **JOSEPH COWMAN**. (q. v.)

vi.   **SAMUEL** b. in 1766. (q. v.)

vii.   **HENRIETTA** md. Oct. 14th, 1804, **GERARD HOPKINS**. (q. v.)

viii.   **SARAH** md. **ELISHA HOPKINS**. (q. v.)

ix.   **JOHN** b. in 1774, d. Jany. 26th, 1799.

PHILIP, second son of **Samuel** and **Elizabeth** (Thomas) **Snowden,** md. Dec. 1st, 1791, **PATIENCE,** dau. of **Joseph Hopkins,** she d. Oct. 16th, 1822, having had issue: **ELIZABETH** b Oct. 8th, 1792, d. Nov. 7th, 1795; **SAMUEL** b. Jany. 13th, 1794, of whom presently; **MARY ANN** b. May 28th, 1796, md. ———— **HUSBANDS,** and d. Aug. 10th, 1824; **JOSEPH HOPKINS** b. April 26th, 1798, d. Oct. 14th, 1801; **RICHARD** b. March 19th, 1800, (q. v.); **ELIZABETH** 2d, b. May 13th, 1802, d. April 24th, 1804; **PHILIP THOMAS** b. June 26th, 1802; **CAROLINE** b. Jany. 4th, 1807; **JOHN P.** b. Feby. 25th, 1809, d. Aug. 20th, 1819; **JAMES** b. Oct. 6th, 1811; **ISAAC** b. Sept. 9th, 1813; and **WILLIAM** b. May 20th, 1815.

SAMUEL, eldest son of **Philip** and **Patience** (Hopkins) **Snowden,** b. Jany. 13th, 1794, md. Jany. 18th, 1822, **MARY RICHARDSON,** and had issue: **JOHN T.** b. Dec. 21st, 1822; **MARCELLUS P.** b. June 16th, 1824; **RICHARD H.** b. Nov. 19th, 1827; **PHILIP M.** b. June 14th, 1831; and **SAMUEL** b. Oct. 13th, 1833.

RICHARD, third son of **Philip** and **Patience** (Hopkins) **Snowden,** b. March 19th, 1800, md. June 17th, 1829, **MARY,** dau. of **Isaac** and **Letitia West,** of Sandy Spring, and had issue: **SARAH AMANDA** b. Dec. 11th, 1829; **ELLEN JANE** b. Aug. 19th, 1831; **HENRY ALLEN** b. Aug. 9th, 1833; and **CHARLES EDWARD** b. Oct. 19th, 1836.

SAMUEL, third son of **Samuel** and **Elizabeth** (Thomas) **Snowden,** b. in 1766, md. Dec. 1st, 1796, **ELIZABETH,** dau. of **John Cowman,** and d. May 26th, 1823, having had issue: **SAMUEL** and **ELIZABETH** twins, b. Oct. 27th, 1797, Samuel d. June 29th, 1798; **JOHN** b. Jany. 25th, 1799, d. Sept. 19th, 1826; **SAMUEL** b. Sept. 13th, 1800, d. s. p.; **RICHARD** b. July 26th, 1802, d. March 26th, 1813; **MARY** b. March 2d, 1804, md. **THOMAS TYSON; MARTHA** b. June 28th, 1810, d. Sept. 1st, 1836; and **REBECCA** and **JOSEPH** twins, b. Dec. 17th, 1814.

JOHN, youngest son of Richard and Elizabeth (Thomas) Snowden, inherited "Birmingham Manor," md. at the age of 40 RACHEL, dau. of Gerard and Mary (Hall) Hopkins, and had issue:

i.   RICHARD PHILIP d. unmarried.

ii. ANNA MARIA b. in 1787, md. JOSEPH R. HOPKINS, and d. Mch. 27th, 1864.

iii. GERARD HOPKINS b. Apl. 27th, 1788, md. and had an only son, JOHN b. Nov. 11th, 1827, d. July 7th, 1828.

iv. JOHN T. d. unmarried Jany. 13th, 1813.

v.   MARGARET md. ———— HOPKINS.

vi. REZIN HAMMOND b. Sept. 8th, 1796, of whom presently.

vii. RACHEL md. Judge JOHN S. TYSON. (q. v.)

REZIN HAMMOND, youngest son of John and Rachel (Hopkins) Snowden, b. Sept. 8th, 1796, inherited "Birmingham," md. Nov. 24th, 1829, MARGARET, dau. of John McFadon, who d. July 30th, 1858, and her husband July 23d, 1866, having had issue:

i.   JOHN b. Nov. 24th, 1830, of whom presently.

ii. WILLIAM b. Apl. 1st, 1833. (q. v.)

iii. RICHARD PHILIP b. Nov. 13th, 1834. d. Nov. 23d, 1863.

iv. ANTOINETTE b. Nov. 2d, 1836.

v.   JULIUS b. May 16th, 1838, d. at Upperville, Va., Dec. 11th, 1855.

vi. HARRY WILSON b. Apl. 12th, 1841, md. Sept. 7th, 1865, SOPHIA, dau. of Rev. T. B. Sargeant, and has had issue: ACHSAH b. Mch. 25th, 1869, d. Mch. 29th, 1869.

vii. MARIA LOUISA b. June 9th, 1843, md. June 30th, 1869, Professor ALFRED M. MAYER, the distinguished scientist, and has had issue: BRANTZ b. June 1st, 1870, d. Dec. 22d, 1871; and JOSEPH HENRY b. Jany. 12th, 1872.

JOHN, eldest son of Rezin H. and Margaret (McFadon) Snowden, b. Nov. 24th, 1830, md. June 16th, 1857, SARAH E., dau. of Basil Hopkins, and d. Aug. 16th, 1872, having had issue: MARGARET b. May 21st, 1858; JOHN b. Jany. 17th, 1860; ELIZABETH HOPKINS b. May 8th, 1861; BASIL HOPKINS b. Jany. 14th, 1863; HARRY FENWICK b. Aug. 30th, 1865, d. Dec. 6th, 1865; HERBERT b. July 3d, 1868; SARAH ENGLISH b. June 28th, 1870, d. Sept. 1st, 1870; and VIRGINIA HOPKINS b. Nov. 20th, 1871, d. July 8th, 1872.

WILLIAM, second son of **Rezin H.** and **Margaret** (**McFadon**) **Snowden**, b. Apl. 1st, 1833, inherited "Birmingham," and resides there. He md. Mch. 29th, 1857, **ADELAIDE**, dau. of **Dr. Gustavus Warfield**, and has had issue: **REZIN HAMMOND** b. May 31st, 1858, d. Nov. 9th, 1863; **GUSTAVUS WARFIELD** b. Mch. 4th, 1862, d. in infancy; **MARY THOMAS** b. June 27th, 1860, d. Nov. 10th, 1863; **JULIUS** b. Nov. 23d, 1863; **WILLIAM** b. Apl. 13th, 1866, d. at the age of 8; **LOUISA VICTORIA** b. Mch. 13th, 1868; **MARIA ANTOINETTE** b. June 3d, 1870; **ADELAIDE WARFIELD** b. June 24th, 1872; **SOPHIA CARROLL** b. Feby. 24th, 1875; and **EUGENIA** b. in 1877.

STABLER.

WILLIAM STABLER, b. in 1767, md. June 4th, 1789, **DEBORAH PLEASANTS**, and d. Jany. 24th, 1806, leaving issue:

i. **THOMAS PLEASANTS** b. Nov. 5th, 1791, of whom presently.

ii. **EDWARD** b. Sept. 26th, 1794. (q. v.)

iii. **JAMES P.** b. Sept. 14th, 1796. (q. v.)

iv. **CALEB BENTLEY** b. Jany. 24th, 1799. (q. v.)

v. **WILLIAM HENRY** b. April 13th, 1802, md. **ELIZA**, second dau. of **William** and **Martha** (**Patrick**) **Thomas**, and has had issue:

    i. **MARTHA** b. Feby. 9th, 1826, md. **THOMAS MOORE REESE**. (q. v.)

    ii. **JOSEPH** b. Jany. 24th, 1827.

    iii. **HENRIETTA** b. Jany. 27th, 1829, md. **NICHOLAS SNOWDEN**. (q. v.)

    iv. **LUCY** b. Sept. 11th, 1830.

    v. **WILLIAM** b. March 16th, 1832.

    vi. **ELLEN** b. Feby. 16th, 1834.

THOMAS PLEASANTS, eldest son of **William** and **Deborah Stabler**, b. Nov. 5th, 1791 md. June 2d, 1813, **ELIZABETH P.** youngest child of **Gerard** and **Margaret** (**Thomas**) **Brooke**, and had issue:

i.   **BROOKE** b. April 25th, 1814.

ii.   **SARAH** b. Jany. 31st, 1816.

iii.   **GEORGE** b. May 18th, 1818, md. Nov. 22d, 1843. **MARY W.** dau. of **Phineas** and **Rachel Paxson**, and has had issue: **ELIZA W.** b Sept. 17th, 1847; and **WILLIAM** b. Aug. 20th, 1849, all now deceased.

iv.   **JOHN** b. April 13th, 1820, md. May 8th, 1851, **ALICE ANN**, dau. of **Joseph E. Bentley**, and has had issue: **FLORENCE** b. June 24th, 1852; **ALICE EVELYN** b. Aug. 14th, 1854; **CORA** b. Oct. 6th, 1856; **ANNA B.** b. Feby. 24th, 1859; **FANNIE** b. Oct. 15th, 1860; **ELIZA BROOKE** b. May 15th, 1863; **JOHN, Jr.** b. Nov. 15th, 1865; and **ALICE BENTLEY** b. Jany. 8th, 1868.

v.   **DEBORAH** b. April 7th, 1822.

vi.   **JAMES** b. May 30th, 1827.

vii.   **HOWARD** b. Aug. 5th, 1829, md. Nov. 25th, 1858, **ESTHER G.** dau. of **James** and **Esther G. Moore**, and d. July 18th, 1876, having had issue: **MILTON** b. Aug. 21st, 1859; **CLARA** b. Nov. 1st, 1861; **LEONARD** b. Aug 17th, 1863; **AUGUSTUS** b. Sept. 18th, 1865; **LOUIS H.** b. May 18th, 1868; and **LILIAN** b. Aug. 26th, 1872.

viii.   **WILLIAM** b. July 11th, 1831, d. Nov. 19th, 1832.

ix.   **WILLIAM HENRY** b. May 6th, 1833.

x.   **DEBORAH** b. June 27th, 1836, md. Nov. 22d, 1864, **SAMUEL M. RUSSELL**, of Burt Creek, Frederick County, Md.

xi.   **THOMAS P. Jr.** b Aug. 30th, 1840.

EDWARD, second son of **William** and **Deborah Stabler**, b. Sept. 26th, 1794, md. **ANN ROBINSON**, third dau. of **Bernard** and **Sarah Gilpin**, and had issue:

i.   **MARGARET** b. Nov. 19th, 1824, md. May 7th, 1846, at her father's residence, **JAMES S.** son of **James S.** and **Amelia Hallowell**, and has had issue: **EDWARD STABLER** d. in childhood; **ANNIE STABLER**; **ALICE**; **JAMES B.**; **FLORENCE**. **JULIA** d. in childhood; and **JULIA** 2d.

ii.   **ALBAN GILPIN** b. May 9th, 1826, md. **JULIA DULANEY BENNETT**, and has no issue.

iii.   **CATHERINE** b. Jany. 20th, 1828.

iv. **SAMUEL JORDAN** b. May 12th, 1830, md. **ALICE FRONK**, and has had issue: **HENRY BROOKE**; **LUCY** d. in childhood; **KATE**; and **MARGARET**.

v. **PHILIP THOMAS** b. Sept. 21st, 1831, md. **CORNELIA NICHOLS**, and has issue: **JENNIE**.

vi. **BERNARD GILPIN** b. Feby. 2d, 1834.

vii. **EDWARD, Jr.** b. March 16th, 1836, md. **ELIZA BUTLER**, and has had issue: **EMILY B.**; **LOUISE**; and **HELEN**, the latter deceased.

viii. **JORDAN** b. Jany. 16th, 1840, md. in 1877, **CAROLINE E. SEMPLE**, of Philadelphia.

ix. **ARTHUR** b. Dec. 25th, 1842, md. **ANNA McFARLAND**.

JAMES PLEASANTS, third son of **William** and **Deborah Stabler**, b. Sept. 14th, 1796, md. 1st Oct. 13th, 1816, **ELIZABETH**, dau. of **Bernard** and **Sarah (Thomas) Gilpin**, who d. Feby. 16th, 1823, having had issue: **PLEASANTS** b. Aug. 4th, 1817; **JOSEPH** b. Nov. 14th, 1818, d. in infancy; **JOSEPH** 2d, b. June 30th, 1820; **DEBORAH** b. Nov. 12th, 1821, d. March 25th, 1822; and **ANN** b. Jany. 26th, 1823, d. in Nov. 1827.

   JAMES P. STABLER md. 2d Jany. 13th, 1830, **SARAH B.** dau. of **Isaac** and **Hannah Briggs**, and d. Feby. 13th, 1840, having had further issue: **FRANCES** b. March 31st, 1831, d. April 6th, 1836; **ELIZABETH G.** b. May 18th, 1834; **FRANCIS D.** b. April 9th, 1837; and **JAMES P. Jr.**, b. June 12th, 1839.

CALEB BENTLEY, fourth son of **William** and **Deborah Stabler**, b. Jany. 24th, 1799, md. Aug. 17th, 1825, **ANN**, dau. of **Thomas** and **Ann Moore**, and has had issue:

i. **CHARLES** b. Oct. 28th, 1826, md. June 16th, 1853, at Mr. Samuel Ellicott's residence, **SARAH E.**, dau. of **Mahlon** and **Elizabeth Kirk**.

ii. **MARY M.** b. June 11th, 1828, md. May 9th, 1848, **WARWICK P. MILLER**, and has had issue: **ANNIE** b. May 4th, 1849; **FREDERICK** b. July 9th, 1850; **ROBERT H.** b. Aug. 29th, 1851; **CORNELIA** b. Dec. 17th, 1854; **ISABEL** b. Sept. 11th, 1856; **CALEB STABLER** b. Feby. 21st, 1859; **WARWICK P., Jr.** b. Oct. 28th, 1860; **BERTHA** b. Feby. 14th, 1863; and **MARY JANET** b. Nov. 18th, 1865.

iii. **ROBERT MOORE** b. Mch. 15th, 1830, md. **HANNAH B. TAILOR**, and has had issue: **CAROLINE T.** b. Oct. 5th, 1860; **CLARKSON T.** b. Mch. 2d, 1862; **ALBERT** b. Aug. 30th, 1863; **MARY M.** b. Feby. 5th, 1865; **ALICE T.** b. Oct. 24th, 1866; **EMMA T.** b. Sept. 18th, 1868; **LYDIA B.** b. Aug. 19th, 1870; and **FLORENCE** b. Nov. 23d, 1873.

iv.   FREDERICK b. Dec. 19th, 1831, md. **MARTHA R. BROOKE**, and has had issue:
       TARLTON BROOKE b. Mch. 26th, 1868; **ROSE MILLER** b. May 18th, 1869; and
       CALEB b. June 14th, 1872.

v.   **WARWICK** b. Nov. 29th, 1833.

vi.   **ASA M.** b. July 2d, 1837, md. **ALBINA OSBORN**, and has had issue: **NEWTON** b.
       Jany. 10th, 1868; **MORTIMER** b. June 10th, 1869; **LLEWELLYN** b. Aug. 20th,
       1872; and **CAROLINE MILLER** b. Mch. 23d, 1874.

vii.   **DEBORAH B.** b. May 3d, 1843.

TALBOT.

RICHARD TALBOT, of Anne Arundel County, Md., d. in 1663, leaving
a wife who afterwards md. **WILLIAM RICHARDSON**, and issue, as
follows:

i.   **RICHARD.**

ii.   **EDWARD** md. Mrs. **ELIZABETH COALE**, widow of Wm. Coale, and dau. of
       Philip Thomas, and d. in Jany. 1692-3, leaving issue by his wife who d. in 1725;
       ELIZABETH who md. a **MACINTOSH**; and **JOHN**, who had issue: Cassandra, Eliza-
       beth, and Lucey.

iii.   **ELIZABETH** md. 1st a **LAWRENCE**, and after his death, md. December 10th, 1686,
       RICHARD GALLOWAY, Sr.

iv.   **JOHN** md. **SARAH** ——, and d. in June, 1707, leaving issue: **ELIZA**, **RICHARD**,
       and **DANIEL**.

TILGHMAN.

Col. **EDWARD TILGHMAN**, of Wye, son of Richard and Anna Maria
    (Lloyd) Tilghman, b. July 3d, 1713, was a member of the Stamp
    Act Congress of 1765, and one of the committee which drew up the

remonstrance presented to Parliament. He md. 1st **ANN**, dau. of **Major William Turbutt**, and had issue: **ANNA MARIA** md. **BENNET CHEW**. (q. v.)

Col. **TILGHMAN** md. 2d, in 1749, **ELIZABETH**, third dau. of Samuel and Mary Chew, and had further issue:

i. **RICHARD**.

ii. **EDWARD** b. Feby. 11th, 1750-1, an eminent lawyer of Philadelphia, md. in 1778, **ELIZA-BETH**, dau. of Chief Justice Chew, and d. Nov. 1st, 1815, having had issue: **EDWARD** b. Feby. 27th, 1779, md. **REBECCA WALN**, and had issue: Edward, Rebecca, Elizabeth, Ann, and Jane; **BENJAMIN** b. Jany. 1st, 1785, md. **ANNA MARIA McMURTREE**, and had issue: Edward, William M., Benjamin, Richard, Maria, Elizabeth, and Ann; **ELIZABETH** md. **WILLIAM COOKE**; and **MARY** md. **WILLIAM RAWLE**, and had issue: William Brooke, and Elizabeth.

iii. **BENJAMIN**.

iv. **ELIZABETH** md. **RICHARD TILGHMAN**, and had issue: **RICHARD EDWARD**.

v. **ANNA MARIA** md. 1st **CHARLES GOLDSBOROUGH**, and had issue: **CHARLES** b. July 15th, 1765, Governor of Maryland in 1818; and **WILLIAM TILGHMAN** b. in Dec. 1766, d. s. p.

Mrs. **ANNA MARIA GOLDSBOROUGH** md. 2d, Rt. Rev. **ROBERT SMITH**, first Protestant Episcopal Bishop of South Carolina, and had further issue: **ROBERT** and **WILLIAM**.

Col. **EDWARD TILGHMAN** md. 3d in 1759 **JULIANNA CARROLL**, and d. Oct. 9th, 1785, having had further issue: **MATTHEW**, **BENJAMIN**, **MARY**, and **SUSANNA**.

TODHUNTER.

JOSEPH TODHUNTER, md. **ELIZA ONION**, and had issue: **MARY ANN** md. **SAMUEL ELLICOTT**, (q. v.); **ELIZA** md. **EVAN PHILIP THOMAS**, (q. v.); **KATE** md. **JONATHAN THOMPSON** of N. Y., and has issue: **LILLY**; **MINNIE** md. **WILLIAM WESTCOTT**; and **JOSEPH**; **EDMONDSON** md. **EMMA FRANCES KEYWORTH**, and has had issue: **JOSEPH** d. in infancy; **MARY G.**; **STEPHEN** and **ROBERT**; **JOSEPH** d. s. p.; **CHARLES**; **WILLIAM**; **ALISON** md. —— **CLEVELAND**; and three children who d. in childhood or infancy.

TYSON.

RYNER TYSON, of Germany, being converted to the doctrines of Friends, by William Penn, emigrated to Pennsylvania with him. He had issue: **MATTHIAS,** of whom presently; **JOHN, PETER, ABRAHAM, DERRICK, HENRY, ISAAC, ELIZA** and **SARAH.**

MATTHIAS, eldest son of **Ryner Tyson,** had issue: **RYNER; ISAAC,** of whom presently; **JESSE;** and **ELIZABETH.**

ISAAC, second son of **Matthias Tyson,** md. **ESTHER SHOEMAKER,** who d. Sept. 8th, 1796. Her husband pre-deceased her, having had issue: **ENEAS; ELISHA** b. Feby. 8th, 1750, of whom presently: **DOROTHY; ELIZABETH; NATHAN; JACOB; SARAH** md. **ISRAEL KNIGHT,** (q. v.); **GEORGE; JESSE,** (q. v.); and **TACY.**

ELISHA, second son of **Isaac** and **Esther (Shoemaker) Tyson,** b. Feby. 8th, 1750, removed to Baltimore, md. 1st, Nov. 5th, 1776, **MARY,** dau. of **William** and **Hannah Amos,** who d. in 1811, and 2d, Oct. 22d, 1814, **MARGARET COWMAN,** by whom he had no issue. He d. Feby. 16th, 1824, having had issue by his first wife:

i.   **ISAAC** b. Oct. 10th, 1777, of whom presently.

ii.   **ESTHER** b. Feby. 23d, 1779, d. in childhood.

iii.   **LUCRETIA** b. Jany. 9th, 1780, md. **JOHN W. WILSON,** and had issue: **ELISHA T.** b. March 14th, 1801, d. Sept. 1st, 1804, **ISAAC** b. July 2d, 1802; and **WILLIAM** b. April 9th, 1805.

v.   **WILLIAM** b. Oct. 2d, 1782, md. **ELIZA,** dau. of **Jonathan** and **Sarah Ellicott,** and had issue: **SARAH E.** b. Sept. 10th, 1804, md. **LLOYD NORRIS; JONATHAN** b. May 4th, 1806; **WILLIAM; SAMUEL; CHARLES; MARY ELIZABETH EDWARD; JANE MARTHA NATHANIEL;** and **LETITIA.**

v.   **MARY** b. Sept. 4th, 1785, md. **ENOCH CLAPP.**

vi.   **NATHAN** b. Nov. 4th, 1787. (q. v.)

vii.   **JAMES** b. Mch. 4th, 1790, d. in childhood.

viii.   **SARAH** b. Aug. 19th, 1791, d. in childhood.

ix.   **ELISHA** b. Jany. 28th, 1796, md. **SARAH S. MORRIS.**

x.   **DEBORAH** b. March 12th, 1798, d. May 12th, 1801.

ISAAC, eldest son of **Elisha** and **Mary** (**Amos**) **Tyson**, b. Oct. 10th, 1777, at Jericho, in Harford County, Md., md. 1st, Nov. 8th, 1797, at Sandy Spring Meeting House in Montgomery Co., Md., **ELIZABETH**, dau. of **Evan** and **Rachel Thomas**, who d. May 12th, 1812, having had issue:

i.   **PHILIP THOMAS** b. June 23d, 1799, Geologist of the State of Maryland, md. Jany. 8th, 1824, **REBECCA WEBSTER.**

ii.   **DEBORAH** b. May 12th, 1801, md. Nov. 15th, 1825, **CHARLES ELLIS**, of Philadelphia, and d. May 9th, 1828, leaving issue: **EVAN T.** b. Aug. 10th, 1826; and **DEBORAH T.** b. Feby. 19th, 1828. **CHARLES ELLIS** md. 2d, **MARY**, dau. of Luke and Ann Morris, and d. leaving issue by her: **NANCY M.** md. **WM. M. ELLICOTT**, Jr. (q. v.)

iii.   **MARY** b. Aug. 8th, 1803.

iv.   **EVAN THOMAS** b. Nov. 8th, 1805, d. March 31st, 1826.

v.   **RACHEL THOMAS** b. Nov. 9th, 1807, md. Oct. 14th, 1855, **JOHN JACKSON**, of Philadelphia, who d. April 14th, 1855, leaving issue: **HENRIETTA** md. **ERNEST TURNER**; **WARNER**; and **LYDIA.**

vi.   **HENRIETTA THOMAS** b. Nov. 12th, 1809, md. June 7th, 1838, **JOHN SAURIN NORRIS**, and d. Feby. 27th, 1871, leaving issue: **ISAAC TYSON**; **JOHN OLNEY**; **MARY** md. **GEORGE PERRY**, who has since deceased, leaving one child, **Henrietta**; and **HENRIETTA.**

ISAAC TYSON md. 2d, in 1815, **PATIENCE MARSHALL**, and d. Jany. 30th, 1864, without further issue.

NATHAN, third son of **Elisha** and **Mary** (**Amos**) **Tyson**, b. Nov. 4th, 1787, md. Sept. 27th, 1815, **MARTHA**, dau. of **George** and **Eliza Ellicott**, and d. shortly after celebrating the Golden Anniversary of their wedding day. His wife d. a few years afterwards leaving issue:

20

i.   **JAMES ELLICOTT** b. Aug. 21st, 1816, md. **HARRIET JOLLIFFE**, who d. having had issue: **FRANK; ELIZABETH**, and **MARTHA** d. in childhood.

ii.   **ELIZABETH BROOKE** b. Mch. 30th, 1818, md. **JOHN M. SMITH**, and has issue: **GILBERT**, a widower with one child; **THOMAS** md. in 1877 **HELEN PARRY**; and **MARTHA** md. in 1877 **SAMUEL HOPKINS**. (q. v.)

iii.   **HENRY** b. Nov. 18th, 1820, md. **MARY GILLINGHAM**, and d. Sept. 1st, 1877, leaving issue: **NANNIE, ALICE; MADGE; ESTELLE**, and **BEATRIX**.

iv.   **ISABELLA** b. Mch. 17th, 1823.

v.   **ANNA** b. Feby. 26th, 1825, md. —— **KIRK**.

vi.   **MARY** b. Aug. 11th, 1826, d. in the same year.

vii.   **ROBERT** md. 1st, **JANE GAMBRILL**, and after her death 2d, **SARAH SMITH**.

viii.   **LUCY**.

ix.   **FREDERICK**.

JESSE, sixth son of **Isaac** and **Esther** (Shoemaker) **Tyson**, md. 1st April 1st, 1790, **MARGARET**, dau. of John and Elizabeth Hopkins, who d. June 20th, 1804, having had issue:

i.   **ESTHER** b. March 22d, 1796, d. Aug. 19th, 1797.

ii.   **JOHN SHOEMAKER** b. Nov. 7th, 1797, md. **RACHEL**, dau. of John and Rachel Snowden, and d. leaving issue a son, **JOHN S.** who md. **MARY ROBERTS**; and several daughters.

iii.   **MARGARET** b. July 4th, 1802.

iv.   **ANNA** b. May 10th, 1804.

JESSE TYSON md. 2d. May 22d, 1806, **SARAH**, dau. of Henry and Ann Ridgely.

VANDERHEYDEN, FRISBY, RANDOLPH.

MATTHIAS VANDERHEYDEN, of New York, md. ANNA MARGA-
RETTA, dau. of Col. Augustine Hermann, of Bohemia Manor, Md.,
to which place he removed after his marriage. They had issue several
sons, all of whom d. s. p., and the following daughters:

i.   JANE md. —— COUTS, of Scotland, and had issue: JAMES.

ii. FRANCINA md. 1st, EDWARD SHIPPEN, of Philadelphia, and had a dau. MARGARET
     md. JOHN JEKYLL, of Boston. Mrs. SHIPPEN md. 2d, Col. HYNSON, of
     Chestertown, Md.

iii. AUGUSTINA b. in 1685, md. JAMES HARRIS, and d. in 1775, leaving issue:
     MATTHIAS.

iv. ARIANA b. in 1690, md. 1st, Feby. 9th, 1712-13, JAMES FRISBY.

JAMES and ARIANA (Vanderheyden) FRISBY had issue:

i.   SARAH b. Dec. 7th, 1714, md. Sept. 9th, 1730, JOHN BRICE, and had issue: ARIANA
     b. June 19th, 1732, md. Sept. 4th, 1750, Dr. DAVID ROSS; SARAH b. June 3d,
     1735, md. in 1761 JOHN HENDERSON; JOHN b. Sept. 22d, 1738; ANN b. in
     1744; JAMES b. in 1746; BENEDICT b. in 1749; EDMUND b. in 1751; and
     ELIZABETH b. in 1757, md. 1st, LLOYD, and 2d, WALTER, DULANY.

ii. ARIANA MARGARET b. Sept. 18th, 1717, md. WILLIAM HARRIS, and had a son
     JAMES, d. s. p.

iii. FRANCINA AUGUSTINA b. Aug. 16th, 1719, md. 1st, in 1738, WILLIAM STEVEN-
     SON, and had a son WILLIAM; and 2d, Dr. DANIEL CHESTON. (q. v.)

Mrs. ARIANA FRISBY md. 2d, THOMAS BORDLEY, (q. v.), and
3d, in Nov. 1728, EDMUND JENINGS, of Annapolis, where they
resided until 1737, when they removed to England. Mrs. JENINGS
having been inoculated for the small-pox died of that disease in Apl.
1741, having had issue by her third husband: EDMUND b. in 1731, d.
in 1819; and ARIANA md. JOHN, son of Sir John Randolph, Knt., (of
whom presently.) He was Attorney General of Virginia, and d. in
1784 at London, having removed to England at the breaking out of
the Revolutionary War, being a prominent loyalist.

JOHN and ARIANA (Jenings) RANDOLPH had issue:

i. EDMUND, of whom presently.

ii. SUSAN BEVERLY md. Major GRIMES.

iii. ARIANA JENINGS md. Capt. JAMES WORMELEY, and had issue with others:
RALPH RANDOLPH b. Oct. 29th, 1785, a Rear Admiral in the English Navy, who
d. June 26th, 1852, at Utica, N. Y., leaving issue:

    i. Mary Elizabeth b. in London, July 26th, 1822, is a well-known novelist, Authoress of
"Forest Hill," "Annabel," "Our Cousin Veronica," and numerous Magazine
articles; md. Randolph Latimer, of Baltimore, and is now resident at Newport, R. I.

    ii. Katherine Prescott b. Jany. 14th, 1830.

EDMUND, only son of John and Ariana (Jenings) Randolph, b. Aug.
10th, 1753, espoused the side of the Colonies in the Revolution;
appointed by Washington his Aide Aug. 15th, 1775; Attorney General
of Virginia in 1776; elected a delegate to Congress in 1779, and took
an active part in its proceedings until 1782; was Governor of the State
of Virginia from 1786 to 1788; a member of the Convention that
formed the Federal Constitution in 1787, opposed that instrument as then
proposed, but magnanimously gave it his support after its adoption, and
when it was submitted to the Virginia Convention voted in its favor;
was Attorney General of the United States 1789-90, and Secretary of
State in Washington's Cabinet 1794-5. He md. Aug. 29th, 1776,
ELIZABETH, dau. of Robert Carter Nicholas, and d. Sept. 13th,
1813, leaving issue: LUCY; PEYTON; EDMONIA; and SUSAN BEVERLY.

WALKER.

THOMAS WALKER, of the town of Leeds, in England, came to New
York about the year 1790, and settled at West Farms; the family
seat being now incorporated in New York City limits. He had two
sons: THOMAS E. of whom presently; and JOHN J. md. RACHEL, dau.
of Philip E. and Eliza Thomas, and d. leaving an only son, EVAN PHILIP
WALKER.

THOMAS E. son of **Thomas Walker**, was a merchant of New York City, md. in 1826, **ANN,** dau. of **Philip E.** and **Eliza Thomas,** and had issue:

i.   **PHILIP EVAN THOMAS** Attorney-at-Law, b. in 1828, d. in 1854.

ii.   **ALBERT** b. in 1829, d. in infancy.

iii.   . **ELIZABETH ANN** b. in 1830, md. in 1859, **DAVID TWEEDIE,** of Glasgow, Scotland, and has issue: **THOMAS E. W.** b. in 1860; **ANNE** b. in 1862; **M. STANLEY** b. in 1864; and **MARY** b. in 1869.

iv.   **THOMAS GEORGE** b. in 1832, a merchant by profession, md. 1st, in October 1860, **LUCY BOWMAN HOLBROOK.** a descendant of Nathaniel Bowman, who came from England about 1630, and was one of the original settlers of Watertown, Mass. She d. in 1871, having had issue: **HOLBROOK** b. in 1861. d. in March 1862; **ARTHUR LUCIAN** b. in 1863; **MARION** b. in 1866; and **LOUIS BOWMAN** b. in 1869. After the death of his first wife, **THOMAS G. WALKER** md. 2d in April 1873, her cousin **LOUISE JONES BOWMAN,** and has further issue: **LUCY** b. in 1874.

v.   **WILLIAM GEORGE** b. in 1834, d. in infancy.

vi.   **WILLIAM THOMAS** b. in 1836, d. in infancy.

vii.   **GEORGE EDMONDSON** b. in 1837, an Attorney-at-Law, md. in 1866, **JANET E.** dau. of the **Hon. James W. White,** one of the Justices of the Superior Court of New York City, and his wife **Rhoda E. Waterman,** a grand-daughter of Gen. Joshua Whitney, the founder of Binghampton, New York, and has issue: **GERALD GRIFFIN** b. in 1869; **KATHRIN ANN** b. in 1870; and **CECIL THOMAS** b. in 1872.

viii.   **LEWIN WETHERED** b. in 1839, md. in 1876, **SOPHIE LIEBENAU.**

ix.   **HARRIET** b. in 1842, d. in infancy.

x.   A son b. in 1846, d. unnamed.

WARFIELD.

Dr. Charles Alexander Warfield was b. Dec. 14th, 1751, at "Bushy Park," in the upper part of what was then Anne Arundel County, where he resided until his death. He was graduated at the University of Pennsylvania, and was one of the originators of the Medical School of the University of

Maryland. He had a very large practice, extending over several of the Counties. In early life he was a prominent member of the "Whig Club," and on hearing of the arrival of the "Peggy Stewart" at Annapolis loaded with tea, went with the Club to that town, determined to destroy the vessel and its cargo. Samuel Chase, the Signer of the Constitution, who had been employed by Mr. Anthony Stewart, the owner of the vessel, as his lawyer, met them opposite the State House, and attempted to divert them from their purpose. Finding that his speech was having some effect upon them, Dr. Warfield interrupted him, pronouncing it submission and cowardice in the Club to hesitate, and called on them to follow him to the vessel. It is said that Mr. Stewart was compelled to kindle the torch which Dr. Warfield carried, and to set fire to his vessel by threats of hanging him if he refused. This act had an extensive influence in deciding the course Maryland took in the Revolution.

Dr. **WARFIELD** md. Nov. 21st, 1771, **ELIZA**, dau. of **Major Henry Ridgely**, and d. Jany. 29th, 1813, having had issue:

ANNA who md. **SAMUEL THOMAS.** (q. v.)

HENRY RIDGELY b. Sept. 14th, 1774, d. at Frederick, Md., in March 1839, unmarried.

iii. **HARRIET** d. in infancy.

iv. Dr. **PEREGRINE** b. Feby. 8th, 1779, md. May 13th, 1806, **HARRIET SAPPINGTON**, and d. s. p. July 24th, 1856. His wife d. the 27th July of the same year.

v. **ELIZA** md. **RICHARD SNOWDEN**, of "Oakland." (q. v.)

vi. Dr. **GUSTAVUS**, of whom presently.

vii. **CHARLES ALEXANDER** b. Nov. 1st, 1787, md. Feby. 25th, 1812, **ELIZA HARRIS**, and had issue: SALLIE b. Nov. 30th, 1812, d. at Sykesville, Md., April 12th, 1817; CHARLES ALEXANDER b. Feby. 15th, 1815, killed in the C. S. A. during the Civil War; EDWARD HARRIS b. Nov. 10th, 1817; PEREGRINE b. in 1819, and HENRY b. in 1821, all now dead.

viii. **LOUISA VICTORIA** md. her Brother-in-law **RICHARD SNOWDEN**, of "Oakland" (q. v.)

Dr. **GUSTAVUS**, sixth child of **Dr. Charles Alexander Warfield**, was b. March 31st, 1784, md. Oct. 27th, 1810, at "Whitby Hall," to **MARY**, dau. of **Evan W. Thomas**, by the venerable Bishop White of Pennsylvania. Dr. Gustavus Warfield was an eminent Physician, and actively engaged in practice for nearly sixty years. He d. having had issue:

i.   CHARLES ALEXANDER b. at "Whitby Hall," and d. there, aged 11 years.

ii.   MARTHA ANN b. at "Bushy Park," md. there Dr. WILLIAM G. KNOWLES. (q. v.)

iii. ELIZABETH RIDGELY b. at "Bushy Park," md. RICHARD NICHOLAS, son of
      Richard Snowden, of Oakland. (q. v.)

iv.   MARY THOMAS b. at "Bushy Park," md. EDWARD P. SNOWDEN. (q. v.)

v.   EMMA WARFIELD b. at "Longwood Cottage" after Dr. Warfield's house was burnt, md.
      June 11th, 1846, at "Longwood," Rev. Dr. THOMAS J. SHEPHERD, Pastor of the
      First Presbyterian Church, Philadelphia.

vi.   LOUISA VICTORIA b. at "Longwood," which was re-built in 1821, and resides there with
      her mother.

vii. Dr. EVAN WILLIAM b. May 25th, 1825, at "Longwood," md. Nov. 9th, 1848, SALLIE ANN
      WARFIELD, and had issue: GUSTAVUS b. Nov. 24th, 1849; OLIVIA GRIFFITH b.
      Jany. 14th, 1852; LOUISA VICTORIA b. May 11th, 1853; MARY THOMAS b. June
      13th, 1855; CHARLES DORSEY b. Feby. 24th, 1858, d. June 30th, 1858; EVAN
      WILLIAM b. Apl. 12th, 1859; CHARLES DORSEY b. Dec. 29th, 1860; and CLARA
      b. Sept. 3d, 1863, d. in 1867.

viii. GUSTAVUS d. in infancy.

ix.   EUGENIA GRAY md. Nov. 25th, 1858, Dr. WILLIAM HENRY STINSON, of Balti-
      more, who d. at "Falling Water," his country seat, Dec. 19th, 1864, leaving issue: MARY
      WARFIELD; WILLIAM HENRY b. Jany. 19th, 1862, and ISABELLA WARFIELD.

x.   ISABELLA md. May 17th, 1853, at "Longwood," CHARLES DORSEY WARFIELD,
      and has issue: CHARLES ALEXANDER b. Apl. 27th, 1854; GUSTAVUS b. Dec.
      13th, 1855; MARY EMMA b. Sept. 27th, 1857; HENRY RIDGELY b. Sept. 12th,
      1859; EUGENIA GRAY b. Aug. 4th, 1861; PEREGRINE b. Jany. 15th, 1864;
      HARRY RIDGELY b. Nov. 8th, 1869; and ARTHUR b. Oct. 3d, 1871.

xi.   ADELAIDE md. WILLIAM, son of Rezin H. Snowden, of "Birmingham." (q. v.)

xii. GUSTAVUS d. in infancy.

ARMS FROM AN ILLUMINATED PEDIGREE.

WETHERED.

The genealogy of this family extends directly back to A. D. 1400, and indirectly several centuries further; their grant of arms was the third issued by the Herald's College, dating about A. D. 1523. They claim descent from a Withred, who was King of the Saxons of Kent from A. D. 686 to 725, and this claim is made probable by the fact that the monarch's court was held at the old castle of Berkhampstead, which adjoins land for centuries in the possession of the Wethered family. One of the name was Archbishop of York A. D. 700, and is noted as the first who gave written charters; and another was Archbishop of the same See A. D. 1225.

We begin the pedigree with **JAMES WETHERED**, of Ashlyns, in Hertfordshire, whose son **JOHN** had issue with others, a son **JOHN**, who had issue: James, of whom presently: Agnes md. in 1542 Saunder Abery; and Sisley md. in 1545 George Evely.

JAMES, only son of **John Wethered**, md. **ALICE** ———, and had issue: MARGARET b. in 1539: JONE b. in 1541, d. in infancy: EDMUND b. in 1542: JONE b. in 1545, d. in 1557: and FRANCIS b. in 1547, was a member of Parliament in 1619, md. in 1571 AGNES ———, and had issue, a son FRANCIS, of whom presently.

FRANCIS, son of Francis and Agnes Wethered, md. MARGARET BARGELAW, and d. in 1667. leaving issue surviving:

i. ELIZABETH b. in 1660 md. HENRY GUY, of Tring. M. P., who was a Groom of the Chamber, and Clerk of the Treasury; and had issue: HENRY; and ELIZABETH md. Sir ANDERSON de PENDELEY, Knt. of the Papal Order of the Golden Spur.

ii. THOMAS b. in 1666, md. in 1626 ELIZABETH ——, and d. in 1671, having had issue: FRANCIS d. s. p.; and SAMUEL, who was a Colonel in the Army, and left three sons: Thomas, who sold the family estate to Lord Tankerville, and d. in Italy; William; and Samuel, who engaged in mercantile business in London, and became quite wealthy. Unfortunately becoming interested in the South Sea Bubble, he lost all his fortune, and it is said died of mortification consequent on his failure, in 1719. He had md. Dolly, eldest dau. of Sir William and Lady Susanna Lewin. (q. v.) and had issue: Samuel, of whom presently; Lewin, Governor of Cape Coast Castle, Africa; George; Richard, (q. v.); Henry, lost at sea; Sarah; and Mary.

In 1720 Mrs. Dolly (Lewin) Wethered removed to America, and settled at Jamaica Plains, near Boston, New England, taking with her, her children Samuel, Richard, Henry, Sarah, and Mary. She removed to Maryland on the information of her son Richard, who wrote his mother that the people there were much more like their friends in England, than the New Englanders, and the climate far more genial.

SAMUEL, eldest son of Samuel and Dolly (Lewin) Wethered, returned to England, md. —— THORNTON, and had issue: WILLIAM, of whom presently; SAMUEL a Colonel in the Army; JOHN; THOMAS; SARAH md. —— LAW, Army Commissary at Fort Cumberland, in America; CATHERINE md. Capt. DIXON, of the British Army; and DOLLY md. Sir ARTHUR LOFTUS.

WILLIAM, eldest son of Samuel and —— (Thornton) Wethered, was a Colonel in the Army, and one of the officers in Braddock's ill-fated expedition against Fort Duquesne. He md. —— COCHRANE, and had issue: SAMUEL and WILLIAM both in the British Navy, and lost at sea in the Rockingham; THOMAS, Commissary General of the Army, md. —— KIRWIN, and had issue: THOMAS, a Surgeon in the Army, and HENRIETTA md. Dr. BERNARD DUFFY; and MARY.

RICHARD, fourth son of Samuel and Dolly (Lewin) Wethered, md. ISABELLA, dau. of Col. William and Isabella (Pearce) Blay, of Blay's Range, Kent County, Md., and had issue:

n

i.   **WILLIAM** removed to Virginia, md. ———— **HURT**, and had a son, **PEREGRINE** md. ———— **TURPIN**, and had a son **Turpin**.

ii.   **JOHN** d. in childhood.

iii.   **SAMUEL.**

iv.   **JOHN** md. **MARY**, dau. of Judge J. **Sykes**, of Delaware, and had issue

    i.   **PEREGRINE**, of whom presently.

    ii.   **SAMUEL** md. **ELIZA**, dau. of Col. George **Yeates**, of Kent Co., and had issue: John D.; George Yeates md. Ann Irwin Matilda; Lewina; Elizabeth, Sarah; and Samuel md. Elizabeth Evans, and had issue: George, Mary, Eliza and Hugh

    iii.   **LEWIN** b. Feby. 17th, 1787. (q. v.)

    iv.   **MARY.**

    v.   **SARAH ISABELLA.**

    vi.   **ANN CATHERINE** md. **ROBERT C. LUDLOW**, U. S. N. (q. v.)

    vii.   **CATHERINE MATILDA** md. **GEORGE JEFFRIES**, who changed his name to "**JAFFREY**," and had issue: Matilda d. in 1850; and Mary md. Capt. H. Field, U. S. A.

    viii.   **HARRIET C.** md. Admiral **WILLIAM B. SHUBRICK**, U. S. N., and had issue Mary md. Dr. George Clymer, Surgeon U. S. N., and had a dau. Mary W. B. Shubrick; and Harriet d. in 1850.

    ix.   **CAROLINE.**

PEREGRINE, eldest son of **John** and **Mary** (**Sykes**) **Wethered**, md. **HANNAH MEDFORD**, and d. in 1857, having had issue:

i.   **JOHN LATHAM** md. Jany. 16th, 1862, **CHARLOTTE**, dau. of George and Margaretta (Ringgold) Spencer, and had issue: **MARGARETTA SPENCER**; **MARY ELIZABETH** and **JOHN LATHAM.**

ii.   **MARY ELIZABETH** md. **WILLIAM JANVIER**, who d. April 26th, 1876, having had issue: **WILLIAM, JOHN WETHERED**, and **MARY C.**

LEWIN, third son of **John** and **Mary** (**Sykes**) **Wethered**, b. Feby. 17th, 1787, md. **ELIZABETH**, dau. of Elias and Mary (Thomas) Ellicott, and had issue:

i. PEREGRINE b. Aug. 10th, 1806, md. LOUISA MARIA, dau. of Lambert and Alethea (Ireland) Wickes, and had issue: LEWIN; and ANN ELIZABETH md. June 2d, 1857, WILLIAM NICOLS EARLE WICKES, and had issue: Louisa Maria and William N. E. d. in infancy, and Lewin Wethered.

ii. CHARLES ELIAS b. Nov. 7th, 1807, ISABELLA BATHURST, and had issue: CHARLES b. in 1837, d. in 1840.

iii. JOHN b. May 8th 1809, member of Congress, md. in 1835. MARY, dau. of Philip E. Thomas. In 1844 Professor Samuel F. B. Morse perfected his invention of the Electric Telegraph, and a line of wire was laid between Washington and Baltimore. Mr. Wethered was then in Congress, and present when Morse announcing that the circuit was completed, and the line ready for messages, asked "who shall have the honor of sending the first message?" Some one suggested the President (Tyler;) cries of no! no! showed his unpopularity; and the Professor smiling, repeated "Well then, gentlemen, who shall it be?" A gentleman said "Mrs. Dolly Madison, President Madison's widow;" this met the approval of all present, and Mrs. Madison was sent for. When she came, she asked "what is it you wish me to do, gentlemen?" Some one replied, "to send a message to Baltimore and get a reply in a few minutes." After expressing her disbelief and wonder at this statement, Mrs. Madison selected Mrs. Wethered as her friend in Baltimore, and sent the message, a fac-simile of which appears among the Addenda of this book, and which was the first ever sent by Telegraph.

iv. SAMUEL b. Feby. 22d, 1811.

v. MARY LEWIN b. Dec. 2d, 1812, md. WILLIAM G. THOMAS. (q. v.)

vi. ANN POULTNEY b. Nov. 26th, 1814, md. HENRY CARVILL, and had issue: MARY and JOHN.

vii. LEWIN b. May 8th, 1819, d. March 11th, 1826.

viii. ELIZABETH b. Feby. 2d, 1822, md. Hon. D. N. BARRINGER, who was Minister at the Court of Spain in 1850, and d. leaving issue: LEWIN; ELIZABETH; PAUL; MOREAU; and SAMUEL.

ix. JAMES SYKES md. MARY WOODWORTH, and has had issue: LEWINA; CAROLINE; MARY, and WOODWORTH.

WILLSON.

HENRY WILLSON, of Baltimore County, had issue:

i.   **HENRY** b. June 19th, 1747, of whom presently.

ii.   **PRISCILLA** b. Oct. 29th, 1749, md. Nov. 7th, 1769, **JOHN WORTHINGTON.**

iii. **RACHEL** b. Nov. 9th, 1751, md. **SAMUEL HARRIS.** (q. v.)

iv.   **ELIZABETH** b. March 13th, 1754.

HENRY, only son of Henry Willson, b. June 19th, 1747, md. Jany. 3d, 1771, **MARGARET,** dau. of William and Margaret Harris, and had issue: **HENRY** md. **ANTOINETTE POUJARD; WILLIAM; SAMUEL; PRISCILLA** md. **JOHN McFADON; MARGARET** md. **ROBERT ANDREWS; RICHARD; JOHN; THOMAS; GERARD;** and **ELIZABETH** md. ———— **WILLSON.**

ADDENDA AND CORRIGENDA.

Facsimile of the First Telegram.

" Message from Mrs. Madison.   She sends her love to Mrs. Wethered."

M   E   S   S   A   G

F   R   O   M   M

R   S   M   A   D   I

S   O   N   S   H   E   S   E

N   D   S   H   E   R   L

O   V   E   T   O   M   R

S   W   E   T   H   E   R

E   D

Marriage Certificate of Philip Thomas and Ann Chew.

MARYLAND, ss :

Whereas Philip Thomas of Ann Arundel County & Ann Chew the Daughter of Samuel Chew. Having Publickly declared their Intentions of marriage with each other at two monthly meetings of the People called Quakers and after due Deliberation no just Impediment to the accomplishment of the same being found it was approved of by the said meetings and they left to their Libertie to appoint Time and Place convenient for the Consummation thereof.

These are therefore to Certifie that on the Eleventh Day of the Sixth month called August Anno Dom 1724 at the House of the sd. Samuel Chew. The said Philip Thomas & Ann Chew appeared in a Publick and open assembly of the said People and others mett Together chiefly for the end and Purpose aforesaid and did then & there Solemnly Declare that they took each other in marriage in the Presence of Almighty God & before that Assembly with mutual promises to be unto each other Faithful & Loveing until Death

In testimony whereof the said Philip & Ann have hereunto subscribed their names as Husband & Wife (She according to the custom of marriage assuming the name of her Husband) and, we who were Present at the said Declaration of Marriage & Subscription have hereunto Set our names the Day and year aforesaid.

P THOMAS
ANN THOMAS

Sam¹ Chew Jr
Mary Chew
Mary Thomas
Samuel Thomas Jr
John Thomas
Eliz Snowden
Mary Galloway
Nath⁰ Chew
Sar⁰ Richardson

Samuel Harrison
Eliz⁰ Bond
John Chew
Eliz⁰ Holland
Samuel Chew
Ann Thomas
Sarah Lock
Marg¹ Birkhead
Tho. Smith
Ann Chew
Rich⁰ Galloway
Ab⁰ Richardson

Samuel Chew
of Maidstone
Jno Galloway
Marg¹ Richardson
Joseph Richardson
Richard Richardson
Daniel Richardson
Eliz⁰ Smith
Priscilla Johns
Richard Johns
Kensey Johns
Hen. Childs
Peter Sharp
Rob¹ Roberts

Gerrard Hopkins
Eliz⁰ Johns
Sarah Hall
Mary Hall
Sarah Harrison
Mary Chew
Dorothy Brooke
Ann Chew
Sarah Bond
Abra. Johns
Ann Rawlings
Sarah Gover
Elizabeth Birc-
head

Elizabeath
Robeartson
Sarah Robeartson
Rebekah Rich'son
Marg¹ Hopkins
Sarah Richardson
Mary Hall
Mary Richardson

Will of Philip Thomas.

Addressed "For Mother Thomas at heer hous on ye Poynt."

In ye name of God Amen + I Phillip Thomas of ye County of Anna-
rundell In ye provence of Maryland being weake in body but of sound
& perfect memory & being made sensible of ye unccertainty of this mortall
Life & ye sertainty of Deat have Thought convenant to will & bequeath
of my worldly Istate as folloeth in this my last will & testament

Irs.   I Bequeath my soull to my Redeemer & my Body to the dust
       from whence it came

Irs.   I will & bequeath unto my two Sonns Philip Thomas And Sam^{ll}
       Thomas five hundred acars of land lying att ye Clefts in Calvert
       County in ye foresaid Province of Maryland caled Beakely & ye
       same to bee equallie divided betwene them or to bee sold by
       them as my said suns shall think fitt

Irs.   I will & bequeath unto my beloved & faithful wife Sarah Thomas
       all ye poynt of Land called fullers-poynt being one hundred &
       twenty acars & lying in The County of Annarundell aforesaid to
       be disposed of or Imployed or sold for ye only use of & behoofe
       of my wife as shee shall think good

Irs.   I give & bequeath unto my said wife five hundred acars of Land
       called ye playns lying in puttapsco River in ye County of Balte-
       more in ye province of Maryland to bee disposed Imployed for
       ye only (*profit*): (or) yous of my sd wife ass shee shall think
       good during her naturall life & after to bee delivered to my sun
       Sam^{ll} as his posesion

Irs.   I give & bequeath unto my said wife, all my personall Estate, both
       moveable & immoveable, viz: goods marchandise plate money
       sarvants chattles Eaither In this province or Else whear except
       what before two my two suns & what after shall bee mentioned
       or disposed of by mee

Ips.   I give & bequeath unto my sun Sam^ll Thomas four Cowes or heaifers to bee delivered to him forth withafter my decese & one feather Bead

Ips.   I give and bequeath unto my Dafter Martha Thomas four Cowes or heaifers to be delivered unto heer forth with after my desccase & one feather bead.

Ips.   I give & bequeath unto my grand Child Mary the Dafter of John Mears five Eues to be delivered to the Sd John Mears forth with after my desease to be kept by him for ye yous of ye said Mary

Ips.   I give & bequeath unto my two grandchildren Phillip and Elizabeth ye sun & Dafter of Wm Coale nine eues & one Rame to be delivered unto ye sd Wm Coale forth with after my Deseas for ye yous of ye sd Phillip & Elizabeth

Ips.   I give & bequeath unto my wife afore sd ye Rent Rents & Revenues of two houses y^t I have in Bristol During heer naturall Life and after to bee sould and the produce thear of to bee equally divided between my five Chilldren viz Phillip Sam^ll Sarah Elizabeth and Martha

Ips.   I give & bequeath unto ye Coman stock for the Relefe of pore frends Caled quakers four hundred pounds of tobacco to bee payd forth with after my deseas

Ips.   I will & declare my trew & loveing wife Sarah Thomas afore sd to bee my (*whle*) & sole Executrix of this my Last will & testament.

Ips.   I will & desieir y^t if itt shuld soe hapen y^t aney difference or contravarsey shuld arise after my desease betwene aney of my children and my wife concarning ye primises aforesd y^t then itt bee broght Before & a Judged of by ye body of frends Comonly Called quakers & what theay shall agree upon in that behalfe is by mee Rattefied & a Lowed of to stand in Law to all Intents & porposes

Ips.   I will & declare this to bee my last will & testement hereby Disanuling & making voyd all other wills or Testements by me formerly made In withness whearof I have here unto sett my hand & seal Dated this ninth day of ye seventh month Called September Anno
            1674

Singd Sealed & Delivered   PHILLIP THOMAS.
    in ye prs^t of us
JOHN RICKE   Probated
MARMUEDUKE NOBLE   July 10th 1675

ADDENDA.

CHEW.

On page 55, line 24, after **HENRY** (second son of **Joseph** and **Eliza Chew**) add: md. **ELIZABETH** ——, and had issue two sons: **HENRY**, who removed with his father to one of the lower counties of Maryland, and **JOSEPH** b. Aug. 24th, 1719, resided at Deer Creek in Harford County, Md., md. in 1745 **SARAH** ——, and had issue:

i.   **ELIZABETH** b. July 18th, 1747, md. Nov. 24th, 1768, **JOHN HOPKINS**.

ii. **SUSAN** b. Dec. 25th, 1749.

iii. **THOMAS** b. June 8th, 1752, md. **ELIZABETH**, dau. of **William** and **Cassandra Morgan**, and had issue: **Edward M**.

On page 56, line 5, after **Mary**, read "md. in 1726-7 **Gilbert Crockett**," and omit the last 7 words in line 6.

On page 60 omit the account there given of **RICHARD**, fifth child of **Samuel** and **Mary Chew**, and instead insert the following:

RICHARD, third son of **Samuel** and **Mary Chew**, b. in May, 1716, md. Jany. 5th, 1749-50, **Mrs. SARAH (Lock) CHEW**, widow of his cousin Samuel Chew, of John, and d. June 24th, 1769; his wife d. Feby. 1st, 1791, having had issue by her 2d husband:

i.   **MARY** b. Dec. 27th, 1750, md. Feby. 10th, 1767, **Dr. ALEXANDER HAMILTON SMITH**, and had issue: **UPTON**, and **SARAH**.

ii.   Maj. **RICHARD** b. Apl. 10th, 1753, of whom presently.

iii.   Capt. **SAMUEL** b. Dec. 9th, 1755, d. Feby. 1st, 1785.

iv.   **LOCK** b. Nov. 14th, 1757, d. s. p. in 1794.

v.   **FRANCIS** b. July 10th, 1760.

vi.   **SARAH LOCK** b. Nov. 20th, 1761, md. —— **LANE**.

vii.   **PHILEMON LLOYD** b. July 23d, 1765.

Major RICHARD, eldest son of **Richard** and **Sarah** (**Lock**) **Chew**, b. April 10th, 1753, md. 1st. Feby. 4th. 1773. **MARGARET**, dau. of **James John Mackall**, who d. May 20th, 1779, aged 24, having had issue :

i.   **RICHARD** b. Oct. 4th, 1773, of whom presently.

ii.   **MARY MACKALL** b. Sept. 17th, 1776, md. —— **BRINGMAN**, and had issue : MARGARET md. Dr. **FRY**.

Major CHEW md. 2d. **FRANCES**, dau. of **Thomas Holland**, of Calvert County, Md. She d. Sept. 26th, 1799, and her husband June 6th, 1801, having had further issue :

i.   **THOMAS HOLLAND** b. Oct. 27th, 1781. (q. v.)

ii.   **WILLIAM H.** b. Aug. 7th, 1784, d. Sept. 11th, 1799.

iii.   **SARAH** b. March 16th, 1787, d. Dec. 28th, 1790.

iv.   **PHILEMON** b. Feby. 20th, 1789, md. **MARIA**, dau. of **Gen. John Brooks**, and d. leaving issue : **RICHARD B. B.**

v.   **SARAH LOCK** b. in 1790, d. in infancy.

vi.   **FRANCES** b. April 19th, 1793.

vii.   **BETTIE H.** b. Sept. 17th, 1795, d. Sept. 19th, 1797.

viii. **SAMUEL LOCK** b. July 17th, 1797, d. Feby. 12th, 1798.

ix.   **BETTIE H.** 2d, b. May 15th, 1799, d. Oct. 10th, 1800.

RICHARD, eldest son of **Major Richard** and **Margaret** (**Mackall**) **Chew**, b. Oct. 4th, 1773. md. Dec. 20th, 1804, **ELIZABETH**, dau. of **Leonard Hollyday**, and d. June 20th, 1831. having had issue :

i.   RICHARD b. Sept. 21st, 1805, d. s. p. Sept. 23d, 1832.

ii. SARAH AMELIA HOLLYDAY b April 21st, 1807, d. unmarried.

iii. MARGARET MACKALL b. Feby. 1st, 1809, of whom presently.

iv. LEONARD HOLLYDAY b. Nov. 13th, 1810, md. AMELIA BEALL HOLLYDAY, and d. s. p.

v.   JAMES JOHN b. Feby. 20th, 1813, d. s. p. Oct. 1st, 1847.

vi. MARIA LOUISA b. May 27th, 1815, d. in Aug. 1835.

vii. ROBERT WILLIAM BOWIE b. March 13th, 1819, md. May 21st, 1846, MARY VIR-GINIA LEVERING, who d. in Sept. 1863, and her husband d. s. p. in Apl. 1868.

viii. MARY ELIZABETH b. March 17th, 1820.

MARGARET MACKALL, second dau. of Richard and Elizabeth (Hollyday) Chew, b. Feby. 1st, 1809, md. March 20th, 1831, Dr. ROBERT W. GLASS, who after her death md. ISABELLA HAMILTON, and d. Nov. 4th, 1875, having had issue by his first wife:

i.   JOSEPH b. in 1832.

ii. ELIZABETH C. b. Aug. 27th, 1835, md. 1st, Nov. 27th, 1856, DANIEL CARROLL DIGGES, and 2d, Oct. 13th, 1870, Dr. LLEWELLYN CROWTHER. By her first husband she had issue: MARGARET CHEW b. Jany. 1st, 1858; and DANIEL CARROLL b. Sept. 5th, 1859, d. Oct. 24th, 1876.

iii. RICHARD CHEW b. in Oct. 1837, d. in the C. S. A. Dec. 7th, 1863.

iv. MARGARET L.

THOMAS HOLLAND, eldest son of Maj. Richard and Frances (Holland) Chew, b. Oct. 27th, 1781, md. 1st, ELIZABETH, dau. of Walter Smith, of Calvert County, Md., who d. Dec. 30th, 1825, and her husband md. 2d, Feby. 7th, 1828, MARY DAVIS, who d. Aug. 11th, 1829, leaving an only dau. MARY ELIZABETH F. b. Feby. 28th, 1829. THOMAS H. CHEW d. March 16th, 1840, having had issue by his first wife:

i.   RICHARD b. Sept. 26th, 1806, d. April 19th, 1809.

ii. SUSAN SMITH b. Dec. 5th, 1807, d. Sept. 9th, 1809.

iii. FRANCES ANN b. May 2d, 1810, d. Aug. 21st, 1822.

iv.   **WALTER SMITH** b. Aug. 13th, 1811, md. Jany. 7th, 1840, **MARTHA J. REID**, of Wilkinson County, Miss., and has had issue:

    i.   **ANN REID** b. Nov. 23d, 1840.

    ii.   **THOMAS HOLLAND** b. Jany. 29th, 1843.

    iii   **SARAH ELLEN** b. May 17th, 1848.

    iv.   **RICHARD FLOWER** b. April 15th, 1851.

    v.   **ELIZABETH SMITH** b. June 14th, 1853.

    vi.   **JAMES REID** b. Aug. 26th, 1856, d. Aug. 15th, 1860.

    vii.   **WILLIAM SCOTT** b. Sept. 15th, 1858, d. March 23d, 1861.

    viii.   **FREDERICK FREELAND** b. Nov. 9th, 1861, d. May 31st, 1863.

v.   **JOSEPH SMITH** b. July 15th, 1814, d. Aug. 27th, 1822.

vi.   **PHILEMON** b. July 2d, 1816, of whom presently.

vii.   **DANIEL RAWLINS** b. Nov. 25th, 1819, d. July 16th, 1820.

Dr. PHILEMON, sixth child of **Thomas H.** and **Elizabeth (Smith) Chew,** b. July 2d, 1816. md. Nov. 26th, 1839, **REBECCA CHEW FREE-LAND,** and has had issue:

i.   **THOMAS HOLLAND,** Jr. b. Jany. 23d, 1842.

ii.   **ELIZABETH** b. April 12th, 1843, md. **Dr. T. B. POINTDEXTER.**

iii.   **MARIA LOUISA** b. Dec. 28th, 1844, md. **SAMUEL G. SMITH.**

iv.   **SUSAN HAWKINS** b. April 21st, 1846.

v.   **JOSEPH WALTER** b. March 15th, 1849.

vi.   **WILLIAM FREELAND** b. Nov. 20th, 1851.

vii.   **EDWARD** b. Oct. 25th, 1855, d. in 1870.

viii.   **MARY CECELIA** b. March 17th, 1858, d. in 1868.

On page 61, omit lines 19 and 20, and insert the following pedigree

JOHN, second son of **Samuel** and **Sarah (Lock) Chew,** md.   — —. and d. May 26th, 1785, leaving issue:

i.   JOHN LANE b. in 1762, of whom presently.

ii.   SAMUEL md. Nov. 1st, 1803. ANN SMITH, and had issue: WILLIAM PACE b. Nov.
      21st, 1806; SARAH ANN b. June 21st, 1808; HORACE b. May 12th, 1812;
      and EDWARD R., who d. Nov. 8th, 1829.

iii. NATHANIEL LANE.

iv.   WILLIAM LOCK md. REBECCA ———, who d. June 12th, 1840.

JOHN LANE, eldest son of Samuel Chew, b. in 1762, md. MARY R.
WILSON, who d. in 1802, her husband d. in 1832, having had issue:

i.   ELIZABETH b. in 1788, d. unmarried in 1870.

ii.   JOHN b. Dec. 3d, 1790, of whom presently.

iii. EDWARD b. in 1794, md. ——— SPARROW, and d. leaving issue: THOMAS EDWARD
      b. in 1840; and JOHN LANE b. at, and occupied the old homestead "Lombardy
      Poplar," Anne Arundel County, Md.

JOHN, eldest son of John Lane and Mary (Wilson) Chew, b. Dec. 3d,
1790, entered the U. S. Navy about 1805, and served for many years,
acting as Recruiting Officer in the service, with headquarters at Philadelphia and New York. He resigned in 1817, and joined the Mexican
Expedition of Gen. Espoz y Mina, acting as his Chief of Staff.
After the failure of that attempt he returned to the United States and
entered the merchant service as captain of a vessel in the trade between
Baltimore and the Mediterranean ports. Retired from the sea in 1826,
removed to North Mississippi in 1835, and engaging in cotton planting,
amassed a considerable fortune. He md. May 28th, 1828. MARY ANN
SMITH, of Calvert County, Md., who d. July 10th, 1876, her husband
d. Feby. 24th, 1872, having had issue, with seven other children who d.
in infancy.

i.   GLORVINA b. May 15th, 1830, d. unmarried.

ii.   JOHN CALHOUN b. May 28th, 1838, md. 1st, July 11th, 1861, ZILPHIA GUTHRIE
      FULLER, and had issue: JOHN MARSHALL b. May 17th, 1862. Mrs. CHEW
      d. Aug. 8th, 1863, and her husband md. 2d, Feby. 1st, 1876, THEODORA R.
      SEIXAS.

iii. FRISBY FREELAND b. Oct. 9th, 1839, md. Sept. 26th, 1861, JULIA A. FULLER,
      and has issue: FREELAND FULLER; FRANK NATHAN; JOHN BEVERLY; and
      MARY ANN.

iv. ROBERT EDWARD b. Oct. 28th, 1844. md. Oct. 25th, 1865. MARY PUGH GOVAN, and has issue: JULIA HAWKS; EDWARD GOVAN; FRISBY FREELAND. RALPH; WILLIAM ROBERTS; FRANK; and CARRIE.

Page 62, omit line 9, and insert:

ANN, eldest dau. of Larkin and Hannah (Roy) Chew, md. WILLIAM JOHNSTON, and had issue: JOSEPH; LARKIN md. MARY ROGERS; JUDITH md. ROBERT FARISH; ROBERT md. ANN COOK; JOHN d. unmarried; BENJAMIN md. DOROTHY JONES; JAMES md. MARY WARE; WILLIAM md. ANN FLINT; HANNAH md. FRANCIS COLEMAN; RICHARD md. DOROTHY W. BEVERLY; and ELIZABETH md. JOHN BENGER.

Same page omit line 11, and insert:

LARKIN, fifth child of Larkin and Hannah (Roy) Chew, md. MARY BEVERLY, and had issue:

i. ELIZA BEVERLY md. 1st. BEVERLY STANARD, and 2d, MOSES BUCKNER. By her first husband she had issue:

  i. WILLIAM.

  ii. LARKIN, of whom presently.

ii. MARY md. 1st, JOHN SMITH, and had one son, and 2d, OLIVER POWLES.

LARKIN, second son of Beverly and Eliza (Chew) Stanard, md. ELIZABETH, only dau. of Robert and Molly (Parrot) Chew, and had issue:

i. BEVERLY CHEW md. MARY B. FLEMING.

ii. Judge ROBERT resided at Richmond, Va., md. JANE CRAIG.

iii. MARY B. md. EDMUND FOSTER.

iv. Col. JOHN md. CAROLINE MATILDA, dau. of John and Ann (Fox) Chew.

v. THOMAS md. —— PENNY, of Louisiana.

23

vi.   HUGH md. Mrs. ANN SIMPSON.

vii.   ELIZABETH md. Dr. WOOLDRIDGE.

viii. KITTY md. CHRISTOPHER BRANCH.

ix.   LAVINIA d. unmarried.

x.   CAROLINE MATILDA CHEW md. LATON STANARD.

xi.   COLUMBIA md. —— PRATT.

xii.   LUCY ANN d. in infancy.

Page 63, line 29, omit the first four words, and insert:

JOHN, second son of **Robert** and **Molly** (**Parrot**) **Chew,** md. **ELIZABETH SMITH,** and had issue:

i.   ROBERT SMITH md. ELIZABETH FRENCH, and had issue JOHN JAMES md.
      ELLEN PATON; GEORGE FRENCH d. unmarried; ANN ELIZA md. Lieut. MINOR,
      U. S. N.; and ROBERT md. —— SMITH, of Washington.

ii.   MARY BEVERLY md. SETH BARTON.

iii. ELIZABETH md. Dr. JAMES FRENCH.

Page 63, line 29, omit the last five words, and insert:

JOSEPH, youngest child of **Robert** and **Molly** (**Parrot**) **Chew,** md. **MARY WINSLOW,** and had issue: ROBERT BEVERLY d. unmarried; JOHN WINSLOW md. ELIZABETH VOSS; ALBERT G. lived at Louisville, Ky., md. —— MORRIS, of Baltimore, Md.; ADELINE md. in Kentucky; JOSEPH; and WILLIAM.

Page 63, omit line 30, and insert:

MARY BEVERLY, second child of **John** and **Margaret** (**Beverly**) **Chew,** md. Col. **JOSEPH BROCK,** of Spottsylvania, Va., and had issue:

i.   JOHN md. ANN CURTIS.

ii. ELIZABETH md. 1st, J. T. LEWIS, and 2d, BEVERLY STUBBLEFIELD, or STRIBBLEFIELD.

iii. MARY md. JOHN CARTER.

iv. CATHERINE d. unmarried.

v.   JOSEPH a Captain U. S. A., md. ANN, dau. of John and Ann (Fox) Chew, and had issue :

   i.   JULIA ANN CHEW md. SILAS WOOD, of New York.

   ii. CADWALLADER WILLIAM d. unmarried.

   iii. MARY d. in infancy.

vi. WILLIAM md. 1st, ——— BARNES, and 2d, BETSEY POWLES.

vii. SUSAN md. BEVERLY ROBINSON.

ELLICOTT.

On page 72. ELIAS, thirteenth child of Elias and Mary (Thomas) Ellicott, md. SARAH, dau. of Dudley and Deborah Poor, and d. in 1873, having had issue :

i.   SARAH md. in 1867, HENRY TRACY ARNOLD, of New York.

ii. ADELAIDE VICTORIA.

iii. HENRY d. in infancy.

iv. MARGARET md. Dec. 15th, 1868, Dr. ALFRED A. WOODHULL, U. S. A.

v.   MARY LOUISA d. May 12th, 1873.

FAIRFAX.

On page 74 omit the first paragraph, and insert:

This family was seated at Towcester in Northumberland, at the Conquest, and is supposed to be of Saxon stock. The pedigree begins with Richard Fairfax, son of John, and grandson of Henry Fairfax, of Shapenbeck, who in 1204 possessed the Manor of Askham and other lands in Yorkshire; he had issue a son and heir William living in 1212-13 md. Alice, dau. and heir of Nicholas de Bugthorpe, and had a son and heir William, High Bailiff of York in 1249, bought the Manor of Walton, and md. Mary, widow of Walter Flower, and had a son and heir Thomas living in 1284, md. Anne, dau. and heir of Henry de Sezevaux, Mayor of York, and had issue: William and Bego d. s. p., and John living in 1312 md. Clara, dau. and co-heir of Roger Brus, of Walton, and had a son and heir Thomas md. Margaret, dau. of John Malbis, and had, with two daus. Anne md. —— Martin; and Clare md. 1st, —— Palms, and 2d, Sir William Malbis; a son and heir William md. Ellen, dau. of John Roucliffe, of Roucliffe, and had issue: Thomas, his heir; John; Margaret, Prioress of Muncton; Mary and Alice, nuns of Sempringham. Thomas was living in 1350, md. Elizabeth, dau. of Sir Ivo Etting, Knt., of Gilling, and had issue: William, his heir; Thomas; Guy; John; and Richard.

William md. Constance, sister and co-heir of Peter, fourth Baron de Mauley, and had issue: Thomas, his heir, Richard; and Bryan, who was Parson of Longtoft, and Precentor of York Minister in 1423-4.

Thomas was living between 1385 and 1396 md. Margaret, widow of Sir Robert Roucliffe, Knt., and sister and heir of Richard Friston, of Marston, and had issue: Richard, his heir; Guy, George; Thomas; John; and Nicholas.

Richard, living between 1400 and 1430, md. Eustace, dau. and heir of John Carthorp by his wife Elisabeth, dau. and co-heir of Sir William Ergham, Knt., and had issue: William, his heir; Bryan, a Priest; Sir Guy, of whom presently; Richard, a Priest; Sir Nicholas, a Knight of Rhodes; Miles; Margaret; Anne; and Ellen, a Nun of Muncton.

William d. in 1452-3, leaving a son Thomas, d. in 1504-5, leaving a son Sir Thomas, K. B., d. in 1520-1, leaving a son Sir Nicholas, d. in

1570, leaving a son Sir William, whose son Sir Thomas was created in 1629 Viscount Fairfax of Emely in the Peerage of Ireland, md. Catherine, sister of Henry first Viscount Dunbar, and d. in 1636, leaving two sons, Thomas, second Viscount md. Alathea, dau. of Philip Howard, and had a son Thomas, third Viscount, whose only son Charles md. Nov. 17th, 1729, Elizabeth, dau. of Hugh fourth Lord Clifford of Chudleigh and widow of William Viscount Dunbar, and had issue which became extinct in the male line in the same century; and Henry whose son Henry had an only dau. and heir Frances who md. in 1697 David, Earl of Buchan. We now return to Sir Guy, third son of Richard and Eustace (Carthorp) Fairfax, who was appointed Judge of the Court of King's Bench, Sept. 29th, 1478, built the Castle of Steeton, md. Margaret, dau. of Sir William Rither, of Rither, and d. in 1495, having had issue: Sir William, his heir; Thomas, a Serjeant-at-Law; Guy; Nicholas; Ellen md. Sir Nicholas Welstrop; and Maud md. Sir John Waterton, Master of the Horse to King Henry VI.

Sir William was appointed a Judge of the Court of Common Pleas, May 21st, 1510, md. Elisabeth, sister of Thomas first Earl of Rutland, and granddaughter of Anne, Duchess of Exeter and sister of King Edward IV., and d. in 1514-15, leaving issue: Sir William, his heir; Ellen md. Sir William Pickering, Knight Marshall of England; Elizabeth md. Sir Robert Oughtred; Anne md. Sir Robert Normanville, Knt. of Kilnwick; and Dorothy md. ——— Constable, of Hexby.

Sir William was High Sheriff of York in 1535, md. in 1518, Isabella, dau. of John Thwaites, who brought him the Manor of Denton, and Askwith in Wharfedale, and Bishop Hill and Davy Hall within the walls of York. He joined the Pilgrimage of Grace, but appears to have been pardoned his share in that outbreak, and d. Oct. 31st, 1557, having had issue: Guy, d. s. p.; Thomas, of whom presently; Francis; Edward; Henry; Gabriel, who inherited under his father's will, "Steeton," and the most part of his paternal estate, md. Elizabeth, dau. of Robert Aske, and was ancestor of the Fairfaxes of Steeton; Anne md. Sir Henry Everingham, of Saxton; Mary md. Robert Rockley of Rockley; Bridget md. Sir Cotton Gargrave of Nostell; Ursula md. Ralph Vavasor, of Hazlewood; and Agnes md. Edward Elloft, of Farnell and Nottingley.

Thomas, eldest surviving son of Sir William and Isabel (Thwaites) Fairfax, inherited his mothers property at Denton, Nun Appleton, Askwith, Acaster, and in the City of York; was knighted by Queen Elizabeth in 1576, md. Dorothy, dau. of George Gale of Asham Grange, and d. in 1599, having had issue: Thomas, of whom presently; Henry, Fellow of Trinity College, Cambridge, in 1613, d. s. p.; Charles, who was a Colonel in the

army, a pupil of Sir Horace Vere, and killed at the siege of Ostend ;
Edward, of Newhall, the poet, and author of " Godfrey of Bulloigne," the
best English translation of Tasso's " Jerusalem Delivered," who d. in 1632 ;
and two daughters, Ursula and Christiana.

On page 75, line 5, insert " 18th," between " Oct." and " 1627."

On the same page, the order of the sons of the first **Baron FAIRFAX**
should be as follows: **FERDINANDO; HENRY; WILLIAM; CHARLES;
JOHN; PEREGRINE; THOMAS**; and three who d. young.

On the same page, **URSULA**, dau. of **Ferdinand Lord Fairfax**, by his
second wife, md. **WILLIAM CARTWRIGHT**, of Aynho, Northamp-
tonshire, and had issue: **WILLIAM**; and **RHODA** md. **Lord HENRY
CAVENDISH.**

On page 76, omit lines 10 and 11, and insert, had issue: **HENRY**, 4th
Lord, of whom presently; and **BRYAN** b. Oct. 6th, 1633, md. April
22d, 1675, **CHARLOTTE**, only dau. and heir of **Sir Edmund Cary** by **Anne**,
sister of the Earl of Macclesfield, who d. Nov. 14th, 1709, her husband
d. Sept. 23d, 1711, having had issue: **BRYAN; FERDINANDO**, and **CHARLES**
M. A. Christ Church College, Oxford in 1712: who all d. s. p.

On the same page, line 14, after " presently," insert: **BRYAN**, Commissioner
of Customs, d. Jany. 9th. 1747-8: **BARWICKE; DOROTHY** md. 1st,
ROBERT STAPLETON, of Wighill, and 2d, **BENNET SHERRARD**, of
Whissenden, and d. in Jany. 1743-4: **FRANCES** md. —— **RYMER;**
ANNE md. Sept. 2d. 1690, **RALPH**, son of **Sir Ralph Car**, of Cocken, and
d. July 3d, 1699: and **URSULA** and **MARY** who both d. unmarried.

On the same page, line 26, change the date to Dec. 9th, 1781.

On the same page, omit lines 27 to 30 inclusive, and insert:

ii.   **HENRY COLEPEPPER** d. unmarried Oct. 14th, 1734.

iii. **MARGARET** md. Rev. **DAVID WILKINS, D. D.**, and d. s. p.

iv.   **FRANCES** b. in 1703, md. **DENNY MARTIN**, and d. Dec. 13th, 1791, leaving issue Rev. **DENNY** and Gen. **PHILIP**; who both assumed the name of "**FAIRFAX**," and inherited in succession the English estates of the family.

v.   **ROBERT** b. in 1706 succeeded as 7th Lord Fairfax was a Major in the Life Guards, M. P. for Kent in 1754 and 1761; md. 1st, Apl. 25th, 1741, **MARTHA**, dau. and co-heir of **Anthony Collins**, of Baddow. She d. in 1744, leaving a son who d. in 1747; and her husband md. 2d, in 1749 a dau. of **Thomas Best**, of Chatham, who d. s. p. in 1750, and Lord Fairfax d. s. p. July 15th, 1793, leaving his English Estates by Will to his nephew Rev. Denny Martin.

On the same page, lines 33, 34 and 35, read:

HENRY baptized Sept. 15th, 1685, d. s. p. at York, Nov. 22d, 1759; **THOMAS** baptized Mch. 13th, 1687, d. in infancy; **RICHARD** baptized July 31st, 1690, buried Oct. 29th, 1690; **WILLIAM**, of whom presently; **BRYAN**; **DOROTHY**; and **ANNE**. **WILLIAM** b. in 1691, was Virginia Agent of his cousin, the 6th Lord Fairfax.

LEIPER.

On page 117 James and Thomas Leiper had a brother Andrew who settled in Virginia, md. and d. leaving issue: Andrewetta md. Edward Williamson; and Frances md. Thomas Crouch.

On page 118, line 3, after "md." insert: by Rev. Dr. William White, Nov. 3d, 1778, to

CORRIGENDA.

On page 6, line 30, instead of "Caemarthenshire" read: **CAERMARTHENSHIRE**.

On page 9, line 14, instead of "Caermarvonshire" read: **CAERNARVONSHIRE**.

On page 9, line 16, instead of "ap Owen" read: **ap HOWELL**.

On page 13, line 13, instead of "Rice ap Griffith" read: **Sir RHYS ap THOMAS**.

On page 28, line 23, read: **JOHN** before "Qwyman."

On page 29, line 34, instead of "Zoralya" read: **ZORAYDA**

On page 30, line 7, instead of "dau. of James and Deborah (Snowden)" read **dau. of Roger and Mary**.

On page 30, line 10, **omit** all after "1754."

On page 36, line 11, instead of "1866" read **1876**.

On page 43, line 14, after "Deborah, &c." read: **md. RICHARD THOMAS.** (q. v.)

On page 43, line 20, after "Aug. 9th, 1801" read: **md. JAMES P. STABLER.** (q. v.)

On page 47, line 16, instead of "Sportlande" read: **SPOTLANDE**.

On page 53, line 6, instead of "Maurice" read: **ANTHONY MORRIS**.

On page 53, line 13, instead of "Susan" read: **ELLEN**.

On page 53 in the sons of James and Mary (Gibson) Carey the order should be: **JAMES; GEORGE GIBSON; HENRY GIBSON; and ALEXANDER GIBSON**.

On page 53, line 17, after "deceased" read: **leaving two children**.

On page 53, line 18, after "Grace Gibson" add: **and has issue: GIBSON; GRACE; and MARY**.

On page 62, line 19, instead of "Sistai" read: **SISTRAI**.

On page 78, line 7, instead of "Farquhard" read: **FARQUHAR**.

On page 87, line 4, after "1805" read: **MARIA, dau. of Benjamin and Eliza Poultney**.

On page 92 insert among the children of Gerard T. and Dorothy (Brooke) Hopkins the following: **x. RACHEL b. May 19th, 1822**.

On the page 93, line 19, instead of "John" read: **JOHNS**.

On page 97, lines 8 and 12, instead of "Flodoard" read **FLODOARDO**.

On page 104, line 13, instead of "George Wardour" read: **GEORGE A. WARDER**. And instead of "has" read: **d. leaving**.

On page 112, line 30, instead of "of whom presently" read: **(q. v.)**

On page 115, line 31, instead of "Clendenning" read: **CLENDINNING**.

On page 116, line 8, instead of "Angustus" read: **AUGUSTA**.

On page 141, line 24, after "Edward" add: **P.**

On page 142, line 7, **omit** the word "Snowden."

On page 152, line 7, after "Beatrix" add: **and MARTHA ELLICOTT**.

INDEX

OF PRINCIPAL PERSONS, AND SURNAMES.

NOTES.

On page 65, line 14, I promise an account of three younger sons of JOHN CHEW; this has not been received, and I doubt his having had such issue. On page 73 WILLIAM M. ELLICOTT, Sr., had a fourth son, Dr. LINDLEY d. s. p. in 1876. On page 93, line 24, the issue of MILES WHITE were all by his first wife, a lady of North Carolina. On page 94, the arms given, are those of LADY CATHERINE (Howard) RICE's brother of the whole blood, ancestor of Lord Howard of Effingham. On page 182, line 16, read: GEORGE and MARY (Gibson) CAREY. Copies of the illustrations in this book may be obtained from the author.

www.ingramcontent.com/pod-product-compliance
Lightning Source LLC
Chambersburg PA
CBHW030823270326
41928CB00007B/867